BREWED IN THE TRADITIONAL MANNER

This book is dedicated to the memory of
Bill and David Clarke, brewers of Hook Norton.

BREWED IN THE TRADITIONAL MANNER

The story of Hook Norton Brewery

Rob Woolley

BREWIN BOOKS

56 Alcester Road,
Studley,
Warwickshire,
B80 7LG

www.brewinbooks.com

Published by Brewin Books 2015

A CIP catalogue record for this book is available
from the British Library.

ISBN: 978-1-85858-539-0

Printed in the UK by
Hobbs The Printers Ltd.

Contents

James and David Clarke (Dave Morris).

Introduction

ONCE, every town had its own brewery, but after more than a century of mergers and takeovers, less than forty of these nineteenth century brewery businesses survive to uphold this tradition.[1] The Hook Norton Brewery Co Ltd, a small independent company situated in the south Midlands, is one of the survivors; which has brewed its distinctive beers in the heart of the English countryside for more than 160 years. History is made by the actions of men and it is the decisions taken and implemented by John Harris, the brewery's founder, and his successors, which chart the growth of the company from its humble beginnings to its position today, as one of the country's few remaining centres of beer production.

'Brewed in the Traditional Manner' is not just the story of the company's growth and development, but the story of a family who, through successive generations, have upheld the traditions and values set by its founder. The book is focussed on the growth and development of the Hook Norton Brewery, presenting a case study of the business. This, by definition, allows a more in-depth investigation and the opportunity "to specify the particular in the context of the general".[2] The book is an independent study and provides a base line for any future research.

Using this model, the story is set against the framework of the broader background of a changing brewing industry in Great Britain and recounts how national decisions have shaped and influenced the company's development.

Beer has a special place in the history of the British Isles. Before the availability of clean drinking water, ale and then beer, formed an essential part of the staple diet of the population. From mediæval times and before, men, women and children alike, all drank alcoholic beverages. A foreign visitor to England in 1598 commented that, "Beer is the general drink and exceedingly well tasted, but strong and what soon fuddles." [3]

During the eighteenth century beer was a cheap but bulky commodity to transport but, because overland transport charges were high in the pre-railway age, a brewer using dray wagons was limited to an economical marketing area of about five miles from his brewery. It has been suggested by Peter Mathias that in rural areas, where population was scattered, the high transport costs would limit the possibilities of further expansion. [4]

These were problems still faced by rural brewers like John Harris in the middle of the following century, even though the railway had reached both Chipping Norton and Banbury by 1855. In the absence of alternatives, the Mathias model provides a basis for understanding how Harris's business developed. This book traces the growth of his business, from his first customers to the time when he 'broke out' of a local market centred on the village and built up an enlarged trading area. No longer 'locked into his market', Harris was able to create a large secure customer base by 1876. [5]

Times have changed; beer is no longer an essential part of the diet and competes now with the growing popularity of wine and spirits for the custom of today's social drinkers. The standard works outlining the history of the brewing industry relate that during the second half of the nineteenth century and into the twentieth century, the acknowledged method by which brewery companies grew and established their businesses, was through the acquisition of tied house properties, particularly in urban areas like London. [6] The development of the Hook Norton Brewery's business, until 1914, did not follow this pattern; it built its secure base on an alternative business plan based on the private trade. When this collapsed at the beginning of the First World War the company was forced to look for alternative outlets and found salvation in the shape of the Working Men's Clubs of Coventry, a trade that continued until the beginning of the present century.

The structure of the book is thematic rather than chronological. There are four main chapters which form the core of the work; each devoted to a separate theme related to a specific aspect of the brewery's development. These are: the running of the business, the production, distribution and retailing of beer. Treating the material thematically provides a vehicle for describing the history and development of each theme in depth, focussing on that aspect of the business. Each chapter covers a period of about one hundred years from 1846 to 1951. The fifth and final chapter, a postscript, concludes the story, bringing it up to date by concentrating on the developments overseen by the three generations of the Clarke family who have run the business since 1951.

The Hook Norton Brewery Archive, a collection of the company's old documents, forms the basis of the primary source material used in the writing of this book. These documents, dating from the nineteenth and early twentieth centuries, include letter books, stock books, wage books, maps, plans and a set of nineteenth century pamphlets and books about brewing, including Moritz and Morris, *'A Text Book of the Science of Brewing'* (1891) and Faulkner, *'The Theory and Practice of Modern Brewing'* (1888), both of which were purchased by Alban Clarke towards the end of the nineteenth century. A further set of documents held at the brewery, form part of the company's records and include the deeds of brewery properties, the brewing books and minute books of the directors' meetings and unreferenced quotes have been taken from these sources. The recollections of Hook Norton villagers who had connections with the brewery, as well as those of the Clarke family have been used to support both printed and primary source material. The company's annual reports to shareholders were also consulted at Companies House in Cardiff.

It is now almost forty years since I lived in Hook Norton and first became interested in the history of the village. The brewery was just one avenue for exploration as I set about collecting information about the village's past. It was not until deciding on a topic for a postgraduate degree that I finally focussed on the Hook Norton Brewery. During these early years of my research I was given every encouragement by Bill Clarke, who not only made available a wide range of brewery documents, but allowed me to take them home overnight, so I could make copies and analyse the information. Without this facility the book would not have been possible. I would like to acknowledge my gratitude to him and for the help and encouragement he gave me.

I would also like to acknowledge the help and assistance given me during this early research by my late mother and friends Amanda Shaw and Peter Ellmer. At the County Record Office, Shirley Barnes, then County Archivist fielded my enquiries, unearthed documents and through correspondence helped me to build up a picture of the village's past. At this early stage of my research, her help was invaluable. I would like to acknowledge the help and time given up by Hook Norton villagers who shared their recollections with me, to talk about life in the village during the first half of the twentieth century. There are too many to mention here by name, but in the context of this book, the recollections of Fred Beale, Percy Hemmings, Harold Wyton, Leslie Matthews and Nan Cross have proved invaluable. I would also like to thank Audrey Haney for allowing me to use the photographs taken by her late husband, Jack, Derek Rayner for sharing his expertise on the workings of steam wagons, Dave Morris for the use of his picture of James and David Clarke, Ian Hayward for allowing me to use the letter from the Coppage Archive, Robert Humphreys of the Parliamentary Beer Group for the use of the picture of David Clarke and the Hook Norton Brewery Company for allowing me to use photographs from the company's archive. Unless otherwise stated, all other photographs come from my own collection.

The first steps towards this history of the Hook Norton Brewery were taken during 2000 with the commencement of a postgraduate degree at the University of Wolverhampton. The guidance provided by Professor Malcolm Wanklyn and Dr Paul Henderson helped to shape the way in which the wealth of material I had amassed was organised and presented. I would like to acknowledge their invaluable contribution to the project.

With the degree successfully completed five years later, work on *'Brewed in the Traditional Manner'* began in earnest. The thesis was re-written and extended beyond 1913, taking the story of the brewery to 1951. This required a second phase of research and I would like to acknowledge the invaluable help given me by Ken Oultram who joined me on several early morning journeys to Hook Norton to complete this work and to Barbara Hicks, for her assistance in tracking down the answers to outstanding questions, however obscure, during the latter stages of writing the book.

'Brewed in the Traditional Manner' has had a long history but it was always intended that the book should grow out of postgraduate research work. This has only been possible through the continued support of successive generations of the Clarke family who have allowed me access to the company's archive. I would like to acknowledge the support given initially by Bill when I began my research, by David and his wife Paula when I was involved in postgraduate research and more recently as this book took shape, by James, the current Managing Director. Without their help and support over a period of more than forty years this project would not have come to fruition.

I would also like to acknowledge the help and support of my family. First, to my brother, Professor Guy Woolley, for his constructive comments on the content, which have helped to shape the book. I would also like to thank my daughters for stoically enduring the many conversations about brewing and the Hook Norton Brewery at the dinner table when there were probably more entertaining topics to be discussed and finally, I am especially grateful to my wife Kay for her help and support throughout the project. She has fulfilled many roles, having helped with the research, proof reading chapters, making suggestions and being the sounding board for ideas as the writing progressed.

R.M.W. St Peter's Day 2014

Notes

1   Email Correspondence with Ian Loe of CAMRA 21/11/2006. In 2006 there were 550 licensed brewers in the UK, of which 35 had their origins in the nineteenth century or earlier.

   Email Correspondence with Ian Loe of CAMRA 8/3/2001. There were only four brewpubs (brewing Victuallers) brewing in 1974 when CAMRA published its first *Good Beer Guide*. They were 'The Old Swan' in Netherton, Dudley, the 'All Nations' in Madeley, Telford, the 'Three Tuns' in Bishops Castle, south Shropshire and the 'Blue Anchor' in Helston, Cornwall.

2   Walton. J.K. and Walum. J. (eds) *Leisure in Britain 1780-1939*. MUP 1983. p.2. and Waller P.J. *Town, City and Nation England 1850-1914*. OUP 1983. pp.10/11. Quoted in Jennings. P. *The Public House in Bradford 1770-1970*. Keele 1995. p.2.

3   Burnett. J. *Liquid Pleasures – Beer*. Routledge. 1999. pp.112-113.

4   Mathias. P. *The Brewing Industry in England 1700-1830*. CUP 1959. p.xxii.

5   Mathias. P. 1959. p.xxii.

6   Gourvish. T. & Wilson. R. *The British Brewing Industry 1830-1980*. CUP 1994. pp.267-8.

Beer and the Brewing Process

THE PROCESS by which beer is brewed has remained virtually constant throughout history. This account is based on the pamphlets produced by three nineteenth century brewers and the stages they describe would have been equally recognisable to those who brewed two hundred years before them and those two centuries later.

The traditional ingredient used in the brewing of beer is malt, but before it can be used, the malt is crushed or ground, to form a grist. The crushed malt is then transferred to the mashtun.[1] Mashing is the action by which malt grains are stirred in hot liquor (water) so that the grains become, 'Completely wetted; [with] care being taken that all clots or balls are broken in pieces, otherwise malt within them [will] remain dry, and of course yield nothing to the water'.[2]

The mashtun is a round wooden vessel with a false or moveable bottom fixed about an inch above the real bottom. The false bottom consists of a number of plates.

There are a myriad of small holes in the false bottom and this allows the liquor to percolate through the grain into the space between the two floors and prevents the malt grains from clogging up the plumbing taking wort (sweet unfermented liquid) away to the copper. The provision of a false bottom also makes it easy to clean after each brew.[3]

In modern breweries the 'mashing' is done mechanically, but in the past this was achieved by manually stirring with a 'mashing rule' or oar.

Malt Storage: Sacks in 1975 and bulk silo in 2012.

6am: The start of mashing. c1975.   *Adding hops to the copper. c1975.*

If done manually the process was labour-intensive and in London in particular, Irish labourers, through their efficient working practice became specialists at the job.[4] Stirred, the mash is then allowed to stand allowing the soluble starch contained in the malt to be converted by enzymes to maltose.[5] When the wort is run off into the copper the contents of the mashtun are sprayed continually with hot liquor, allowing it to permeate through the mash, washing further 'extract from the malt'.

Coppers vary in both shape and size depending on the brewery. Once in the copper, hops are added to the wort and boiled. At the end of boiling the contents of the copper is run into the hopback, a large vessel with a false bottom used to separate the wort from the hops.[6] The wort being too hot to begin fermentation is allowed to cool. This is done in the flat cooler, a very large shallow vessel with raised edges. In nineteenth century breweries, these were placed in 'some airy situation' so that cooling took place as quickly as possible, but to ensure that the required drop in

Racking beer into casks. c1975.

temperature could be achieved reliably, irrespective of weather conditions, the wort was passed over the refrigerators, a system of pipes carrying a constant flow of cold water which through heat exchange brought the wort down to the required temperature.[7]

Once cooled, the wort passes into the Fermenting Vat (or gyle-tun), a deep round or square vessel, in which it is mixed with yeast (also referred to as 'balm') so that fermentation can begin. This takes several days before the process is complete. The final stage of the process before racking the beer into casks is cleansing, by which the yeast is removed from the beer.

Notes

1   Bushnan. J.S. *Burton and its Beer*. 1853. Ch.VI p.132.
2   Ham. J. *The theory and Practice of Brewing from Malted and Unmalted Corn.* 1829. 'Mashing'.
3   Ham. J. 1829. 'Mashing'.
4   Ham. J. 1829. 'Mashing'.
    Bushnan. J.S. 1853. p.133.
    Mathias. P. *The Brewing Industry in England 1700-1830*. CUP. 1959. p.38.
5   Monckton. H.A. *The History of English Ale and Beer*. Bodley Head. 1966. p.19.
6   Hawkes. S.M. *The Swan Brewery, Walham Green*. c1850. p.12.
    Bushnan. J.S. p.134.
    Ham. J. 1829. 2. 'Boiling'.
7   Bushnan. J.S. 1853. p.134.

Photographs taken at the Hook Norton Brewery between 1975 and 2012.

Notes on Terms

Weights, measures and money

The traditional British monetary system was based on pounds (£), shillings (s) and pence (d). Twelve pence made a shilling and there were twenty shillings to the pound. A penny was comprised of two halfpennies (ha'pennies) or four farthings. In February 1971 this changed with the introduction of decimal currency.

Throughout this book I have retained the use of pounds, shillings and pence to record monetary transactions. No decimal equivalents have been given as the relative values of, for instance a 10 shilling note (10/- or 10s) would not be accurately represented by its decimal equivalent 50p. This is reflected in the table below which shows the values of ten shillings at twenty five year periods between 1850 and 1975 based on the value of 50p in 2007.

1850	1875	1900	1925	1950	1975
£41.19	£33.78	£38.79	£20.44	£12.35	£3.02

Source: www.measuringworth.com *(using RPI)*

Similarly I have used imperial measurements of weight when describing quantities of raw materials used in the brewing process. Quantities of malt are expressed in terms of the number of bushels or quarters used in the mashing process, with eight bushels making a quarter (qtr).

Cask Sizes

Butt: 108 gallons, Puncheon: 72 gallons, Hogshead: 54 gallons
Barrel: 36 gallons, Kilderkin: 18 gallons, Firkin: 9 gallons, Pin: 4½ gallons

'Charles made his way to the bar.
"Pint o' Hook Norton" he ordered.'

'Kissing Christmas Goodbye'. Agatha Raisin
Cotswold Murder Mysteries (M C Beaton)

Chapter 1
The Business of Brewing

John Harris c1824-1887 (HNBC).

The Move to Hook Norton

There has been malting in the Scotland End area of Hook Norton for several hundred years, supplying the village with malt for its brewing needs. Of those who have plied this trade, John Harris is the best known, but until recently there has been no convincing explanation as to why he came and set up business in the village. It has been assumed that he arrived in Hook Norton sometime during 1849 and began brewing, with his widowed mother providing the working capital, but this was not how it happened.[1] His arrival in the village was not quite as triumphant as this premise suggests and it would take the intervention of fate, in the form of the tubercle bacilli and the death of a cousin before John Harris could establish himself during the final weeks of 1846.

The catalogue of events that eventually brought him to Hook Norton began when his cousin James and his wife moved to the village from Deddington with their children. James was a yeoman farmer and in 1841 had land on 'Faint Hill'.[2] Perhaps looking for a more substantial holding Harris acquired the farm and maltings in Scotland End, securing the deal in June 1845.[3]

Sadly his tenure of the farm was short and lasted little more than a year. Early in 1846 James was 'certified' as having phthisis, now an archaic term, but then used to describe the degenerative illness, consumption, which we now recognise as pulmonary tuberculosis. James died nine months later on 21st October and was buried in the Baptist burial ground three days later. James was 41 years old.

Within a fortnight of his death, the executors of his Will instructed the Banbury auctioneers, Salter and Williams, to place an advertisement in the Banbury Guardian for the sale of all his farm livestock and harvested crops.

> To be sold by auction by Salter and Williams on Friday November 13th on the premises of the late James Harris. The valuable flock of half-bred Lambs, short horned cattle, draught and nag horses, pigs, rick of wheat, quantity of wheat, thrashed rick of barley, straw to be spent, rick of prime hay,

two oak timber trees felled last season, farming implements
and other effects.

    The above stock will be found to be clean, sound, young
and healthy. Corn and hay well harvested, without rain and
the produce of good land. The sale will commence with the
lambs at Half past twelve-o-clock.

The sale took place 23 days after James's death. Tantalisingly, John
Harris's presence is absent from the documentation relating to his
cousin's illness and subsequent demise. Whether John came to Hook
Norton to help out on the farm during his cousin's final months or made
known his interests in the farm is unknown. Neither is it known on what
terms he rented the farm, but the speed with which the executors
instructed the auctioneers to expedite the sale of James Harris's farm
stock suggests that they had a tenant waiting to move in.

    John Harris was twenty one when he took over the farm and maltings
during the final weeks of 1846 and there appears to have been no
hostility to his arrival.[4] He was the youngest son of Henry and Elizabeth
Harris. The family lived in the small hamlet of Chilson, near
Chadlington, six miles south of Chipping Norton.[5] John had three older

Chilson.

siblings, sisters Ann and Mary, and a brother, Henry. The family were farmers and when his father died in July 1843, the running of the family farm fell to John and his older brother Henry. His cousin's death provided John with the opportunity to begin his own business. When information was collected during the final weeks of 1846 for the following year's edition of the Post Office Trade Directory, John Harris had already established himself as the village maltster. Within four years, he held the monopoly on malt production in Hook Norton and was trading as a maltster and farmer.[6]

Harris's business activities were centred on farming and malt production, yet the nature of much of it was seasonal. Information gleaned from later documents suggests that he was probably involved in mixed farming, having some cattle, pigs and growing cereal crops, with horses providing the motive power. Barley grown through the summer months was malted during the winter. His own, and barley bought in from other local farmers, supplied his and local malting needs. With village communities at Sibford, Swalcliffe, Tadmarton and Bloxham all supporting their own maltsters, the relatively isolated position of Hook Norton meant that Harris's market, supplying 'home brewers' was probably restricted to the immediate village, outlying farms and the smaller nearby villages of Swerford and Wigginton. Although few contemporary papers survive from this period, the 1856 Brewing Book shows that he employed pale malts in most of his brewing, using dark malt only for Porter.

We can only speculate why John Harris added brewing to his business portfolio; the most common way of entering the brewing trade was through dealing in brewer's raw materials or associated businesses. William Tetley of Leeds was a maltster, wine and brandy merchant and brewing victualler. The profits amassed from this business provided the capital for him to move into wholesale brewing. Gales Brewery began when Richard Gale, a corn merchant, purchased the "Ship and Bell" in Horndean, Hampshire, with its associated brewing facilities in 1847 and set up in business as a brewer. Cobbs' of Margate and Deal were contract brewers in naval ports, but began in business as brewing victuallers and may have entered brewing via their malting business. Others entered the brewing business because their trade brought them into contact with brewers. William Bass, for example, began as a carting contractor, moving casks of beer in Burton, before becoming a brewer in 1777. Harris's entry into the brewing trade was a natural extension of his farming and malting business and the step from occasional cottage brewer to wholesale brewer was not large, a matter of scale of production and an extension to his business activities in a way that offered him the possibility of all the year round commercial activity.[7]

The family oral tradition handed down by the members of the Harris-Clarke family, suggests John Harris started brewing in 1849. In more recent times, this tradition was reaffirmed by the late Bill Clarke who was quite adamant that '*they*' had said he started brewing in 1849. Such tradition undoubtedly came from Bill's parents and uncle, themselves all members of John Harris's close family and it is most likely that the information came from John Harris himself and has since been perpetuated by the family.[8]

It has also been suggested more recently that commercial brewing began in 1856.[9] This is based on an entry in the first surviving brewing book dated November 24th 1856. Being the first brew in the book, and being numbered one, indicated the commencement of commercial brewing, but this argument cannot be sustained. Harris's Stock Book for the period 1855-1879 provides detailed information about quantities of beer sold both monthly and annually during 1855. The entries for 1855 represent the first information about John Harris's business and suggest he had been involved in commercial brewing for several years prior. Other records suggest an intermediate date for the commencement of commercial brewing. In the census return for 1851, John Harris described himself as a 'Maltster and Farmer of 52 acres and employing two labourers'. During the same year he supplied Gardener's Trade Directory for Oxfordshire with the same information, reaffirming he was a maltster. The directory was published the following year. When in 1900 the Prospectus for the Share Issue for the new company was published, it contained the following sentence, 'This Company [HNBC]

has been formed to take over and carry on the old-established concern…
founded by the late John Harris in the year 1851.' The same information
was repeated in the Banbury Guardian in 1902 marking the opening of
the 'new brewery'. These statements, however, contradict John Harris's
own advertising through the Trade Directories and it seems more likely
that his commercial enterprise dates from 1852 when he provided
information for the new edition of Lascelles & Co's Directory and
Gazetteer of Oxfordshire. His updated entry reads, 'John Harris
common brewer and maltster'. Maybe not coincidently, he also
purchased the farm site during September that year for £350 from John
Parish, acting in his role as an executor of the Will of James Harris. The
purchase being funded possibly by his mother's money, as the oral
tradition suggests.[10]

Based on the available information found in the brewery deeds, the
family oral tradition, the evidence from two trade directories and a
census return, it is now possible to suggest a process by which Harris
made the transition from maltster and farmer to common or wholesale
brewer. His first business was malting and farming, but was probably
involved in small scale brewing to provide beer for his own domestic use
and the needs of his farm workers, especially at harvest. No details of
Harris's early brewing survive, but the following account describing how
a Staffordshire farmer, brewing once a month, went about his business
gives some insight into what life on Harris's farm in Scotland End may
have been like.

> You'd have friends and neighbours dropping in every day and
> people'd say 'Would you like a jug of beer?' Always a jug, never
> a glass. There were two jugs always kept for beer, one was the
> quart jug and the other was the pint jug. Nobody had less than
> a pint and the majority had a quart. The workmen, they
> always took a bottle of beer each into the fields every morning,
> and a bottle every dinner time, and they were those square
> bottles that held about a pint and a third…He brewed once a
> month, in the old furnace they did the washing in, the copper.

It was a small furnace that was in, and he had a larger one put in that'd hold forty gallons. By the time it boiled away, it was down to thirty six gallons. The barrel was 36 gallons. That's how much he brewed at a time… He filled the boiler with water in the evening time, about 6 o'clock, as soon as we'd finished the milking, and he boiled it. It'd take about two hours to boil, and then he'd put it on top of the malt in what he called the mash tub.

This mash tub was simply a large barrel with the top or bottom knocked out of it. It held about 50 [or] 60 gallons. That was bagged up he called it, covered up for the night to keep warm. Then in the morning as soon as he'd milked, he drew the water and malt mixture off, and put it in the boiler…then he added some hops and whatever sugar he added and it was boiled…that was boiled from about 8 o'clock to about 12 o'clock, all morning…well it boils up like milk, so what he did, he had two buckets…when it boiled he would take a bucketful out and put it on one side. When it began to boil up again he'd take another bucketful out and tip the first bucketful back in to cool it…he used to mind the beer himself…he had to mind the beer, in case it boiled over…if it boiled over there was a row and we were all for it.

While he were minding, he took the dregs, the wet brewer's grains out of the mash tub, washed the tub and put it ready for the beer. Then at about 12 o'clock, he would take the beer out of the boiler and cool it down the old milk refrigerator till it was reasonably warm…and then it was put into the cleansed mash tub and the barm that's used to work it added…It'd stay in the mash tub three days. After that it settled and he drew it off into the barrel with a big wooden tap…he didn't seal the barrel straight away because very often it was still working…but after two or three days he would seal the barrel…and that would last a month.[11]

Maybe Harris also had visitors who, having enjoyed a jug of his beer, became his customers, buying beer from him from time to time, until in 1849, as family tradition suggests, the demand was such that he began seriously to consider brewing commercially. By brewing on a semi-commercial basis, he was able to evaluate whether there was a sustainable market that would allow him to brew beer on a full time basis. By late 1851 he was convinced that a profitable wholesale brewing business was possible and agreed to buy the farm a year later to secure ownership of the site.

Site plans of John Harris's farm show that his first brewhouse was situated between two cottages. One served as a store and the other as a dwelling house.[12] These premises fronted the public road, being situated approximately where the present brewery and the remainder of Harris's 1872 brewery now stand. The malthouse, with its own well, stood at right angles to these buildings.

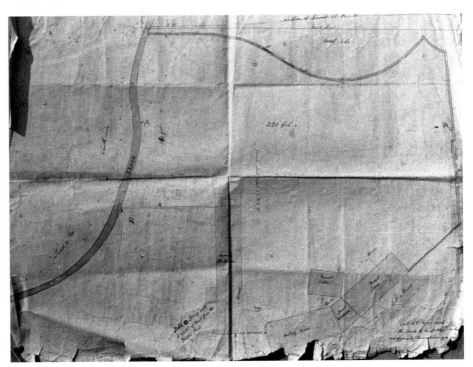

Plan of the site John Harris bought for £350. c1846 (HNBC).

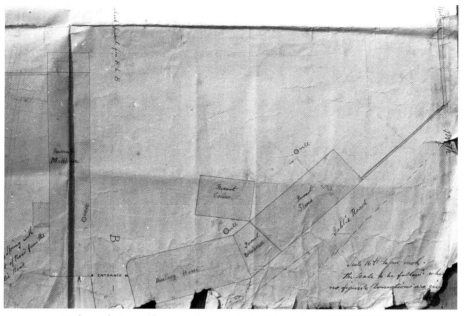

Enlarged view of layout of the main buildings in c1846 (HNBC).

The passing of the Beer Act in 1830 signalled the beginning of a period of free trade that was to last for fifty years. The Act ended restrictive licensing of public houses and a new type of drinking house was created – the beerhouse.[13]

As part of the Act, the Chancellor of the Exchequer removed all excise duty from beer while leaving that on malt and hops unchanged. The measures of the Beer Act provided Harris with a financial incentive, for although he was taxed on all the malt he produced, his beer was free of duty and after costs were deducted, he stood to make a net increase in his overall profit.[14]

From the 1850s, skilled workers benefited from a rise in real wages and it has been suggested that this fuelled an increase in beer consumption.[15] Harris benefited from this increased demand and from 1861 demand for his beer grew significantly and continued to do so for the next fourteen years. Tastes in beer changed with the growing popularity of mild beers. Porter beer had been the drink of the eighteenth century but by the mid nineteenth century demand for it had fallen dramatically. This change suited the smaller brewer, like Harris, as mild beers needed less time to stand before being sold and as a consequence less capital was tied up in stock.[16] John Harris took advantage of these new trends and mild beers figured prominently in his sales for the first thirty years of trading.

When John Harris began commercial brewing, his business consisted of himself and two labourers. With such a simple business structure Harris's day to day instructions would have probably been given by word of mouth. With Harris himself as the focus of a day's work, the two labourers would have been directed to work in whichever area of his venture they were needed.[17]

Frances Elizabeth Chaundy (HNBC).

The growing success of his business is not only reflected in the sale of barrels of beer, but also through Harris's census returns. In 1861 John and his wife Frances Elizabeth and their six month old son, John Henry, were living in the cottage adjacent to the brewery. They had a domestic servant, twenty year old Ann Cross. John styled himself simply as a brewer and maltster and employed Richard West as his clerk to look after the paperwork.

At this stage John Harris appears to have been actively involved in the daily running of the business. To cope with the growing trade Harris employed his first traveller/drayman, Richard Howse. A decade later Harris still ran the farm and described himself as a 'Brewer, Maltster, Farmer of 22 acres, employing travellers, a clerk, brewer, 9 men and [a] boy' having apparently sold thirty acres of land to fund the expansion of his brewery. He had become a major employer in the village with most of his employees drawn from the immediate area. At some point before the 1871 census return, Harris offered employment to his twenty year old nephew Walter Bowl and towards the end of the decade he also took on his sister's other younger son, Alban Clarke. Bowl and Clarke were half brothers and worked together in the brewhouse as 'brewer's assistants'. Not only was the business flourishing but his family had also grown. John Henry was now ten and had two sisters, Frances Elizabeth and Mary.

Harris was 56 years old in 1881. In addition to his thriving brewing and malting activities, he now farmed 145 acres, employed sixteen men and two boys, but only seven of them, including his two nephews, appear to have been living in Hook Norton. With an enlarged workforce and increased sales, the structure of the business became more complex, but the basic 'functional structure' [18] remained simple. This allowed Harris to assume a managerial role and make the executive decisions, while delegating responsibility to those working in each of the five different departments. In 1871 Thomas Edgington[19], had been the clerk, dealing with the paperwork but ten years later George Groves had replaced him. Groves was a significant addition to the work force, initially described as a 'Brewer's clerk', he rose to become the Company Secretary, working

John Harris and his family (HNBC).

for the brewery for more than fifty years. With Bowl and Alban Clarke, assisted by John Wyton working in the brewery overseeing production, John Turvey and William Cox were found, respectively in the cellars and the maltings and Richard Howse, the traveller/drayman was employed to work from the stables.[20]

The success of the business gave John Harris the opportunity to move from the cottage adjacent to the brewery to a larger property in Scotland End, more in keeping with his position as a successful brewer. His success, however, came at a price. During 1875 he was diagnosed with 'adult on-set' or as it is now known, type 2 *diabetes mellitus*. Diabetes is not a single disease, but a syndrome with many causes and was first described by the ancient Egyptians in 1500BC. There is no record of how the condition affected Harris, or without the modern understanding and treatment, he was able to control the levels of sugar in his blood. The preferred treatment of nineteenth century physicians was to prescribe a low carbohydrate diet, which controlled both feelings of thirst and excessive urination. It may be, however, as a brewer, that he used a method where urine was added to a flask and fermented with a piece of yeast. After twenty four hours the specific gravity of the liquid was taken; the amount of glucose in the blood being the difference in specific gravity before and after fermentation x 0.23.[21]

The business after John Harris

John Harris died on the 16th November 1887. His death was simply recorded on page 5 of the Banbury Guardian along with other recent deaths in the area. He was 63 years old. The management of his estate was left to his executors, as trustees of his Will, rather than directly to his son John Henry.[22] The decision appears to reflect Harris's understanding of the situation; that his son's interests were in farming, rather than brewing. To maintain the continuity of brewing the trustees were directed by Harris's Will, dated 21st October 1887, to ensure that,

> no sale shall be made of any part of my real or personal Estate used or employed in the carrying on of my business of a Brewer and Maltster and Farmer as long as [the] business can be profitably carried on…in such name and by means of such managers and agents as they shall think fit and to employ therein the whole or any part of the capital which shall be employed therein at my decease.

Even though John Henry's interests were in farming, it was his father's expressed wish that his son should be employed in assisting with the running of the business at an agreed salary and have the first option of purchasing it at a 'fair and reasonable price'. A codicil, attached to the will, written a week before Harris's death, further authorised the trustees to manage the business and acquire as and where necessary licensed properties to enhance the business. The timing of the Will and its Codicil, giving specific details regarding the future of the business, suggests that Harris was probably involved in discussions with his family outlining his intentions, to provide a *holding situation*, by which the business could continue until a satisfactory permanent arrangement for its future was agreed.[23]

Harris left his trustees charged with the overall strategic management of the business. Actual day to day decisions involving the running of the brewery were the responsibility of Alban Clarke, who became 'Managing Brewer'. His responsibilities included not only brewing, but the overseeing of the whole process, from the purchase of barley, malting, mashing, fermentation and racking and distribution. It was during this period that Alban Clarke began a period of self-education, widening his knowledge of the brewing business by purchasing the latest brewing text books and taking the Brewer's Journal.

The trustees of Harris's Will were his widow, Frances Elizabeth, his son John Henry, his brother-in-law John Chaundy and nephew Henry Harris. The trustees were not passive managers during their period in charge. They were responsible for the purchase of two licensed properties, and for commissioning three building projects to improve facilities at the brewery. From the surviving documentary evidence from this period it appears that John Henry Harris acted as their representative in any business transaction as it is his name that appears on the legal documents for the purchase of The Gate Inn (1888) and Sun Inn (1891), bought for £905 and £800 respectively. Similarly when quotations and contracts were drawn up for building work to be carried out by Alfred Groves of Milton under Wychwood [24], it was to John Henry that the papers were addressed. It was he who signed the contracts for additions to the maltings (March 1894) and who received the plans for the alterations to the stables. Although not involved in the daily running of the brewery, John Henry adopted his father's title of 'brewer, maltster and farmer' and during the early years of the twentieth century he acted as the company's representative on the Banbury and District Licensed Trades Association and was one of the vice-presidents of the association.

The business was run by the Trustees for a period of eight years following John Harris's death, the brewery still carried the founder's name and the only discernable difference was that company correspondence was now signed on behalf of 'John Harris Exors'.

A series of apparently unrelated events during the last decade of the nineteenth century give some insight into the process by which a permanent solution to the long term future of the management of the brewery was reached with the incorporation of the Hook Norton Brewery Company Limited in 1900. John Harris had not anticipated that circumstances would place Alban Clarke in the position of sole 'managing brewer', as he had hoped that both his nephews, Walter Bowl and Alban Clarke, would 'continue to give the same assistance as Managers [to the] business, which they have for a long time given' and as family members, they were to be paid a mutually agreed annual salary.[25] Between them, the half brothers had gained considerable practical experience, and the reference to them as 'managers' suggests that Harris had delegated an increasing degree of responsibility to them as time passed, so ensuring continuity in the future management of the business, but the partnership did not last.

During John Harris's life, both Bowl and Clarke had lived at their uncle's house, but by 1891, Bowl had moved out and was living in the village with his 76 year old mother Ann, a woman of independent means, and he was working as the senior 'Brewery Commercial', a position he held for a number of years. There is no documented explanation for Bowl's change in employment and we can only speculate on the reasons for his departure. It is also not clear when Bowl ceased working for the brewery, but by 1899 he appears to have retired and is listed in Trade Directories as one of the 'Private Residents' living in Hook Norton.

Bowl's departure from the brewhouse left a significant gap, with the day to day running of the business left to Alban Clarke. This provided him with the opportunity to play the leading role in fashioning the future of the Company. There is no direct evidence that John Henry Harris and Alban Clarke had devised a 'master plan' for the future of the brewery, but subsequent events do suggest that the move towards incorporation was planned.

In 1895 there was a fundamental change in the status of the business. On 1st October that year, at the High Court of Justice – Chancery Lane, legal proceedings were brought by John Henry Harris, Henry Harris and Alban Clarke, against Frances Elizabeth Harris (the younger), her sister Mary Ann and their mother.[26] The context within which these proceedings were set is unclear, as the papers pertaining to the case have been lost. The only known surviving documentation is a summary of the outcome found in the brewery archives and conveyances resulting from the case, which are held with the brewery deeds.

The outcome, however, is clear. In his Will, John Harris instructed that his Trustees should, after paying his 'funeral expenses and testamentary expenses and debts and legacies bequeathed...invest the residue of the said moneys in any investments authorised by law for trust funds... [and] pay the income thereof to my Wife during her life'. After her death their two daughters were to be paid 'one equal fourth part' of the trust fund, 'together with interest at the rate of Four pounds per centum per year', with the remainder being paid to his son John Henry.[27]

For John Henry Harris to fulfil his father's wishes and purchase the business it was necessary for him first to re-negotiate his mother's position as 'beneficial owner' of her husband's estate. She had a 'life interest in [his] real and personal estate' and a suitable alternative was needed to guarantee her an annual income.

The ensuing agreement involved her three children agreeing to pay an annuity of £400 and in return, 'all income, profits and annual production ...to accrue from the estate of John Harris' were conveyed to them. This included the brewery, maltings and the farm. With the legal status of the brewery resolved John Henry came to an agreement with his sisters 'as [joint] beneficial owners', to mortgage their third share of the business to him. The agreements involved the sisters mortgaging their interests in the 'freehold hereditaments' – the Brewery and all the buildings concerned with its working 'to secure sums of £2,226/14/6, with interest'.

Following the legal settlement in 1895, and against a background of changing social and economic values, the strategic management of the business became the responsibility of John Henry Harris, his two sisters and Alban Clarke. The name of the company was changed from 'John Harris Exors' to 'J.Harris & Co'. As Managing Brewer, Alban Clarke continued to take responsibility for the day to day running of the brewery as well as monitoring the company's financial situation.

The sale of casked beer had been the backbone of John Harris's business and he had recorded the sale of beer in terms of the number of barrels sold. From 1892 Alban Clarke introduced a new system, recording the sale of casks in terms of the revenue generated. The number of barrels sold between 1887 and 1896 increased by 61.7% and from 1892 to 1900 cash from the sale of casks increased by 152%, compared with a national increase in output of 32.2% for the same period.

Sales between 1887 and 1900

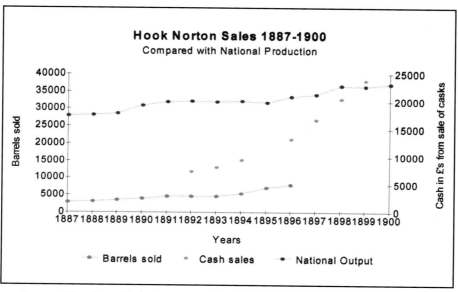

Source: Monckton. H.A. A History of English Ale and Beer. 1966. Appendix D. HNBC Archive: Stock Books 1876-97, Sales Ledger 1892-1911.

A consistent feature of Clarke's management was his cost analysis of processes or parts of the business in a move towards greater efficiency or savings. In 1891 he analysed the 'amount of trade done' in the period since his uncle's death. His analysis showed an increase in 'business done' of £3,145/19/4¾d, but the company's book debts for the same period also showed an increase, up by 38%. The balance sheets for the following two years are not available, but Clarke collated figures for the sales of cask beer. In 1892 and 1893 these differed by only one pound in the respective yearly totals, but the following year cask sales rose by £1,403. This trend continued for a decade, but between 1895/6 and to the turn of the century the annual increase in cask ale sales began to decline. This fall continued throughout the first decade of the new century, except for the years 1900/01 and 1903/04 when cask sales rose by almost £3,000. Even though the sale of cask beer contributed a diminishing proportion of the total yearly income, it continued to be a major source of income for the brewery, although by 1910 sales had fallen since 1892 by nearly 20%.

A change in the system of accounting was introduced by the new management in 1895 to synchronise the brewery's financial year with the traditional agricultural year. This ran from the 1st October to 30th September so as to coincide with the availability of new raw materials. The company balance sheet, favoured by John Harris, was abandoned in favour of the 'Gross and Nett Profit Accounts' prepared for the Surveyor of Taxes. These provide information not only about gross and net profit, but also details of stocks of beer and materials in hand, interest on mortgages, and costs incurred in the general running of the business.

The London firm of Messrs Hoskins and Son were entrusted with preparing of the brewery's trading accounts. These accounts showed during the last five years of the nineteenth century, the total yearly sales grew by almost 74%. Initially annual net profits rose almost by three fold, but then, and for the following three years, profits fluctuated. While overall sales continued to grow, the annual increase in sales began to flag. In 1896/7 sales had increased by 33% in the year, but in the following two years these fell to just over 20% and for 1899/1900 it was down to only 0.6%.

By the turn of the century the company no longer relied solely on cask beer for its revenue, as bottled beers and wines and spirits began to make a growing contribution to the business. Bottled beers were introduced during 1892 and represented a small, but significant contribution to the total beer sales, replacing the stone jars used during the nineteenth century. The first decade of the new century saw the sales of bottled beer increased by 105%, although this represented only about 7% of the annual yearly total. From 1903/04 sales of bottled beer increased by nearly 80% and were worth £1,967/18/4d in 1911, while all other sources of income reflected a downward trend.

With the growing popularity of bottled beer, the Hook Norton Brewery moved to extend the range of such beers available in its public houses. This was achieved by buying quantities from other local brewers. Entries in the 'Goods Purchased' ledgers for 1904 show the company bought in Dark Stout from Hitchman's Brewery in Chipping Norton. Quantities were relatively small; four or six dozen bottles, specifically for the Reindeer Inn in Banbury. In July the following year the brewery began buying bottled Guinness, on a more regular basis, also from Hitchman's. The usual order was six dozen bottles every fortnight, but in 1906 this was changed and nine of the ten orders placed for bottled Guinness were for four, rather than six dozen bottles. A year later, of the eleven orders placed with Hitchman's, seven were for six dozen bottles, but the Reindeer was no longer the sole destination for sale, as Guinness began to appear in the company's other public houses. With trade declining during 1908 and 1909 the four dozen order became standard. Interestingly, the price of bottled Guinness from Hitchman's between 1900 and September 1913 remained unchanged at 6/8d for four dozen and ten shillings for six dozen.

From the middle of September 1913 the Hook Norton Brewery began importing barrels of Dark Stout directly from the Guinness Brewery in Dublin for bottling. Initially two barrels were sent on the 16th September and again on the 8th October at a cost of £2/1/7d each. Thereafter a regular order of one barrel approximately every fortnight was sent until the outbreak of the First World War. Stout destined for

Hook Norton came via Bristol, where Guinness had long had an agency, being transported by rail to the village for bottling at the brewery. The single barrel order to Hook Norton was superseded by deliveries of hogsheads during the summer of 1941. Rolling these larger casks up to the bottling plant proved to be 'such a labour'. Stout continued to be supplied from Dublin until 1942, after which it came from Guinness's Park Royal plant.

In the national context bottling beer was in its infancy before the First World War. The process was slow, even with machinery. At Hook Norton bottling was done by hand and was a labour intensive task. The financial returns, however, made it worthwhile for brewers to continue production, as sales at Hook Norton demonstrate. After the First World War, sales of bottled beer increased at a faster rate and by 1939 a third of all beer consumed nationally was bottled.[28]

Bottled in Hook Norton.

Another new element added to the business was the wine and spirits trade. From 1st January 1897 the company's licensees were informed by George Groves that they should in future order all their wines and spirits from the brewery. Initially sales of wines and spirits showed an increase, but by 1911 sales had fallen by 8%. The trade was worth on average £3,549 a year between 1900 and 1911, but followed the overall trend of decreasing sales. Another source of income was the rent from the farm and licensed properties owned by the company. Like the drink sales, rents showed a small increase during the first five years of the twentieth century but by the end of the decade they too had fallen.

The New Company

When moves to establish the Hook Norton Brewery Company were instigated in 1900, it was Harris, his sisters and Clarke who were cited as the vendors in the sale of 'J.Harris & Co' to the newly created company which came into being on the 1st April 1900. The company was established with three directors; these were John Henry Harris, Alban Clarke and William Toy, a partner in the firm of solicitors Wilkins & Toy from Chipping Norton. Toy became the company Chairman.

During May the Directors were busy establishing the business. The company seal was ordered and solicitors were instructed to prepare the conveyance and other documents necessary for the acquisition of the freehold brewery site from John Harris & Co. At the same meeting, agreements were also drawn up for the new company to engage five key employees, George Groves, company secretary, John Gibbins, assistant brewer, and three travellers, Messrs Stratford, Brotheridge and Wilkes. It was not, however, until the 21st August 1900 that the conveyancing of the 'transfer of business from John Harris & Co to the Hook Norton Brewery Company' was completed.

Earlier in July, John Henry Harris, his sisters Frances Elizabeth and Mary Ann, and Alban Clarke met with William Toy. It was agreed that the objective of the Hook Norton Brewery Company was 'to acquire and take over as a going concern' the business of John Harris & Co. The business was to be acquired at the agreed valuation of £76,000, including all the existing liabilities, mortgages and debts. The following week, on the 13th July, the three directors met again. Having been informed that the company had been incorporated the previous day the meeting moved onto other business and appointed George Groves as Company Secretary at a salary of £120 a year and Messrs Gillett & Co, in Chipping Norton as the brewery's bankers.[29] The meeting then turned to the company's Prospectus for the proposed Share issue to raise a nominal capital of £52,000. The document was approved, signed by the directors, and George Groves was authorised to issue the Prospectus. The Share capital was divided into two issues. The first and larger issue was for 2,700 – 5½% Cumulative £10 Preference Shares, to raise £27,000. A dividend was to be paid half yearly and would take priority over the Ordinary Shares. The offer was opened to subscription on the 19th July 1900 for three days only.

In preparing the Prospectus for this first Share issue, the company commissioned Messrs. Thomas, Peyer & Miles, Brewery Valuers of London, to present an 'independent survey and valuation of the property… and report on past trading'. This assessed the company's profits for the years ending 30th September, 1898 and 1899 and concluded that the profits for these years were £4,712/14/8d and £4,155/5/1d respectively. This apparent decline in profits and the fall in beer and malt sales were explained by Messrs. Thomas, Peyer & Miles,

> The decline in profits for the past twelve months is more apparent than real, since, notwithstanding that the Beer Sales increased by 17%, the extensive building operations which were already in progress, necessitated the purchase of a considerable quantity of beer from other Brewers, and the manufacturing profit thereon was consequently lost.

At the beginning of August 1900, William Toy and John Henry Harris met to allot the 2,700 Preference Shares in response to the applications they had received. An examination of the 148 applicants shows that the company did not just attract people in the immediate vicinity. There were applications from Alnwick, Birmingham, Brackley, Cheltenham, Coventry, Dorchester, Dudley, Leamington Spa, London and Stratford upon Avon. Applications came from farmers, shopkeepers, tradesmen, bank and insurance workers, engineers, the clergy, solicitors, teachers and nurses, including the matron of the County Hospital in Dorchester. The distribution of shares varied. Ten percent of the subscribers bought just one or two shares, but over half bought either 5, 10 or 20 shares. Farmers and Gentlemen, tended to purchase larger number of shares, typically 50, although a farmer from Middleton Stoney, near Bicester purchased 100 shares.

The largest single shareholder was the company Chairman, William Toy, with a total investment of 239 shares, bought in two separate applications for 130 and 109 shares. He was not the only person from the Hook Norton Brewery to invest in these Shares. John Henry Harris

THE HOOK NORTON BREWERY COMPANY,
LIMITED,
HOOK NORTON, OXFORDSHIRE.

Incorporated under the Companies' Acts, 1862 to 1898.

SHARE CAPITAL - - £52,000,

Divided into:—

2,700 5½ per cent. Cumulative Preference Shares of £10 each - £27,000
2,500 Ordinary Shares of £10 each - - - - - - - £25,000

£52,000

The whole of the Ordinary Shares will be taken by the Vendors or their nominees as fully paid up in part payment of the purchase money.

Issue of 2,700--5½ per cent. Cumulative £10 Preference Shares, payable as follows:—

£1 per Share on Application.
£4 ,, ,, on Allotment.
£5 ,, ,, on 18th August, 1900.

£10

The Preference Shares are entitled to a fixed Cumulative Preferential Dividend of 5½ per cent. per annum and rank both as to Dividend and Capital in priority to the Ordinary Shares.

The Dividends on the Preference Shares will be paid half-yearly, the first being calculated from the dates of payment of the respective instalments.

Directors:

WILLIAM TOY, Esq., Chipping Norton, *Chairman*.
JOHN HENRY HARRIS, Esq., Hook Norton, *Managing Director*.
ALBAN. ALFRED CLARKE, Esq., Hook Norton, *Managing Director*.

Bankers:

Messrs. GILLETT & CO., Chipping Norton.

Solicitors:

Messrs. WILKINS & TOY, Chipping Norton.

Auditors:

Messrs. THOMAS, PEYER & MILES, 2 Adelaide Place, London Bridge, London, E.C.
Messrs. HOSKINS & SON, 143, Cannon Street, London, E.C.

Secretary:

Mr. GEORGE GROVES.

Registered Offices:

THE BREWERY, Hook Norton.

Front page of the Hook Norton Brewery Company Prospectus: 1901 (HNBC).

bought 42, Alban Clarke had 10, George Groves bought 10 and John Gibbins, the assistant brewer had one.

The second Share Issue approved by the Board was for 2,500 Ordinary Shares of £10 each, which as part of the sale of John Harris & Co. were allotted to the Vendors, John Henry Harris, his two sisters and Alban Clarke. These shares were allocated in accordance with their limited liability in the company. This specified that Harris and his sisters Frances Elizabeth and Mary Ann should receive two seventh parts (714) and Alban Clarke one seventh (357), but in practice this was only roughly adhered to. John Henry Harris received 736 shares, his sisters 707 and 705 respectively and Alban Clarke 325.

In the summer of 1903 it was felt necessary to raise money to pay off a proportion of the company's mortgage debt brought about by the deaths of several of the company's mortgagees. A second issue of Preference Shares was ordered. The issue of 1,500 – 5½% B Cumulative Preference Shares 'ranked … after the 2,700 Preference Shares and in priority to the Ordinary Shares'. The full issue was, however, not offered for subscription. The Board deciding to offer only 750, with the proviso that the minimum subscription the company would accept before 'proceeding to allotment' was 200 shares.

The subscription opened on Thursday 14th May for seven days. Eight days later the Board met to discuss the number of applications received. Fifty two people had replied and taken up the full allocation of 750 shares. It was another twenty years later before the remaining 750 shares were issued.

The three-man Board of Directors assumed the responsibilities formerly exercised by the trustees. The day to day matters remained the responsibility of Clarke and Harris and this they split between them with Alban Clarke overseeing brewing and malting and John Henry taking responsibility for the horses, stables, and the farm. The arrangement of joint Managing Directors however, did not endure for long. At the end the first full year of trading, John Henry Harris resigned his position as Managing Director, but retained his place on the Board as a permanent director of the company.

Within the brewery itself a hierarchy can be found with workers identifying their specific job; 'assistant brewer, engine driver-stationary, cellarman and cooper'. Most, however, still referred to themselves as 'brewer's labourer' giving no indication of their roles in the brewing process. Some may have worked in the maltings rather than the brewery and during the summer there was work on the farm during haymaking and harvesting. Within the stables the information is more forthcoming. There are two different roles clearly identified, draymen who delivered beer and two horse keepers, whose job it was to look after the stables and the horses when they were not working. Interestingly the names of the three travellers do not appear in the Wages Book as they were employed on separate agreements and operated from the company offices.

The Structure of the Hook Norton Brewery Company Ltd in 1900

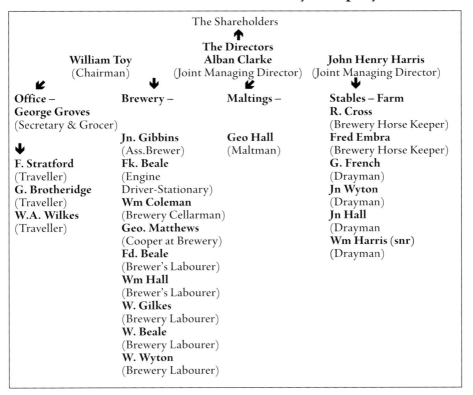

Source: HNBC Archive: Directors Meeting: Minutes 1900-1913. Wages Book 1895-1930.

By the end of the nineteenth century the British economy began to lose its vigour and the nation's reputation as the 'workshop of the world' was seriously threatened by economic activity in both Germany and the U.S.A, although this loss of vigour did not affect the brewing industry immediately.[30] In the five years before 1900, the number of standard barrels brewed nationally increased by more than three and a half million barrels,[31] but in the decade from 1899 to 1909 beer consumption fell by 14% in England and even in the good summer of 1908, there was no revival in demand for beer.

The reasons for the decline in trade were two fold. The first was a general problem. Changing living standards during the second half of the nineteenth century, contributed to the declining consumption of beer. The second was more specific; government intervention through legislation, namely the 1904 Licensing Act, concerned with compensation for the removal of redundant licences, and the 1907 Licensing Bill, eventually leading to the 1910 Finance Act.

Details of the 1907 Licensing Bill were made known towards the end of the year and introduced into the Commons the following May. The brewing industry was shaken to its foundations by the proposals, which it viewed as being imposed by 'a teetotal-ridden Government' acting out of malice. Winston Churchill saw it as 'a measure of plunder to satisfy political spite'. Its intention was to hasten the reduction of on-licences, with the threat of decreased compensation for licences that were refused, but the Bill carried the threat that the State would, after a period of fourteen years, impose a national Licence Committee which would issue licences based on the equivalent of their monopoly value. The Bill was presented in the Commons, where it was passed with handsome majorities on both its second and third readings; only for the Lords to reject it in November 1908. This gave the brewers some respite, but it was short lived as the Bill's measures became incorporated into the 1909 Budget.

In a budget to fund social reform, Lloyd George planned to raise £4 million by increasing the tax burden on the brewing industry. The cost of a brewing licence was increased from a basic £1 to a new tax collected at a rate of 12/- for every 50 barrels brewed beyond the first 100 barrels. Retail licences were trebled and duties on wines and spirits rose from 11/- to 14/9d. The Temperance movement gloated. Leif Jones, a Temperance M.P. confidently declared, 'while the Licensing Bill chastised the Trade with whips, the Chancellor would chastise it with scorpions'. Again the Lords rejected the provisions along with the rest of the Budget. A General Election was called in January 1910 to settle the constitutional crisis. The Government were returned and the budget was reintroduced and passed later that year.

As a result, a new Licensing Act was passed in 1910, consolidated the Acts of 1828 and 1904, but the swingeing clauses of the 1908 Bill were not included. Retail licences were doubled rather than trebled and brewers were able to challenge the rating values of their licensed properties on the grounds of diminished value because of the increased duty. Brewers, including the Hook Norton Brewery, took advantage of this dispensation and challenged the rating valuations of their public houses, arguing the value had been diminished by the additional duty. The brewing trade was in turmoil and many companies felt unable to declare an interim dividend and building work on pubs and breweries ceased. The Temperance threat of the 1907 Licensing Bill and the ensuing 1908 Budget measures, however, did not materialise to the extent brewers had originally feared.[32] Even so, many brewery companies felt unable to declare a dividend in 1910 and reported that the cost of the new taxes represented 60% of their earnings; in Hook Norton it was 75%.[33]

The response of the Directors of the Hook Norton Brewery to the imposition of higher rates of duty was, perhaps predictable. First, Alban Clarke wrote to the shareholders to explain the situation and request their support.

> On comparing the Balance Sheet with the one previously published you will see there has been a considerable falling off in trade when at the same time there has comparatively been a large increase in the amount of duty paid to the Government.

The Company have been compelled to raise the price of liquors to meet the extra burden and consequently there has been less consumption of Spirits. The disastrous summer too, has told seriously against the trade but the main cause of the depression and decline is to be found in the unreasonable taxation of the Brewing Industry threatened by the Budget and it is very evident that if legislation such as the present Finance Bill passes into law the Shareholders in Breweries will stand very little chance of receiving further income on the money invested by them in these securities, therefore it becomes the duty of those people to use every effort in their power to prevent such unfair and unjust measure being passed by this or any Parliament.

The Directors are doing everything in their power to make the business a success, but this cannot possibly be accomplished by them in these terrible times unless the Shareholders assist them by not only patronising the Brewery themselves, but also by using their influence with their friends.

Concerned by the possible impact of the proposed Licensing Bill, 'justly rejected' by the House of Lords, the Directors wrote to reassure their principal mortgagers, including Walter Bowl, that their investment was secure pointing out that 'the shareholders cannot claim a penny against the company unless all liabilities, which include mortgages have been discharged'.

A 5½% dividend was paid in 1909 on the Preference shares, but in such uncertain times, the Directors elected to be prudent. In 1910, (due to high taxation) and again in 1912 they declared that 'there has not been sufficient profit earned during the year' for a dividend to be paid. Only in 1911 could they recommend a dividend being paid on first Preference Shares and that at only 2½%.

In response to the mounting financial problems, the trading figures were regularly inspected and the management focussed on the parts of the business that were not performing satisfactorily. Cutting costs

The Reindeer Inn, Banbury (1975).

became a priority, a principle Alban Clarke had identified in his diary in 1900. The trading figures of agents and travellers came under particular scrutiny. Agencies were closed and it was decided that the Reindeer Inn in Banbury 'be offered to the Banbury Corporation for £4000 on consideration that the Corporation grant the company the premises on a lease on terms to be mutually agreed'. The deal did not materialise and only the interior of the Globe Room was sold off to Messrs Lenygon of London for £1000.

Smaller public houses were also disposed of and in February 1911 six were offered for sale, but other properties deemed to be more profitable were acquired. Cost cutting did not focus solely on the trade. The largest single contributor to annual expenditure, wages and salaries, accounted for on average more than a third of the expenditure each year. Ways to reduce the wage and salary bill were considered and in December 1910, Alban Clarke announced that 'it would be necessary to discharge some of the brewery workmen immediately after the Christmas holidays', but the scale of the intended redundancies is unclear. Only Busby, who acted as chauffeur, was informed, eventually 'that his services [would] not be required'.

The average number of those employed fell from 40 in 1908, to 35 in 1911, but the fortnightly totals show the number of men working varied throughout the year. There were months, like April, July and September when more men were employed than in other months of the year.

There was no restructuring of the men's wages in 1911 either, and rates of pay remained fairly constant with brewery workers like Frank and Fred Beale continuing to be paid 22/- and 20/- respectively a week, although the two office clerks were paid a bonus of two guineas each in recognition of 'extra work done' and their salaries were raised. Changes were made however, to the salaries and commission paid to travellers and agents, based on the principle that that they were 'remunerated in accordance with the value of the business to the Company'. A new formula for payments was devised allowing for a basic salary and percentage allowances for mileage, travelling expenses and commission.

It was not only the brewery workers who were threatened by cost cutting. Two old dray horses, Spot and another, were 'to be sold or otherwise disposed of forthwith' and the horse Sharper from Shipston was also to be 'sold at the earliest opportunity'. The purchase of new fermenting squares, urgently required in the brewery, was 'indefinitely' postponed and the Christmas list of gifts of beer and spirits to free houses was 'curtailed', with game substituted as an alternative which Alban Clarke's shooting parties could provide free of charge.

The Board were understandably concerned about the poor perform-ance of the company and in 1910 turned for help to Percy Flick, who had acted on their behalf for at least a decade as a valuer of licensed properties. He came from a brewing family, having worked for the family business in Banbury as an assistant to the maltster. Later he had set up in business on his own in the town as a property agent, advertising himself as a 'Public House Broker and Expert Licensed Victuallers Valuer'. It was in this latter role that his first recorded dealings with the Hook Norton Brewery occurred in 1899.[34]

Towards the end of 1910 Flick submitted a number of suggestions to the Directors, 'with a view to improving the working of the business in the future'. These were discussed at the AGM and met with approval and Percy Flick was engaged from January 1911 'to assist in the management of the business at a salary of £150 a year, plus 10% on the increase in the net profits'. He, in return agreed to devote at least two days a week to the company's business. Flick's impact was immediate. By the end of January 1911 he had visited both the Witney and Stratford upon Avon agencies and presented a report to the directors, recommending that they should be closed and the areas worked in a different manner. He negotiated with the railways to gain beneficial transport rates and before the middle of the year, reported on the running of the agencies at Kineton, where he found that the discounts were too high, and Quenington, which he found satisfactory. At the end of his first year as an employee, Flick submitted a report at the December meeting of the Directors on the past workings of the company including more suggestions for future reforms of working practices. The report was discussed, adopted and filed. At a second meeting, the following day, he unveiled a new basis for the remuneration of travellers which was discussed. It was resolved to adopt the plan if at all possible. Flick also became the company's travelling representative, overseeing the change of tenants at their licensed properties, visiting agents to discuss their business, with a view to improving their trade figures, collecting cash from customers and selling, on behalf of the company, the Globe Room panels. When, during 1912 there was trouble with the quality of its beer, it was Flick, as the company troubleshooter, who was instructed to gain advice from the Burton brewers and who appointed a temporary brewer to assist in eradicating the problems.

The increase and decrease in trade between 1900 and 1919

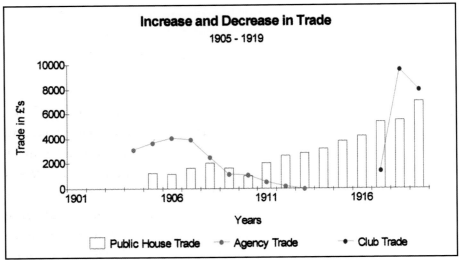

Source: HNBC Archive Trade Ledgers. 1901-1920.

Between 1909 and 1913 there was an increased demand for beer in the country as a whole,[35] but this increase was not reflected in production at Hook Norton.

It is clear from correspondence between Flick, Clarke and William Toy, written between September and December 1912, that the poor trade figures were of great concern to the management. Having spent time reviewing all aspects of the brewery's business Flick wrote bluntly to Alban Clarke.

> I had hoped to have had a chat with you today over Company matters… I am greatly disappointed that I have not been able to show better results. I am convinced the position can yet be saved, but it will need firmer methods and more *scrapping*!…Under present conditions, I fear my help can be of little use to you, and I am over anxious not to let the position beat me. I cannot afford to be unsuccessful. You have been kindness itself to me since I was called in and [have] given me every assistance, which compels me to depart from my usual procedures to write to you personally… and to urge you to use every endeavour, however distasteful, to save the situation. Your own position and interests are so bound up in the Brewery and this makes it harder for me to stand by and see others 'staying the wheels' of progress.

Appreciating the stress the Managing Director had been under, Percy Flick showed genuine concern for Alban Clarke's health in his letter and he was of the opinion that Clarke should not start another year as Managing Director. Alban Clarke's response to this and other matters expressed in the letter are unknown. Yet it would appear that over the ensuing months there were discussions over his position as Managing Director and by December decisions had been taken with a view 'to improve the management of the business'. William Toy wrote to Alban Clarke outlining the procedures that needed to be followed to achieve the proposed improvements. First and foremost these planned improvements needed to be explained to, and then accepted by, the shareholders at an extraordinary general meeting. Furthermore it was also necessary for the shareholders to approve any remuneration to be paid to Flick and Clarke for their respective positions. The contents of Toy's letter were conveyed to Percy Flick, who replied a couple of days later.

> I need hardly say I am willing to fall in with any scheme, that
> commends itself to Mr Toy and yourself for the betterment of
> the Company's position and if you wish me to take the helm
> for a time – you may rest assured that it will be the 'H.N.B.
> Co' first with me, all personal interests must give way to that
> – the concern <u>has</u> got to be <u>made</u> to pay!

At about the same time that the members of the Board were discussing the company's difficulties, a disgruntled shareholder in Brighton, expressed dissatisfaction in a damning letter sent to George Groves at the company offices.

> I thank you for copy of balance sheet for year 1912. It is very
> disappointing – particularly after reading in the London
> Papers in August last that the Company had recently sold the
> Globe Room at Banbury for a sum of £1,000 … If the
> Company is unable to pay dividends, would it not be in the
> interests of the shareholders to sell the whole concern? For the
> inference seems to be growing that the only folk benefiting
> are the Employees and the Government.
>
> Why should we go on enriching the Exchequer as we are
> doing?

At a meeting of the Directors two days before Christmas, both Alban Clarke and John Henry Harris tendered their resignations as Managing Director and Assistant Managing Director respectively. No reasons for their resignations were given but both men remained directors of the company, with Alban Clarke being appointed brewer. The board then agreed to appoint Mr Percy W Flick as Managing Director. Considering Flick had been associated with the company for more than a decade and with his close involvement in the running of the company, his elevation to the Board of Directors is not surprising. His credentials and business pedigree were known and tested and he was the obvious choice to appoint as Managing Director.

It was not only Hook Norton that suffered during the early years of the twentieth century. As prices began to exceed wages in the years following 1900, a general malaise overtook the industry as sales declined. The Managing Director of Greene King observed, 'a tendency amongst the public not to use the Public House as formerly' and acknowledged his company's falling barrelage was due to 'decreased consumption of drink amongst all classes'.[36] The fortunes of the Hook Norton Brewery, like those of the industry as a whole, were severely tested during the years before the First World War.

Dealing with the War, Peace and War again

As hard as the Directors had tried to come to terms with the decline in sales there was an inherent problem in the running of the business which had pervaded the first decade of the company's trading. The ordering and purchasing of stock for the stables and the control of the outride man had been under the dual control of Alban Clarke and John Henry Harris. As a result there was confusion with both men placing orders which at times were duplicated and as a consequence the company's bank balance suffered. One of Percy Flick's first decisions as Managing Director was to take sole control of spending, directing that 'all purchases should pass through his hands' so provision for payment could be made. In the absence of evidence it is difficult to assess how much of a problem was caused by overstocking. Flick's comments suggest this was not an isolated incident he had resolved. The practice of dual control had existed for some years and as a result the financial difficulties experienced by the brewery during the first decade of trading were self inflicted through lax expenditure control.

By taking control of spending Percy Flick was able to reduce expenditure, which had averaged almost £11,000 a year since 1900, by nearly £3,000 in his first three years as Managing Director. His intervention quickly brought a significant improvement in the company's financial situation.

'Grim-visaged war' loured across Europe in July 1914, as Germany prepared to declare its hostile intentions towards first Russia (1st August) and then France (3rd August). In Britain conflict was seen as 'an eventual

Graffiti scribbled on a drawer in the Offices (Elena Woolley).

probability', but *The Times*, fearful of the German Navy being anchored in the French Channel ports, appealed, as a matter of national security, that Britain declare war on Germany. As the annual August Bank Holiday Monday (3rd August) approached the immediacy of war prompted the wealthy to look to the security of their savings, and those less wealthy to ensure that they had enough money to enjoy their 'annual spree'. The result was a run on the banks, causing some difficulties for the Bank of England. The 4% Bank Rate was doubled on 31st July and further raised to 10% a day later. To give the Bank of England 'breathing space' the paying of some bills of exchange were delayed a month and the Bank Holiday was extended to the Thursday (6th August) and amongst other measures to ease the availability of money, postal orders became legal tender for a short time.[37]

As the financial crisis unfolded, the Directors' of the Hook Norton Brewery company met to consider how it would affect the running of their business. With the banks closed and an air of uncertainty about the future, Percy Flick asked the Board to 'postpone the passing of accounts for payment', unless the payment was essential. This was agreed, as was the need to hold sufficient amounts of ready cash to meet the payment of the men's wages.

Before the month of August was out, the brewing industry was subject to direct government intervention and measures were introduced to control the sale of alcohol in order to curb drunkenness. The initial impact on the industry was an increase in the price of beer, reflected in a rise in duty and the increased cost of raw materials. By the end of 1914 the output in the country as whole had fallen by 35%.[38] The effects of these wartime restrictions on the Hook Norton Brewery Company are discussed in the following chapters.

A consequence of the war was a rise in the cost of living and in June 1915 the Directors met to discuss the payment of War bonuses to the men to help meet these increased costs. After much careful consideration it was decided that brewery workers should be offered from 1/6d to 2/0d a week and the boys a shilling. This agreement did not, however, include the Office staff and it was recognised that the increased prices were 'felt just as keenly by them as other workers'. So it was also agreed that 'a general advance' should be made to provide the Office workers with a bonus as well.

The outbreak of war saw a 'great surge of patriotic enthusiasm' and between August 1914 and March 1916 over two and a half million men answered Kitchener's call and volunteered for active service. In January 1916 the government introduced conscription for all single men aged 18 to 40 years, later extending this to also include married men. The introduction of conscription affected the working of the Hook Norton Brewery; throughout 1916 brewery men were called up, three left in June, three in July, Wyatt left in August and two more went in October.

In all nine men left the brewery during the year and all were given a 'gift' of ten shillings when they left to join-up.[39] The loss of these men to the Forces meant that additional work had to be undertaken by those remaining and the malt men were drafted into the brewery to supplement the remaining workforce.[40] In November 1916 as recognition of this extra work Alban Clarke, Jim Rose, H Allen and J Kelly received bonuses and from June 1916, Minnie Hall, Mary Cross and May Harris, were employed in the Office as clerks. They were paid 13/6d a week.

As the food supply situation deteriorated the government introduced further restrictions, limiting brewing output to 28% of the pre-war level, or a third of the output for 1915-16. The new measures set a target of about 10 million standard barrels for 1917-18, although this was not achieved and national output for the year was about half that of the previous year's output of 13.8 million standard barrels. The new measures were to be introduced on 1st April 1917.[41]

Percy Flick addressed a sombre meeting of the Directors in early March called to discuss the impact of the new restrictions. His assessment was grim. He estimated that for the company to continue, the work force expenses needed to be cut by at least 50% and it should be effected at the earliest possible opportunity. To achieve this the three 'girl clerks' from the Office, the travellers and Messrs Stratford and Wilkes would all have to be 'discharged'. The brewery workforce would also have to be reduced to 'eight men and one or two lads'. His plan was provisionally approved and a further meeting was planned to decide on further staffing reductions. For the three 'girl clerks' their employment at the brewery finished on 7th March 1917. The three 'girl clerks' were not the only women working at the brewery. Kate Coppage was also employed by the brewery, although it not clear in what capacity, but she too was given notice and became redundant at the end of March.[42]

When Percy Flick was appointed Managing Director in 1912 he signed only a 'provisional agreement' with the company [43] and it is not clear whether he viewed his position as a relatively short-term appointment, a possibility he indicated in correspondence with Alban

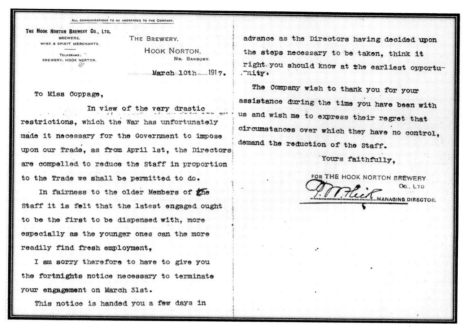

ALL COMMUNICATIONS TO BE ADDRESSED TO THE COMPANY.

THE HOOK NORTON BREWERY Co., LTD.
BREWERS,
WINE & SPIRIT MERCHANTS.

TELEGRAMS:
BREWERY. HOOK NORTON.

THE BREWERY.
HOOK NORTON.
NR. BANBURY.

March 10th 1917.

To Miss Coppage,

In view of the very drastic restrictions, which the War has unfortunately made it necessary for the Government to impose upon our Trade, as from April 1st, the Directors are compelled to reduce the Staff in proportion to the Trade we shall be permitted to do.

In fairness to the older Members of the Staff it is felt that the latest engaged ought to be the first to be dispensed with, more especially as the younger ones can the more readily find fresh employment,

I am sorry therefore to have to give you the fortnights notice necessary to terminate your engagement on March 31st.

This notice is handed you a few days in advance as the Directors having decided upon the steps necessary to be taken, think it right you should know at the earliest opportunity.

The Company wish to thank you for your assistance during the time you have been with us and wish me to express their regret that circumstances over which they have no control, demand the reduction of the Staff.

Yours faithfully,

FOR THE HOOK NORTON BREWERY
Co., LTD
P.M. Flick
MANAGING DIRECTOR.

Letter received by Kate Coppage March 1917, giving her notice (Coppage Archive).

Clarke at the time. The tragic death of Alban Clarke in a cycling accident in early May 1917 changed the situation. Although Flick's agreement with the company remained unaltered, there was no alternative but for him to continue as Managing Director. It was not for another eight years, however, before discussions were finally begun 'to resolve the question of a permanent agreement with the Managing Director'.[44]

Alban Clarke's death was a huge blow to the company. It was not just his expertise in the brew house that was missed. He was the driving force behind the creation of the Hook Norton Brewery Company, and as a director energetically oversaw the building of the new brewery, the incorporation of the company and championed the acquisition of the steam wagon as he led the company into the twentieth century. His interests took him beyond the brewery and he actively involved himself in village affairs.

He had a passion for cricket and during the building of the new brewery he recorded the results of matches involving the touring Australian team alongside his notes and observations on the progress of the building.[45] He enjoyed the rural sports of shooting and fishing and was the moving force behind organising village shooting parties. It was only the illness and subsequent death of Queen Victoria that forced him to cancel a shoot. His shooting partners came from varying backgrounds, and included his friend Pettipher Bennett from Oatley Hill Farm, brewery employees George Groves, John Gibbins and G.H. Brotheridge, the village stationmaster Mr Beechey, the manager of the ironstone working Mr Lightfoot and the local clergyman, Reverend A.W. Russell. It was whilst travelling to Traitor's Ford, near the village of Sibford Ferris, for a Saturday afternoon's fishing, that he met his death following a cycling accident.

Alban Clarke (1858-1917), centre, with a group of his shooting partners (HNBC).

Replacing him would be difficult. In the brewhouse Flick arranged for Mr J.W. Alcock to be re-appointed temporarily, until a new permanent brewer could be appointed. The brewery archives make no mention of the appointment of a new brewer and it may well have been that financial constraints precluded any such appointment. Ultimately the position was filled by Frank Beale, one of the brewery workers, who acted as brewer until his retirement in 1932. Alban Clarke's place on the Board was also left vacant.

Peace and a relaxation of the wartime restrictions on the use of raw materials did not, however, lead to a reduction in prices or a return of pre-war levels of production. Brewers had initially consoled themselves that an economic revival would restore business fortunes and see beer sales improve, but the War took its toll. The combined effects of government controls, the loss of employees to the armed forces and the added burden of limits being placed on the supply of raw materials presented brewers with an uncertain future. As a result some companies either went out of business, or just sold up. During the immediate post war period the wealthier companies took the opportunity to expand their customer base by buying up these failing businesses and between 1914 and 1920 the number of licensed brewers in the United Kingdom fell from 3,746 to 2,914. After 1920, however, circumstances changed and the wealthier brewers faced with falling demand, were forced to rationalise their production capacity, particularly in London and Burton, where over capacity was a problem.[46]

The post war period presented the brewing industry with new challenges as companies strove to re-build their beer sales. People began to look beyond the public house and beer for their entertainment. By the end of the first post war decade, the 'Statist' observed that "The popular hunger for amusement, a natural reaction from the grey atmosphere of wartime and the vast increase of facilities for popular entertainment marked a permanent change in public attitudes" and that "The public house had lost its social importance". In rural England, however, the public house still remained at the 'centre of social activity' in the villages.[47] From early 1920 a lasting decline in the demand for alcoholic drinks set in, and saw the country's output of bulk barrels drop by 20% and the per capita consumption per head fall by 15% by the time war was again declared in 1939.[48]

In Hook Norton, the brewery struggled on. The seriousness of the situation faced by the company is reflected in the annual decrease in both gross and net profits during the years 1918/19 and 1919/20. Gross profit fell and 'Finance and sales statements' were regularly reviewed and show the difficulties that were being faced. In August 1920, Percy Flick reported that the barrelage sales for the previous April and May had been 'quite equal to that of April and May 1919' but fifteen months later the Directors 'observe[d] a considerable fall in the beer trade for the third month as compared with the year 1920'. This was attributed to a reduction in the trade with Coventry, but Percy Flick did not think that the brewery had fared as badly as 'brewers generally', yet sales still continued to fall. In May 1922 the sale of barrels dropped by 47 and in the following month by 'no less than 115', due to the decline in demand for small casks. The following spring the situation was even worse, with 238 fewer barrels being sold and by July 1923 output was down by 360 barrels.

Before the hostilities, malt had sold for about 27/- a quarter and with the effect of the wartime restrictions there was a constant rise in the price. By 1920 the price of malt had risen by 229%, causing financial difficulties not only in Hook Norton. At Gales Brewery, yearly expenditure on raw materials had averaged £2,650 a year for sugar, £2,000 for hops and £7,000 for malt, but in 1920 expenditure rose dramatically with the brewery paying £7,000 for sugar, £5,300 for hops and £26,000 on malt; a total of nearly £39,000. For the first time since 1886, when records were first kept, the Horndean Brewery showed a net loss of £446/8/9d and it was only through a subsidiary part of the company making a profit of £2,000 that the final figure was in the black.[49]

In Hook Norton there were similar problems coping with the rising costs and an inability to increase sales after the 'demise of the old style private trade'. The very future of the business was threatened as the cost of re-stocking with raw materials ate into the company's profits. A gloomy Percy Flick anticipated that he could 'hold out no hopes of recovery under [the] present prices'. At Board meetings during March and June the company's predicament was discussed and 'it was finally resolved to carry on as at present up to September 30th and hope that prices of materials might fall'. The prospects for the brewery looked bleak, and with the uncertainty about the company's future, Percy Flick advised Mrs Clarke that her sixteen year old son, Bill, should not enter the business as 'There was no future for him'. Instead, Bill went off to Gloucestershire, where he spent the next eight years farming.

September 30th 1920 came and went and the business of the Hook Norton Brewery continued as usual. How the predicted financial problems anticipated earlier in the year were resolved is unknown, but an entry in the Minutes of the Directors' Meetings, written twelve years later refers to the repayment of part of a loan made to the company by Percy Flick. The circumstances under which this loan of £3,000 was made are not recorded either, but it poses the intriguing possibility that Percy Flick loaned the company the money to tide it over during the difficulties experienced in the autumn of 1920.

As Company Secretary, George Groves had always overseen the work of the office clerks dealing with orders, their payment and dealing with all the correspondence that this generated, but following the death of Alban Clarke he seems to have taken responsibility for the day to day running of the brewery. With Percy Flick dividing his time between the brewery and his own business in Banbury and William Toy being in Chipping Norton, Groves became the 'go-between' passing company business to and between the two men. On occasions one of the clerks would correspond with Percy Flick, answering a particular enquiry, always addressing him as 'Mr Percy'.

The nature of the correspondence emanating from the brewery office was varied, the majority of it related to customer orders and the payment of bills and examples of these are referred to in later chapters. The problem of bad debt generally had been highlighted by C. Howard Tripp, in his writings for the *Brewer's Journal* in the late nineteenth century. Time had not lessened the problem and it fell to George Groves to chase up the bad payers. If an account was overdue, Groves couched his reply firmly in words that reflected the status of the customer. This firm but tactful reminder was sent to W.H. Littleboy, Esq, Manager of the local Ironstone Mining Company.

> Our financial year ends on 30th inst. after which date our
> books are open to the inspection of the auditors and I am

anxious your account should not be found to be outstanding as it gives occasion for the unpleasant comment which I am sure you would wish to avoid. Will you kindly let us have your cheque for £30/10/6 during the next fortnight.

When the licensee of the Queen's Own in Woodstock fell behind with her account, he firmly requested she paid the outstanding balance of £25/3/0 within a week, but his tone to the licensee of the George Hotel in Shipston on Stour was different and reflected his annoyance that the payment of the outstanding bill had persistently been ignored.

> Dear Sir, Why is it that you ignore our repeated application for payment of our long standing account – 4 guineas. To say the least it is abominable behaviour on your part, having asked us to supply you with goods and now [you] give us all the trouble to get payment. We supply the goods at your request and in good faith and that your intention was to pay. Please send us a remittance for the amount and save any further unpleasantness.

If, however, a customer had a bad debt, he received a blunt and forthright request for the outstanding amount. If payment was not promptly made the account was passed to William Toy and legal action was taken to recover the money.

> I am enclosing our bill against Mr E.J. Stanbra of Wiggington £33/10/6 and Mr W Stanbra of Leas Farm Enstone £9/18/0. Will you please make applications at once for immediate payment and take further proceedings if not paid in each case.

When in the autumn of 1920 the pump supplying water to the Sun and Red Lion public houses failed, it was George Groves who liased with both Messrs Hopcroft and Norris Ltd, the owners of the Red Lion and the builders Messrs Poulton to organise the repair. Poulton's assessment of the problem revealed the old pump was in a bad state of repair and needed at least two new parts. They recommended a new pump should be fitted at a cost of £40, as any repair to the old pump would cost almost as much. George Groves wrote to Hopcroft and Norris to inform them of the situation.

> We understand that the £40 estimate is an addition to their estimate of £5/10/0 for opening and recovering the well. If you can suggest any cheaper means of obtaining a satisfactory supply of water, we shall be glad to hear from you.

It was not, however, until the following July that a cheque for £20/7/6 was received from Hopcroft and Norris, their share of the cost to repair the pump.

The care and maintenance of the company's property was a matter needing to be addressed after the years of wartime restriction and financial difficulties. It is clear that this was taken seriously, but financial restraints meant that repairs tended to be done piecemeal when funds were available for the work. Flick first broached the subject in March 1920 but he experienced difficulties in engaging builders to do necessary repair work, even though there were sufficient funds to cover the expenditure. There is no explanation for Flick's problems with the builders and the matter of repairs appears to have lain dormant for two years before it was discussed again. In 1922 work was needed on both the Queen's Own in Woodstock and the Sun Inn in Hook Norton. There seems to have been some urgency about beginning the work at the Queen's Own as this was sanctioned at a cost of £35 with the proviso that it was 'completed as soon as possible'. The Directors had accepted the builder's estimate of £128 for the work at the Sun, but the initial contract specified the work should be done within three weeks which the builders felt was insufficient and to meet that deadline would mean work would have to be skimped. George Groves wrote to Percy Flick to inform him of the builder's reservations.

> I have seen Busby and his son in reference to the proposed work at the Sun. They say that they could not give an undertaking to complete the work by 31st August and they

decline to give a guarantee as they could not afford to forfeit
the £3 penalty, [but] they would take it on at six weeks.

As a result of George Groves intervention, the work at the Sun was re-
scheduled and the contract was revised, doubling the time allotted for
completion of the repairs in a 'satisfactory manner'.

The business of Directors of the company was not confined solely to
the production and selling of beer. During May 1923 the brewery
received a request from the Chipping Norton Town Council to lease part
of the Red Lion yard in Chipping Norton to the Council for a proposed
market. The brewery's initial response was to reject the request.
Although the yard was small and the current tenant did not make full
use of it, they argued it was necessary to protect the interests of any
prospective tenants of the inn who might want to make more use of it.
The brewery were, however, 'very anxious' to co-operate with the
Council and find a solution, offering to clear 'some of the present
buildings' and create more space. An on-site meeting was arranged
between Percy Flick and the Council's surveyor in late June. It was agreed
that an area at the bottom of the pub yard would be leased to the Council,
but the project dragged on and it was another two years before the matter
was brought to a conclusion.

Before a final settlement could be agreed, changes in the Board Room
were forced upon the brewery with the death of William Toy in May
1924 after a period of ill health. He had been the company's Chairman
and solicitor since 1900 and had taken an active role in setting up the
new business. He was succeeded as Chairman by John Henry Harris, and
his sister, Alban Clarke's widow, Mrs Frances Elizabeth Clarke, as the
holder of the largest number of ordinary shares, was elected to take his
place on the Board of Directors.

In early May 1925 the re-organised Board met to complete the
outstanding business with Chipping Norton Town Council. Terms to be
offered to the council were discussed and it was agreed that the land at
the Red Lion pub yard should be leased for a period of two years at the
nominal rent of 5 shillings a year. In the meantime another piece of land

adjoining the pub yard became available and it was decided that it was to the company's advantage to purchase it, rather than let the Town Council acquire it, as it could be added to the lease to ensure the brewery had control of the whole pub yard. Percy Flick was directed to purchase the land for no more than £50. In the event, Flick secured the land for £42 and the Board revised the lease on the extended yard, increasing it to £3 per annum.

The summer of 1928 proved to be an important period for the business. The issue of outstanding repairs was again addressed. In the months prior to the August meeting of the Directors, Percy Flick made an extensive tour of all the company's properties. He found that a total of twenty two, including the brewery premises were in urgent need of repair, which he estimated would cost £1,261 to put them all into good order. The company finances, although slowly improving were still not robust enough to foot the whole bill and it was decided that work should be carried out on the properties in most urgent need of repair and work was authorized on the six most pressing properties. The others would be done as, and when the finances allowed.

During August the brewery lost one of its most loyal and long serving employees with the death of George Groves. His heath had been ailing for sometime and he was eventually forced to stop working. His death 'left a bit of a gap', and it was during this time that Bill Clarke was recalled from Gloucestershire to join the company, being employed in the first instant, as an assistant in the brewery on the provisional salary of £100 a year.

George Groves had joined the company in 1872 as a brewer's clerk, working with John Harris as he established his fledgling business. In his fifty six years service he saw many changes, being responsible for the efficient running of the brewery office for almost half a century and acting as company secretary for twenty eight of those years. In recognition of his long and loyal service, it was agreed that an honorarium of £50 should be paid immediately to Mrs Groves and that notification of his death was to be placed in the appropriate trade journals. This was not the first instance of a benevolent action agreed by the Board. In 1923 Mr Stratford was unable to earn 'an adequate salary' and at the instigation of Percy Flick he was given a £25 special gratuity. In the same year the private trade was resurrected by Flick for a short time to allow Mr F Veale to 'earn an adequate salary' and in 1931 the wife of John Hall, a former drayman, was granted a 'weekly credit of 7/6d for groceries at Messrs Pilsworth'.[50]

The decade following George Groves's death, heralded a period of change both in the brewery and the boardroom as the older generation who had worked with John Harris and Alban Clarke retired. The loss of Groves necessitated a reshuffle in the boardroom. With the depressed nature of the British economy, the Board felt it would be prudent for Percy Flick to combine his existing duties with those of company secretary, so saving the company the cost of another salary, at least until it became expedient to make a new appointment.[51]

For almost two years Bill Clarke worked in the brewhouse assisting Frank Beale with the brewing, until Beale's health began to fail. During the final week of January 1930 Beale was absent ill and Bill carried through the fermentation of a brew of bitter on his own and during the following week, with Beale still absent, he carried out his first solo brew. Frank Beale soldiered on for a further two years before deciding to retire at the end of September 1932 after forty years employment at the brewery. In recognition of his long service he was given a monthly gratuity of £2.

By the autumn of 1930 the development of Bill Clarke's career within the business became the subject of discussion for the Board. Percy Flick was eager for the bottling plant to be extended and modernised to provide Bill with a 'better chance of progressing in the business', but due to the death of Mr Stratford, Bill was temporarily seconded to help in the offices.

At the end of 1930 two and a half million workers were registered unemployed and a year later that number had reached almost three million due to the economic depression that saw British industry experience a collapse in exports, with coal, iron and steel, wool and cotton and cars all suffering. The impact of this unemployment was a

Bill Clarke 1904-1982 (HNBC).

fall in the demand for beer and production fell nationally by 30%
between 1931 and 1932; this trend was reflected in Hook Norton largely
due to unemployment in Coventry.[52] At a Board Meeting during July
1931, a pessimistic Percy Flick reported 'a considerable falling off in sales'
and he predicted that there 'was little hope of pulling up' sales during
the remainder of the year. These were poor years for the brewery; by
early 1932 there were indications of a small improvement, but it was not
until the middle of the decade that trade really began to 'pick up' and
improve. Even though these were difficult years for the business, Bill

Clarke's salary was still increased to £150 a year from the end of July 1931.

John Henry Harris had been company Chairman since 1924 and the years that he held the position appear to have provided him, for the first time since 1900, with a more active role within the management of the company. Village gossip suggests that there was a degree of animosity between Flick and John Henry during this period. Percy Flick had certainly made his feelings towards John Henry known in his personal letter to Alban Clarke in 1912, being of the opinion that Harris was a 'passenger' who did 'not earn a tithe' of what he was paid. If there was any ill feeling between the two men, there is little documented evidence to support the claim and the Minutes show a Board of Directors concentrating on the business of running the company. There are, however, three recorded incidents where interests might be seen to have clashed. The first in 1915 concerned John Henry's tenancy of the farm. Flick had already expressed his disapproval of Harris's tenancy of the farm, believing the company could charge an independent tenant a more competitive rent. So when John Henry failed to settle the outstanding rent for the farm, which was eighteen months overdue, he was given notice to terminate his tenancy at the end of September. It was pointed out that his behaviour was 'unseemingly in a Director who [was] also a tenant of the Company'. This was not the end of the matter. In October John Henry queried his notice at a meeting of the Board and the matter was deferred and a year later he signed a new tenancy agreement for the 43 acre brewery field at a rent of £86 a year.

In April 1918 Percy Flick had recommended that 'special bonuses' should be paid to members of the office staff. William Toy went on to suggest that both Flick as Managing Director and John Henry Harris should also be paid bonuses, subject to the 'articles of Association'. At the next meeting, Percy Flick reported that under these articles the directors had no powers to pay John Henry the suggested bonus of £50 and the matter was deferred. The final 'spat' between Flick and Harris came shortly after the death of George Groves in 1928 at a Board Meeting called to discuss the draft accounts for the previous year.

Discussions centred on items of expenditure and depreciation and amounts to be written off. As Chairman, Harris suggested that for some items, the amount written off might be written back, with the effect of increasing the net profit. Flick reacted, denouncing 'any such action' and urged the Board to continue with 'the policy of writing down out of profits such items as good will and plant'. He followed this with the recommendation that 'all repairs and improvements to property should be charged against revenues'. With no agreement and views conflicting, it was agreed at the Chairman's suggestion that a meeting with the auditors be convened at the earliest possible date so that the accounts could be discussed in detail. Five days later the meeting was reconvened and the accounts were discussed with a Mr Brown from the auditors and adopted, presumably following the Managing Director's wishes.

John Henry Harris died in December 1934. He had been involved with the management of the brewery since the death of his father in 1887. He took no interest in the actual brewing, but visited the brewery regularly and took a keen interest in the business.[53] Harris farmed in Scotland End and was affectionately known as 'Boss Harry' in the village. The Chipping Norton Advertiser reported that 'his loss [would] be widely felt for his never failing interest in the village.' He was succeeded as Chairman, by his sister Frances Elizabeth Clarke. At the same meeting Bill Clarke was also elected to the Board. Frances Elizabeth remained Chairman until December 1939 when through her own ill health she was forced to relinquish her position, to be replaced by Percy Flick. She retired from the Board in 1942 and her place was taken by her daughters Frances Mary and Nancy. Frances Elizabeth died in 1943 and the brewery was closed during the afternoon for her funeral. With the expectation of being drafted abroad, Nancy Clarke, a nurse, resigned her position on the Board of Directors in December 1944.[54]

The War brought changes. Government restrictions, shortages and higher levels of taxation returned and mirrored experiences of the earlier conflict, but licensing hours remained largely unaltered and temperance protests were less effective and subdued.[55] The impact of these wartime regulations is discussed in the following chapters. The wider impact of the War also had a bearing on Hook Norton and the community as a whole. In response to the bombing of London the village accommodated two hundred evacuee children with their teachers from West Ham and Barking. This doubled the school population of the village, while the army commandeered the brewery stables and dray wagon sheds. A hop store above the old bottle stores became the Officer's Mess, a cook house was created and four large huts were constructed in the fields behind the stables. The first occupants to be billeted in Hook Norton were a company of the Durham Light Infantry during the autumn of 1939. The winter that year was particularly severe with heavy falls of snow and with no heating provided in their billets, they lived in difficult conditions. Early one January morning in 1940 they marched out of the village for Chipping Norton to become part of the B.E.F. in France and were later rescued at Dunkirk. Throughout the period of the war other units of the armed forces made use of the facilities at the brewery stables, perhaps the most memorable being the Gordon Highlanders who came with 'a good pipe band' which marched through the village.[56]

Panelling was removed from these storerooms to make latrines for soldiers billeted at the brewery during the 2nd World War (Elena Woolley).

For the brewery, the presence of military units, not only in Hook Norton but the area as a whole provided a short term outlet for the sale of beer. This transient trade with the military is discussed in Chapter 4.

The routine of wartime brewing was rudely interrupted during February 1944 when the company received a written offer from the Abington Brewery in Northampton, to buy the company.[57] The negotiations were conducted by a Mr Budge, a partner in a firm of solicitors in Towcester on behalf of the Abington Brewery. It appears that he had arranged a meeting with Percy Flick through a mutual contact, a Mr Foot, a local auctioneer. Budge outlined his client's offer to Flick, unfortunately there is no record of Flick's response, but thereafter Mr Budge experienced 'some difficulty' in contacting him. Undaunted Mr Budge approached the Hook Norton Brewery's auditors in London, James Edwards & Co, asking if he could call at their office in Old Jewry. He did not, however, outline the nature of the business he wanted to discuss. Perplexed, the auditors telephoned the brewery and spoke to Bill Clarke who thought it concerned a licensed property owned by Hook Norton, which the Abington Brewery were interested in acquiring. On the 23rd February Mr Budge met Mr Harding, a partner in the firm of auditors, and outlined the Abington Brewery's proposal, mentioning a purchase price of £43,000. He was informed by Mr Harding, that as auditors for the Hook Norton Brewery, his company had no say in the matter unless instructed to do so by the directors. It was agreed though, that Mr Budge would write a formal letter to James Edwards & Co. This would set out the terms of the offer and be forwarded to the directors and Ordinary shareholders in Hook Norton for consideration. Individual copies of this letter were sent to each of the directors, three of whom were also ordinary shareholders and these arrived in Hook Norton at the beginning of March.

The offer was for the purchase of the 'entire holding of Ordinary Share Capital' of the Hook Norton Brewery for £40,000, subject to the company's profitability being satisfactory. Any official response to the offer though is difficult to gauge, as no Board Meeting was called to discuss the matter and it appears that Percy Flick, as Managing Director, acted alone and made the decision to reject the approaches of the Abington Brewery.[58]

Percy Flick's policy as Managing Director was always to keep a tight control of spending wherever possible. Some years this was difficult. At a meeting during August 1928 he drew attention to 'a slight fall in the sales in gross profit and a more serious fall in net profit owing to a slight rise in expenses and heavy unavoidable outlay on repairs'. His great success though, was to reduce expenditure through a policy of austerity. This is perhaps epitomised by the story of a meeting he had with the landlord of the Gate Inn, who wanted the pub's stable doors repaired. When the landlord approached Flick with the request, the riposte apparently, was 'wear the front steps out first, then we'll think about them'. In the decade before he joined the company annual expenditure was in excess of £10,000 a year, but at the end of a difficult first decade, he reduced the average annual expenditure to £7,611 a year and ten years later it was down to an average of £7,000 a year. These improvements in the financial management of the company were the fruits of his frugal financial policy which might have been based on the old saying 'look after the pennies and the pounds will look after themselves'.[59]

Wages and salaries were the company's largest single expenditure, averaging about £5,000 a year between 1901 and 1910. A decade later and under his management, the workforce had been trimmed and the average yearly total was down to £3,077. By 1930 wages were costing about half of what they had twenty years earlier and by 1935 he had reduced the wages bill by almost £3,000. Similar reductions in costs were also achieved on the purchase of Horsefeed and Trade Expenses. Repairs on the brewery and licensed properties averaged about £1,100 a year between 1901 and 1930, rising to £1,214 in 1931 and £1,342 in 1935 as the business climate improved.

Flick's tight control on spending and autocratic style did not endear him to some brewery employees and men left to seek employment elsewhere when he wouldn't increase their pay, and those who crossed him were immediately dismissed. Yet, whenever pay increases for the brewery workers were discussed by the Board, it was Percy Flick who spoke out for a similar rise for the office workers, with whom he seems to have had a better relationship. It was said that the men lived in awe of Flick and when he arrived at the brewery, word soon got around that he was on the premises. At one election the brewery workers had decorated the wagons with posters advertising one of the candidates.[60] When Flick saw these posters he ordered that they be removed as the brewery drew its custom from all walks of life and of political persuasion. Bert Heritage remembered him as 'a very strict man' and 'very sharp' when in conversation.[61] During the First World War Flick kept in touch with brewery men involved in the fighting and passed on news of their well being to those returning home injured or on leave and showed genuine concern for their well being. Although he kept a tight control on the company's expenditure Percy Flick could be more generous with his own money. Percy Hemmings was working in the malthouse drying the malt before it was used in the brewing. Flick asked Hemmings if he could dry a parcel of damp barley for him and this was duly done. A few days later Flick returned to collect his barley, giving Hemmings a tip that amounted to three times the weekly wage he earned at the brewery.[62]

Flick's final years running the company were devoted to seeing the company through the immediate post war years after the imposition of more government restrictions. Raw materials were still in short supply and production was limited to only a percentage of the company's 1939 barrelage and as a result there were beer shortages. The closure of the ironstone quarries in the village and the local railway station in 1951 meant further losses in trade,[63] but his legacy is his firm control of financial matters in the years either side of the First World War, which proved to be crucial to the survival of the business.

Notes

1   Eddershaw D. *A Country Brewery: Hook Norton 1849-1999*. HNBC 1999. p.3 reiterating the family oral traditions.

2   OCRO: Electoral Register for 1841. 'Faint Hill' should read 'Fant Hill'.

3   Deeds of the Brewery. The Vendors were John (Maltster) and William Gilkes (corn dealer of Shillingford, Berkshire). The transaction took place on 21st June 1845.

   James Harris – Death Certificate 21st October 1846 Banbury Guardian 5th and 12th November 1846. The business of the firm of Salter Williams exists only on the pages of the Banbury Guardian. There are apparently no surviving documents pertaining to this company.

4   Horn. P. *Labouring Life in the Victorian Village*. Fraser Stewart Books 1995. p.2 The mind-set of village life in the mid nineteenth century was somewhat different from today's values. Villages were self sufficient and this led to a narrowness of mind by which the people from neighbouring villages were viewed with some hostility and seen as 'foreigners'. Any hostile reaction to Harris's presence in the village could have impeded the development of his business. This lack of hostility could be interpreted to suggest that John Harris was in Hook Norton, possibly running James farm during his final months.

   Oral Tradition. Conversation with Fred Beale. His father referred to newcomers in the village as 'foreigners'. July 1973.

5   Post Office Directory of Berkshire and Oxfordshire 1854, 597, The parish of Shorthampton comprised of the hamlets of Chilson and Pudlicott. In 1851 the population was 309 persons. It was served by a chapel, school, baker-grocer and a beerhouse and four farms. Census Return: Chilson Oxfordshire. 1841.

   National Archives. Will of Henry Harris. Yeoman of Chilson under Wychwood 7/7/1843. PROB 11/1982.

   Post Office Trade Directory 1847. Hook Norton. The information for trade directories was usually collected during the year before publication, suggesting that Harris arrived in Hook Norton in 1846.

6   Census Return Hook Norton: 1851 OCMTRC show other villages in the Cherwell District had maltsters at the time that John Harris set up business.

7   Mathias. P. *The Brewing industry in England 1700-1830,* 1959, pp.255-6.

   Stapleton B. & Thomas J. *Gales: A study in Brewing, Business and Family History*, 2000, pp.32-35.

8   Bill Clarke was referring to his mother (daughter of John Harris), his father (nephew of Harris) and his uncle John Henry (John Harris' son).

9   Eddershaw D. *A Country Brewery: Hook Norton 1849-1999*, 1999, pp.6-7.

10   Gardener *History, Gazetteer and Directory of the County of Oxford,* 1852, p.850; Lascelles & Co: *Directory and Gazetteer of Oxfordshire* 1853. p.189. HNBC Archives: Brewery Deeds. "Confines of messuage malthouse cottages and premises dated 4th September 1852. Mr John Parish to Mr John Harris ... received ... from the within named John Harris the sum of £350." http://www.hook-norton.org.uk/history/economy/

11   Information Sheet: Staffordshire County Museum Service. 1980. Recollections of Mr Brassington Haughton son of the farmer.

12   Oral Tradition. Conversation with W.A. Clarke c1972. Harris is said to have moved in 1865, to the family house in Scotland End. The cottage became the Company Offices and is shown as such on the 1872 ground plan of the brewery. A photograph of the cottage used as the Offices survives, probably taken in mid 1890s, but before 1897 when the present offices were built.

13   Jennings P. *The Public House in Bradford 1770 – 1970.* 1995. p.79.
Stapleton B. & Thomas J. *Gales: A study in Brewing, Business and family history.* Ashgate. 2000. p.33.

14   Monkton. H.A. *A History of English Ale and Beer.* 1966. pp.171-2 & p.205. Appendix B.

A brewing license was required with the fee linked to the number of barrels brewed annually. The maximum fee being £75. See Chapter 3 regarding the taxation imposed for the use of sugar after 1847 due to pressure from West Indian Sugar producers. Duty on Beer and Materials. 1830. Beer Duty ceased.

Hops 2d per lb, Malt 2/7d per bushel. This increased in 1840. Hops was charged at 2d per lb + 5% and Malt at 2/7d per bushel + 5%. In 1847 Sugar was charged at 14/- per cwt.

15   Dingle A.E. *Drink and the Working Class Living Standards in Britain.* 1972, pp.612 & 617.

16   Mathias. 1959, pp.12-13.

17   Child. J. *Organization: A Guide to Problems and Practice.* 1977. p.75.

18   Child. J. 1977. p.76.

19   Census Return: Hook Norton. 1861. Richard West was employed as Brewer's Clerk. The only employee in 1861 to acknowledge employment at the brewery.

20 Census Return: Hook Norton. 1871.

It is not clear who worked on the farm. Householders making returns and giving the occupations of members of their household as 'Agricultural Labourer' did not necessarily specify who employed them.

HNBC Archive: Brewing Books 20/11/1873.

21 Tattersall R. *Diabetes – The Biography*. OUP 2009. pp.2,10,18 & 19.

22 Banbury Guardian. 24/11/1887. Deaths: p.5. November 16th. At Hook Norton John Harris aged 63 years.

23 Probate Registry. Search Ref: 01/04/1172. In the Estate of: John Harris. Will 21/10/1887.

Codicil to the Will. 9/11/1887.

24 Alfred Groves of Milton under Wychwood supplied specifications and drawings for work done on the bottling room and store (1890), additions to the malthouse (1894) and extending the stables (1894).

Correspondence: Alfred Groves & Sons Ltd 6/6/1973. Their records relating to building at the Hook Norton Brewery between 1890-1896 were destroyed in a serious fire on the Company premises in 1935.

25 Probate Registry. Search Ref: 01/04/1172. In the Estate of: John Harris. Will.

26 Summary of Proceedings 'in the matter of the Estate of John Harris deceased'. The High Court of Justice- Chancery Lane 1898 HNO2301.

27 Probate Registry. Search Ref: 01/04/1172. In the Estate of: John Harris. Will 21/10/1887.

28 Monckton. H.A., 1996, p.188.

29 Correspondence with R.J.Webber, Information Officer, The Brewer's Society. 12/3/1983.

'The Brewer's Journal 15th August 1900 shows that John Harris & Co was registered as the Hook Norton Brewery Company Ltd in that year – 12th July.'

30 Hardach. G. The First World War 1914-1918. Allen Lane 1977 pp.2-3.

31 Monckton., 1966, Appendix D. p.222.

32 Gourvish T. and Wilson R. 1994. pp.292-295.

33 Hunt, Edmunds & Co. p10.

Gourvish and Wilson. 1994, pp.277,285,292-294.

34 Eddershaw D., 1999, pp.61-64.

Pearson. L. *British Breweries An Architectural History*. 1999. 174 & 209.

35 Gourvish.T. & Wilson R., 1994, pp.294-295.

36 Gourvish T. & Wilson R., 1994, p.38.

37 Shakespeare. W. *Richard the Third*. Penguin. 1995. Act 1 Scene 1. Richard p55.

Marwick. A. *The Deluge: British Society and the First World War*. OU. 1965. pp.29-31.

The Times: 31/8/1914. Quoted by Marwick. August Bank Holiday Monday was always the first Monday in August. This was changed in 1971 and the holiday was moved to the last Monday of the month.

Keynes. J.M. The City of London and the Bank of England August 1914. Quarterly Journal of Economics. Vol. 29 No 1. November 1914. pp.68-69.

38 Vaizey. J. *The Brewing Industry 1886-1951*. 1960. p.3.

Jennings. P. 1995. p.231.

39 Benson. J. The Working Class in Britain. 1850-1939. I.B. Tauris. 2003. p.150.

www.learningcurve.gov.uk (National Archives) *Britain 1906-1918: Civilians and War 1914-1918*.

Eddershaw. D. 1999 see pp.64-70.

40 Oral Tradition. Adrian Palmer. ABM. Apparently Mr Fred Cooke (snr) had been at school with Percy Flick.

Robson's were taken over by ABM.

www.companieshouse.gov.uk. Associated British Maltsters (incorporated 20/11/1929) in liquidation since 2000.

41 Gourvish T. & Wilson R. 1994. pp.319-321

42 Coppage Archive. Letter from Percy Flick dated March 10th 1917.

43 HNBC Archive: Directors' Meeting Minutes. 23/12/1912.

44 Banbury Guardian. 31/5/1917.

45 The Diary of A A Clarke. 1897.

46 Gourvish T. & Wilson R. 1994. pp.330-31, 346-47. Tetley of Leeds 261 (43%) out of a workforce of 613 joined the armed forces, at Whitbread of London 305 (29%) joined up and Guinness lost 600 men, a sixth of its workforce to the war.

47 Bennison. B. 1995. p.31 Quoted from the "Statist" 14/12/1929.

Agricultural Economics Institute Oxford. Country Planning. OUP 1944 p.88.

48 Bennison. B. Not so Common: the Public House in NE England between the Wars. 1995. p.31.

Gourvish. T. & Wilson R. 1994. p.335.

49 Stapleton. B. & James T. 2000. p.92.

50 Messrs Pilsworth was a grocery store in the village and was still in business in the 1960s. It is now a dentist's surgery.

51 Gourvish T. & Wilson, 1994. p.336.

Sayers R. *A History of Economic Change in England. 1880-1939*. OUP. 1967. pp.52-54.

52 Sayer. R. 1967. p53.

Gourvish T. & Wilson, 1994. p.337. Production had been falling since 1919 and the average output during the 1930.'s was lower than that produced in the previous decade.

Oral Tradition. Conversation with Bill Clarke. 1973.

53 Oral Tradition. Conversations with Fred Beale and Leslie Matthews. 1973

54 Chipping Norton Advertiser: 21/12/1934.

HNBC Records: Companies House Cardiff. 1943.

Nancy Clarke was a nurse and served in this capacity during the last years of the war on a hospital ship.

55 Gourvish T. & Wilson, 1994. pp.356-358.

56 Oral Tradition: Conversations with Nan Cross, former deputy head at the village school and Bill Clarke.

57 Barber N. *Century of British Brewers. 1890-2004*. Brewery History Society. 2005. p.104.

58 Oral Tradition: Bill Clarke recalled that Percy Flick said 'No' and that was the end of the matter.

The Abington Brewery were prepared to employ Bill Clarke as a brewer on his current salary of £550 a year.

59 The Oxford Dictionary of Quotations. 3rd Ed. A corruption of "Take care of the pence, and the pounds will take care of themselves". Attributed to William Lowndes, Lord Chesterfield in letters to his son 5th Feb 1750. OUP 1979.

60 The men were decorating the wagon in the favours of the Tory candidate, a Mr Brassey.

61 Oral Tradition: Conversation with Bert Heritage 1974. Bill Clarke said Flick 'Was mustard!'

62 Eddershaw. D. 1999. p.68.

Oral Tradition: Conversations with Bill Clarke, Bert Heritage, Leslie Matthews and Harold Wyton 1973-76.

Oral Tradition: Conversation with Percy Hemmings. 29/10/1982.

63 Oral tradition: Conversation with Bill Clarke. 1974.

Chapter 2

Brewing Beer in Hook Norton

Bill Clarke, casting the copper c1975.

The Harris Years

1856 had been a poor year, with production down 19%. During November brewing was suspended for most of the month. When brewing recommenced on 24th November, Harris began a new brewing book. This book was not a continuation of the previous months' brewing as the first entry was labelled *'Brewing 1'.* This book signified the beginning of a new period in the development of his business. There is no explanation why brewing should have been suspended. The possibility arises that John Harris may have experienced problems with his brewing plant and needed to replace some or all of the equipment with new, probably larger equipment, particularly as he was to repeat the same procedure sixteen years later when he again re-equipped the brewery.[1]

In the nineteenth century the capacity of a brewery was defined by the size of its mashtun, which was measured in quarters of malt. The quarter (8 bushels) was adopted as the standard, but for commercial purposes a one quarter mashtun was seen as too small and a capacity of ten quarters was judged to be a more appropriate size.[2] The size, however, was peculiar to individual brewers. Allsopp's brewery in Burton on Trent for instance, employed eight mashtuns, the largest of which had a capacity of about 90 quarters producing 13,000 gallons of beer at a time.[3]

The new brewing book established Harris's brewing capacity. In his first brew, he used 18 bushels of malt, but he regularly used quantities of malt ranging between 15 and 19 bushels with the latter quantity becoming the most frequently used. From this use of malt we can estimate that he might have installed a mashtun with a capacity of 3 quarters, but ten years later an examination of the quantities of malt mashed then, suggests it was more likely to have had a capacity of 4 quarters. It was during this period that John Harris first took advantage of 1847 legislation allowing the use of sugar in brewing and began employing it in the brewing of mild and porter beers.

Before he began brewing commercially in 1852 Harris's work had essentially been seasonal; growing barley during the summer and malting it during the winter, but brewing provided him with work throughout the year. Harris's brewing books show him brewing all the year round and during the summer months being able to control fermentation temperatures, a process that caused major problems for his larger competitors.

The 'brewing season' was a practice inherited from the London Porter brewers of the eighteenth century, whose season ran from September to early June.[4] In the mid nineteenth century the inability to control fermentation temperatures during the summer made it necessary for brewers to work only during the cooler winter months on a 'round the clock' basis, building up stocks of beer to meet their summer demand. In Burton, brewers traditionally operated a shorter season.[5] Allsopp's Burton Brewery employed a season from September to April, with brewing taking place day and night. Although they used cooling refrigerators to reduce the temperature of the wort, no mention is made of controlling the fermentation temperature.[6] Allsopp's was not the only brewery to operate a 'brewing season'; Flower and Sons', brewers of Stratford upon Avon, also ceased brewing in the summer. Brewing practice at Flower's determined that through the winter, brewing would happen 'approximately' 30 times a month. As the summer approached the number of brewings was reduced until daytime temperatures made it impractical to ferment the wort successfully. A cessation of brewing meant that 'approximately a quarter' of the workforce was not required for brewing duties during the summer and returned to their villages to work in the fields, the remainder being redeployed to other tasks, including cleaning, repairs, delivery of beer and gardening duties. Even with the installation of refrigeration equipment, it was not until the 1890s that the Flower's brewery was able to carry out successful summer brewing.[7] Both Allsopp's and Flower's were able to brew large enough quantities of beer through the winter to hold in store to cover their summer requirements and could afford to place up to a third of their capital in casks because of the size of their business.[8] For Harris this was not possible. He had neither the capital nor the storage and his operation was not big enough to sustain such levels of investment in stock.

The first page of the 1856 Brewing Book.

Harris's solution lay in his brewing practice. The first entry in the 1856 Brewing Book confirms that Harris was using a thermometer to monitor the temperature during fermentation and a saccharometer to determine the alcohol content.

By exercising control over the fermentation stage of his brewing he was able to maintain round-the-year brewing. This was made possible using the most basic and rudimentary cooling technology, probably a pipe placed in the fermenting vessel and cold water passing through it.[9] It was not only at fermentation that he used water for cooling. During late July 1873 temperatures rose to 70°F, and aware of the need to keep racked beer at an even temperature he improvised by spraying the walls of the store and the tops of the barrels with water to reduce the temperature. By using this simple technology almost twenty years before it was generally adopted by the industry, Harris demonstrated that he was a serious commercial brewer and had discarded any "cottage industry" image that may have existed prior to 1852. With the ability to control fermentation temperatures Harris was able to brew throughout the year and accordingly brewed to demand.[10]

We know very little about John Harris's early years as a Common Brewer.[11] No records have survived for the first few years and the earliest references to his business activities are found in a Stock Book dated 1855, a year in which he sold 548 barrels of beer.

The frequency of Harris's brewing was irregular, and during the winter of 1856-57 there were instances when there was a gap of as much as a month between brewings followed by periods of hectic activity.[12] This, it has been suggested, was due to a lack of demand, but sales actually rose annually during this period. A possible explanation for the irregular brewing pattern during the first part of 1857 was that Harris was away from Hook Norton courting.

The lady in his life was Frances Elizabeth Chaundy, daughter of David Chaundy of Ascott under Wychwood, who like the Harris's, was a farmer. As children John and Frances may have known each other but, now a woman of 33, Frances was living in Brighton at 69, Middle Street.

With John Harris still having a 'hands-on' involvement in the day to day brewing, meeting was a problem. If he was away visiting her, Harris needed to brew sufficient beer to cover any demand during his absence and hence the periods of hectic activity. After June 1857 the irregular brewing ceased and the evidence of different handwriting in the brewing book suggests that Harris had begun delegating the day to day work of brewing to his employees. This was certainly the case in July of the following year. While John and Frances were being married in Brighton at St Nicholas Church, brewing went on as usual in Hook Norton.

It is through Harris's annual use of malt that the development of his business can be followed. During the first two decades of brewing he used widely varying, but increasing quantities of malt. For example, between 1856 and 1860 he used sixteen different quantities, ranging from 3 bushels to 20 bushels (2½ Qtrs) and his usage

St Nicholas Church: Brighton where John Harris married Frances Chaundy on 7th July 1858.

increased by about 12%. During the following decade, Harris used nineteen different quantities, ranging from 6 bushels to 64 bushels (8 Qtrs) in the mashtun and was producing a range of beers, of which XXX, m, Xl, X, x and Porter were the most popular. These beers accounted for more than two thirds of his sales of cask beer. In the years between 1861 and 1872, the pattern of brewing became more settled, suggesting his business was now established, and three quantities of malt, 24 bushels (3 Qtrs), 28 bushels (3½ Qtrs) and 32 bushels (4 Qtrs) were used. These quantities again, were responsible for two thirds of his total output, with 28 and 32 bushels being responsible for half of that total. The most common brewing capacity had risen markedly from the 19 bushels of the previous decade and the quantities of malt used during the period rose by 115%.

Beer sales began to rise significantly from 1863 and although the number of brewings that year (87) was less than those of 1859 (105), Harris still sold 36 more barrels of beer. There is no documented evidence to support the installation of a larger mashtun to cope with the increased quantities of malt used and whether he achieved this increase through the installation of a new mashtun, or by brewing 'a bit thick' and running the existing equipment to its limits is unknown, but from 1863 he began to use 24, 28, 30 and 32 bushels of malt regularly in his brewing.

Throughout the second half of the nineteenth century it was normal practice to add hops to the finished beer during racking, particularly if the beer was to be kept for some time. The addition of a small quantity of hops enhanced the aroma and flavour of the beer and was used particularly with pale ales, rather than mild ales, stouts or porters. The quantity of hops used was small, ranging from a quarter to one pound per barrel and it was important to employ only the best quality and 'thoroughly sound' hops as any impurities would transfer to the beer. There is no record of when Harris began 'dry hopping' his beers, but a note in the 1872 brewing book records he was adding half a pound of hops to each barrel. This practice may, however, have already been in use for some years, as he had been brewing XXXpa since 1859. The practice of dry hopping Hook Norton beers endured until recently.[13]

The combination of growing demand, brought about by the use of a traveller plying for private trade beyond Hook Norton in about 1863 and entry into the tied trade in 1869, made it necessary to brew regularly in larger quantities. By 1872 Harris was using a maximum of six different quantities of malt with 36 bushels (4½ Qtrs) and 40 bushels (5 Qtrs) being most frequently used quantities, but two years later he had come to rely on just two amounts, 28 bushels (3½ Qtrs) and 40 bushels, (5 Qtrs) for the bulk of his brewing.

Between the years 1862 and 1874, the annual quantities of malt used in brewing rose by 67% and this increase created the need for a new maltings and for this, Harris turned to the Birmingham architect, Edward Holmes, who produced plans during the spring of 1865.[14] The new maltings had an upper working floor measuring 76'6" by 45'6" and kiln and malt rooms measuring 36' by 22' and 36' by 15' respectively.

A re-equipped brewery opened in June 1872 and included a larger mashtun with a 6 quarter capacity; its impact was immediate. The number of annual brewings for 1871 (120) and 1872 (125) were very similar, but sales rose by 27%; an increase effectively achieved during the last six months of the year. Unfortunately, however, the brewing books for the final thirteen years of John Harris's life have been lost, so it is impossible to assess how he managed his mashtun during this period of growing demand for his beers, while nationally beer production fell by almost 10%.[15]

The brewing followed a cyclical pattern. His output was 'seasonal' with monthly peaks to meet the demand at haymaking, harvest and Christmas. In October beers for Christmas were produced, including XXXX. This beer was brewed twice a year, in October and March and had to be stored for several months to mature.[16] After the October brewing was completed the number of brewings per month declined until the following March and the next batch of XXXX beer. During the summer demand reached a peak in July and August, corresponding with haymaking and then harvest, but business did not rely solely on the demands of the agricultural year.

Much of John Harris's success was based on his ability to respond to the rapidly expanding demand for beer. Annual beer consumption nationally reached a peak of 40½ gallons per head during the mid 1870s. Thereafter it began to decline.[17] Nevertheless total demand increased as the population of the nation increased by a quarter (7.3 million people) between 1871 and 1901. The number of licensed premises fell by 8.9% over the same period, due primarily to the reluctance of magistrates to renew beerhouse licenses.[18] In only nine of the thirty five years that Harris was brewing, did the annual sales of cask beer fall below the previous year's sales. During the period from 1861-1876 there was sustained growth in sales. In the following eleven years until his death in 1887, sales fell below the previous year on only six occasions, most notably during the last three years of his life, although taken overall the total number of barrels sold each year continued to rise.

A change at the top

When Alban Clarke took over responsibility for brewing after his uncle's death in 1887, his interest in the science of brewing was reflected in his reading matter, for amongst his surviving possessions are, *'The Theory and Practice of Modern Brewing'* (1888) by Frank Faulkner and *'A Text Book of the Science of Brewing'* (1891) by Edward Moritz and George Morris. Both books are autographed by Clarke, the former being dated 'Feb 1889'. They were the latest thinking on brewing science and with the technical articles taken from the *'Brewers' Journal'* they supplemented his already extensive practical knowledge.

The provision of a 'free' mashtun in 1880 offered brewers the opportunity to use malt substitutes which had previously been prohibited.[19] The most common of these were rice and maize. Rice was particularly popular because of its cheapness and high starch content being freed from soluble nitrogenous matter. Brewing using rice was said to produce an 'exceedingly pale beer' and would 'fine very rapidly' giving a 'clean flavoured beer'. The problem was that raw rice needed a higher temperature (190-200°F) at mashing for the 'saccharifying action' to take place and release the starch, compared to that required by malt (140-143°F). With the development and availability of a choice of pre-treated cereal grains during the last two decades of the century, the problems of matching mashing temperatures was removed and treated grain could be mashed with malt at ordinary mashing temperatures.[20]

Alban Clarke took advantage of the 'free' mashtun and malt substitutes. The evidence from brewing book entries for December 1896 and 1898 show that he was using other substances mixed with the malt when brewing certain beers. Flaked rice was used particularly in the production of X and Xl Mild and Pale Ales and quantities of maize were used in brewing XXX Mild, mashing at a temperature of 168°F. Rice and maize were not the only malt substitutes allowed, sugars were also used, added to the copper during boiling.

Three kinds of sugar were in general use, invert-sugar, glucose and cane sugar. The most widely used of the sugars in brewing was invert-sugar, made by treating cane sugar and changing its molecular structure so that it was broken down into dextrose and levulose.[21] The Hook Norton brewing books show, however, that two sugars were being used. 'Invert' was added to the copper when brewing Xl PA and Xl Mild, but during December 1896 the use of glucose, a class of sugars formed from sources of starch, usually maize, rice or sago, was introduced in the brewing of Pale Ale. The use of sugars was said to improve the 'finished beer' by giving it a 'fuller, sweeter flavour', which suited the palette of the late nineteenth century beer drinking public.[22]

The commercial production of invert-sugar involved boiling raw cane sugar in a solution of water with a small quantity of sulphuric acid. Once the conversion of the cane sugar was completed, the sulphuric acid was neutralised with 'whiting'[23] and the solid impurities (gypsum) were allowed to settle. The remaining impurities were removed from the solution by evaporation and passing through charcoal.[24] In Manchester and Salford this process went tragically wrong in 1900. During November two women died in the Crumpsall Workhouse from arsenic poisoning. At their inquest it was stated that there was 'any amount of arsenic' in beer they had drunk. In Liverpool there were reported to be between sixty and seventy cases of beer poisoning in the Mill Road Infirmary and in Stourbridge, Worcestershire, another thirty patients were under observation with the same symptoms.[25] In all over 3,000 cases were reported and there were seventy fatalities. The ramifications of the incident rocked the brewing industry as it ricocheted across the country. Confidence in beer collapsed and there was a 'severe drop' in sales.[26] In an attempt to reassure their customers, breweries sent samples of their beer for analysis and placed adverts with the results in the newspapers. The Hook Norton Brewery, like their competitors, responded to the crisis and placed the following notice in the Banbury Guardian.

> Although it is well known to the Directors that the Ales and Stouts Brewed by the above Company, have been and continue to be Absolutely Pure. They [the HNBC] have submitted samples to the Public Analyst who reports as follows:- I hereby certify that I have examined samples of Beer

that these be replaced. To assess the size of the problem a 'Complaints and Returns Book' was established and reviewed by the Board at every meeting. Although assurances had been given that the problem was being dealt with, the complaints continued through May into June and it was decided to seek a second opinion from brewers in Burton on Trent and to 'engage a capable brewer' to be responsible for the brewing in Hook Norton. Later that month Mr James Alcock from the Central Brewery in Birmingham was 'engaged to assist in the brewing operations of the company for a period of two months at a salary of £63'.[41] An almost immediate improvement in the beer was reported and after a month, Mr Alcock reported to the Board, outlining his suggestions for future brewing operations and for alterations to the brewing equipment.

Although the cause of the problem with the beer had initially been identified as the use of old malt, Alcock recognized that it was all malt stocks that were responsible for the problem. Barley was malted and stored in the malthouse. Without a temperature-controlled environment, the malt was subject to atmospheric conditions and as a result became damp. To overcome this, Alcock introduced the practice of drying the malt on a small kiln the day before it was mashed [42] and after his period in Hook Norton ended it was 'strongly recommended that [this] reform be maintained'. By September 1912, Alcock's changes were being implemented. Normal production resumed and the remaining 173½ quarters of the old malt were sold.

Between 1909 and 1913 beer production increased nationally and an extra three million barrels were brewed.[43] This brief respite brought by the increased demand was not reflected in Hook Norton and the quantities of malt used for brewing and the number of annual brewings continued to fall. Annual quantities of malt fell from 2,156 quarters to 1,260 quarters, during this period and took totals back nearer to the levels brewed twenty years earlier. There was, however, a major difference in the circumstances. In 1893 demand locally was still growing and there was an air of optimism that this would continue into the foreseeable future. By 1914, on the eve of war, that optimism had been extinguished by an unrelenting decline in demand for beer.

New Breweries for Old

The nature of the industry was also changing and with it the internal and external design of the breweries. By 1870, articles were being published suggesting how and where brewing equipment should be placed in the brewery. The principal change in the architecture of the brewery was the 'tower brewery'. Internally these new breweries were technically more advanced with important brewing vessels positioned to allow each process to pass down the tower from floor to floor, taking advantage of gravity and reducing the need for pumping the wort between vessels.

John Harris's Brewery prior to demolition: Spring 1899.

The interest in brewing science and the emergence of specialists, particularly in the fields of brewing architecture and engineering had placed the expertise in the hands of twenty five practices. Architects like George Scammell and William Bradford, added to a growing catalogue of specialist literature, with their books, respectively *'Breweries and Maltings: Their arrangement and construction and machinery'* (1871) and *'Notes on Maltings and Breweries'* (1889).[44] These were different from the pamphlets produced in the early years of the century that described brewing in terms of personal observation and merely alluded to the use of science in brewing. The new generation of books explained in detail the science involved. They were written by men whose experience and qualifications placed them in a position to write authoritatively about the subject. George Scammell for example, was an Associate member of RIBA and a consulting engineer and architect.

Brewers had different reasons for building new premises and these varied; some were to replace premises destroyed by fire, (George Gale in Horndean, Hampshire 1869)[45], others were extensions to existing breweries, (Flower and Sons' of Stratford upon Avon, 1870 & 1874),[46] yet others like R.W. Flick of Banbury commissioned new breweries. Recent research suggests that 634 breweries were built in the forty years between 1865 and 1906, a process that started slowly before reaching a climax during the 1880s.[47]

Technical innovation and a more scientific approach to brewing had not passed John Harris by and with the quantities of malt being employed in his brewing growing by 67% between 1862 and 1874, new, larger, and more 'modern' brewing facilities were required. It might have been expected that he would have turned to someone local, probably in Banbury, to design his new brewery.[48] The town had a long tradition of brewing, but by the late nineteenth century the town's brewing was dominated by the interests of the Hunt family.[49] Between 1865 and 1906 the only new brewery built in Banbury was designed by Charles Johnson and Sons of Bristol.[50] As a result, the expertise and skills that Harris was looking for, to design a new brewery, no longer existed in the town. Such skills were to be found in the cities, London, Manchester and Bristol, not country market towns, not even a 'mature' one like Banbury.[51] Circumstances forced Harris to look further afield and he commissioned Henry Pontifex and Sons, Brewers' Engineers of Charing Cross to design a new 5 quarter brewery. The firm was founded in the early nineteenth century by John Pontifex who had described himself as a brewers' architect. As a company they were regarded as one of the major brewing production plant suppliers of the nineteenth century and capable of building complete small scale breweries. There is no record of the cost of Harris's new brewery, but George Scammell estimated it would cost £2,200 to build a 5 quarter brewery. To help finance his plans it appears that John Harris sold thirty acres of farm land in Hook Norton.[52]

It has been generally assumed that in 1872 John Harris built a new brewery. While the plans show the internal layout of the building and the positioning of the equipment, the lack of any building specifications or other written documented evidence throws some doubt on this assumption. Indeed one of the Pontifex plans carries the title 'Alterations to a 6 quarter brewery', suggesting that the work undertaken was a refurbishment rather than a reconstruction of the premises. The plans were drawn up over a period of approximately five weeks, being dated the 9th May, 30th May and 15th June 1872 and appear to relate to the execution of the work. It maybe no coincidence that John Harris did no brewing during May 1872 and only completed five brews in the following month. During the period between the 9th May and 30th May, it seems work concentrated on plumbing in the main brewing vessels, the coppers, the mashtun, coolers and the various liquor tanks. After the 30th May work shifted towards the fitting of the 'Union' cask cleansing equipment and finally, in mid June the installation of the grist mill elevator. Without the building specifications it is difficult to know what alterations were necessary to the internal structure of the brewhouse to accommodate the new equipment.

The brewery that Pontifex designed for John Harris took advantage of the advances made in brewery design and layout and was based on the tower principle. The plans show the tower having a split level second floor, with the cold liquor back (tank) at a slightly higher level than the grist case, which was directly above the mashtun. The latter was sparged mechanically, although it is not recorded whether this included mechanical mashing. Situated beneath the cold liquor back was the liquor copper which provided hot water for the mashtun. The 'top cooler' was also situated on this floor. The first floor housed the mashtun, the refrigerator and a second cooler. Both the wort copper and the hop back were situated on the ground floor.

The mashtun was fed from a malt mill, driven by a belt system, which stood to its left and delivered crushed malt to the Grist Case by elevator ready for brewing. The plans do not, however, show the extent of the belt system or how it was driven.

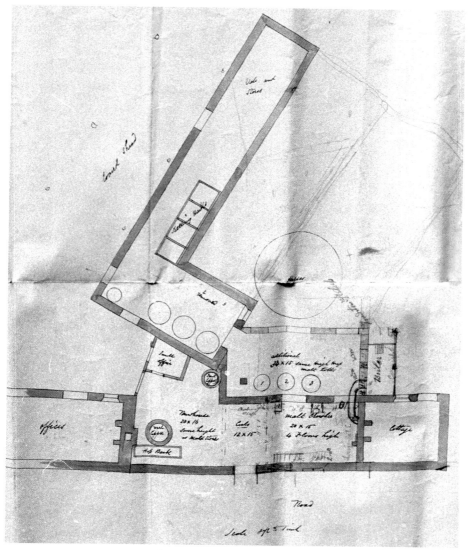

Plan of Harris's Brewery c1872.

The copper on the ground floor was heated directly by a coal fire, rather than steam. Situated to the left of it was the hop back and at the back of the brewhouse was a smaller second copper. The positioning of the 'union' cleansing vessels is unclear as there are no plans showing that part of the brewery, but an undated ground plan shows the fermenting rounds situated behind the tower. The layout of the brewery suggests that it was not a true 'tower' or 'gravitational brewery', like the small tower brewery attached to the Three Tuns in Bishop's Castle (Shropshire), because it was necessary to pump the wort from the hop back to the top cooler on the second floor. Such breweries were known as 'pumping' or 'semi-gravitational' breweries and had the advantage of affording 'far greater facility for future extension of the plant'.[53]

This was an option that Harris took in 1880 by engaging the firm of Arthur Kinder. They were a long established London firm and considered to be one of the three major brewers' engineering practices in the capital.[54] During early May, Harris and Kinder corresponded over the plans for the brewery alterations, arranging to meet in Banbury. The two men met probably on Thursday May 13th, at about 10.30am, in the Red Lion to review the drawings that Kinder had produced. That afternoon Kinder travelled to Hook Norton to make a site survey and decide the positions of the brewing vessels. It was his intention to stay over night and meet Mr Groves, the builder, in Hook Norton the following morning.[55]

The work carried out by Kinder involved the installation of a new larger boiler and a 4HP steam engine, supplied by Gimson and Co, Engineers of Leicester, which was employed to drive a belt system for lifting raw materials, principally malt, and running a new malt mill. Structural changes were made, enlarging the 'tun' room to provide room for up to eight fermenting vessels and roof and floor levels were altered. The biggest structural job however, may have been the enlarging and rebuilding of the portion of Harris's Brewery that remains today, which stood adjacent to the tower. A 'very rough tracing', dated May 17th 1880 and signed by Arthur Kinder himself shows the layout of three floors and staging from which the malt hopper could be charged. There were financial advantages to be gained by dealing with men of the calibre of Arthur Kinder. Having

Delivery Note for materials delivered by rail to Banbury Station 1880 (HNBC).

access to suppliers across the country, he could find the best price for materials, and even with the transport costs, still undercut the local price. As a result orders for iron columns, joists, piping and castings for a pump engine were placed in London and Leicester and sent by rail to Banbury and Chipping Norton Stations, to be delivered by local carriers. The building work was not confined to the brewery. Increased brewing capacity necessitated more storage space. Alfred Groves was instructed to provide plans to enlarge a malthouse to facilitate this need at a cost of £700. In March 1880 he despatched a ground plan of additions for Harris's approval. He suggested that the building should be raised to three storeys high to match existing building and by lowering the ground level two areas for storage 56 feet by 21 and 22 feet by 20 would be created. Groves further suggested that because the roof of the existing beer store was dilapidated and a 'disgrace', that an entirely new roof should be fitted and extended by a further six feet to provide a new larger storage area, some twenty feet wide and stretching the length of the whole building.

By engaging leading figures in their fields, men like Pontifex and Kinder, John Harris reaffirmed he was a serious brewer, and although his business was small and situated in a village, it was an up-to-date modern operation. By using London firms of high reputation he signalled that he wanted the very best; telegraphing an important message to both customer and competitor alike. There was prestige to be gained by using such eminent firms and in so doing he set a precedent that his successors would continue in years to come.

In the absence of the brewing books covering the period between 1874 and 1887 it is still possible to construct a picture of production

John Harris's 1880 brewery dwarfed by the tower of the 'New Brewery' (Elena Woolley).

during the last decade of the nineteenth century. In 1874 John Harris used 5 Qtrs of malt most frequently in brewing, eighteen years later his nephew had increased the size of the mash to 6 or 6½ Qtrs and these two quantities accounted for 88% of all malt used in brewing in 1892. A year later, 6½ Qtrs brews alone accounted for 81% of all malt used, an increase in both the quantity of malt used and the number of annual brewings since John Harris's last entry. It was not, however, until Clarke and John Henry Harris took the brewery out of trusteeship in October 1895 that the quantities of malt used dramatically increased.[56] In the last five years of the century malt consumption increased by 71% with the annual number of brewings reaching its peak of 345 brews in 1899. These were without doubt 'boom' years for the firm. This growth in sales caused 'some difficulty in meeting the increased demand'. The number of brewings per week was increased with the introduction of night time work. The chart below provides an analysis of the Brewing Book entries for the week beginning Monday 5th December 1898 and illustrates how the night shift was organised to achieve this. The working week at the

Date	Brew No.	Beer Brewed	Malt used	Copper	Fermentation Vats
5th December	293	Xl PA	7Qtrs	1 & 2	No.2 Sq No.3 Sq
5/6th December	294	X	7Qtrs	1 & 2	No.7 Sq No.8 Sq
6th December	295	Xl Mild	7Qtrs	1 & 2	No.4 Sq No.10 Rd
7th December	296	Xl Mild	7Qtrs	1 & 2	No.1 Sq No.9 Rd
8th December	297	Xl PA	7Qtrs	1 & 2	No.5 Sq No.6 Sq
9th December	298	X	7Qtrs	1 & 2	No.2 Sq No.3 Sq
9/10th December	299	XXX Mild	7Qtrs	1 & 2	No.4 Sq
10th December	300	X	7Qtrs	1 & 2	No.7 Sq No.8 Sq

Brewing for the week 5th-10th December 1898. Source: Hook Norton Brewery Archive: Brewing Book 1898 – December 5th-10th.

brewery was long, from 6am to 6pm on weekdays and till 4pm on a Saturday. Within a normal week the firm completed eight brewings. This was achieved by brewing daily and on two nights and on some occasions they brewed nine times a week, with the night shifts going on to midnight. All the brewing, both day and night, was carried out by the same group of men, their only concession being that they were allowed to finish their twelve hour day shift early when working nights.[57]

The impact on production during this period meant that the capacity of Harris's Brewery was being stretched to its limits. The mashtun capacity was insufficient to meet requirements and the extra shifts were necessary to meet the growing demand. Any economies of large scale production were restricted by the capacity of the equipment. During this period of hectic production the site underwent substantial redevelopment. It is, therefore, not surprising that from 1894 a planned programme of building to enlarge and improve the existing facilities of the company was begun in preparation for the incorporation of the company in 1900.[58] The plan involved enlarging the existing stables, building of new offices and the construction of a new larger brewery.

The sequence of building was not accidental either, and the plan was driven by the need for increased capacity. By building new and enlarged stables and offices first, the infra-structure to handle the expected increased output was in place before the new brewery was built. The positioning of the new, larger brewery meant that the old offices had to be demolished and replaced by the new building. The new offices were completed during late 1896 and were ready for fitting out in the first months of 1897.[59] A faded pencil note on the Brewery Deeds records that the offices 'stand on the site of the old malthouse'. The offices served a dual purpose. Upstairs were the offices of the company, while in the basement a fledgling wine and spirit business began trading in 1897, with the purpose of supplying the company's licensed properties and travellers.

It is probably no coincidence either, that William Bradford was engaged as architect for the new brewery. In the back of Clarke's copy of Faulkner's 'The Theory and Practice of Modern Brewing' there is a full page

Scotland End Farmhouse, John Harris's original home, later becoming the brewery offices before building began in 1898. Alban Clarke is on the left of the group (HNBC).

advertisement for Bradford's practice and Clarke had already done business with Bradford, using one of his patent cowls on the malting kiln. By engaging Bradford, Clarke followed his uncle's example and went for a leading London brewery architect.[60]

During May 1898 William Bradford visited Hook Norton to finalise the list of brewing plant required and was urged to begin seeking tenders for the work. Surprisingly the building work did not go to Alfred Groves of Milton under Wychwood, the company that had done much of the previous building work for the company. Instead it went to William Bloxham, builders of Warwick Road in Banbury, with a separate contract being placed with Messrs Buxton Thornley of Burton on Trent for brewing equipment.

No plans of Bradford's new brewery have survived, but an undated 2D photo-litho artist's impression of the new brewery was supplied by William Bradford, showing the new brewery overlooking a large open space. The building commands the centre of the picture with the copper house, offices and maltings to the left and the stables on the right. A dray wagon stands in the space before the brewery while another leaves the brewery site, passing the maltings (now the Visitor's Centre). Two men stand in the brewery doorway talking and in front of Harris's old brewery men are moving casks. On the far left of the picture a man and a woman stand talking, one has a bicycle and in the opposite corner a plaque advertises Bradford's business. To promote their business, the directors commissioned a poster from E.S. and A. Robinson of Bristol during 1904, taking Bradford's photo-litho as the centre piece. Robinson's, however, made changes.

The black and white picture was coloured and additions were made to the people working in front of the brewery. Another dray wagon, fully loaded, was added to the centre foreground. The newly purchased steam wagon was placed to the right of the dray wagon and the man and woman with their bicycle were replaced by two men talking in front of the maltings. Other workers are shown working in the area in front of the brewery. Bunches of hops and malt are used on either side to support the central picture and brewery labels advertise India Pale Ale and Double Stout. The company's name and the nature of their business completed the poster. Since the 1970s reprints of this poster have been

William Bradford's Photo-litho impression of the new brewery to be built in Hook Norton c1898.

available from the brewery and the central picture has been used by the company on bill headings and more recently as labels on bottled beer. A copy of the poster is reproduced on the back cover of this book.

Work on the New Brewery began on the 29th July 1898 with the digging out of the foundations for the Copper House and to save the cost of a labourer, a tram line was laid to move the rubble. Unlike John Harris's building projects, brewing went on as usual and was not curtailed. Some brewing sessions were re-scheduled to accommodate the construction work and on occasions brewing took place in the evening, going on until midnight or the early hours of the morning. In the months between July 1898 and May 1900, the company averaged twenty eight brewings a month and achieved more than thirty in eight of the months within this period. Not all beer they sold was brewed in Hook Norton. Small orders for kilderkins of Dark Stout were purchased from Phipps Brewery in Towcester and the Northampton Brewery until the small second copper from the old brewery was re-sited in the present Copper House, specifically for the purpose of brewing stout. Bottling ale was also purchased from Bass in Burton on Trent.

With the brewery being built around the new equipment, brewery employees appear to have worked in precarious surroundings. Frank Beale worked in the brewery under these difficult conditions. His son recalled some of his father's experiences.

> I remember him so well saying they could almost feel the walls shaking [and] sometimes they were working for a while with it just swaying; they'd perhaps installed the equipment but were building round [it]. It was a very clever and well organised operation. It must have been.[61]

Fortunately, there appear to have been no serious injuries during the construction of the brewery, but this may have been more by luck than judgement. In February 1900, for instance, men were hoisting a malt roller to the top of the building when the tackle broke. It fell crashing through a temporary roof, narrowly missing two men. A letter was sent to William Bradford recounting the incident. It concluded, 'You'll be pleased to know the roll sustained no damage before being fixed.'

The main copper from Harris's old brewery was removed in early February 1899 and a month later a new slate roof had been erected over the cold liquor tank. By April the builders began shoring up the front of the brewery building, supporting the walls on stout wooden pillars so new footings for the front of the 'New' brewery could be dug. During the same month the new 'wort copper' was set in place and work began on putting the hop back together. A few days later, however, Clarke noted in his diary that the mashtun had dropped a few inches because supporting walls had been removed. While production seems to have continued without undue trouble and the first brew using the new equipment went through successfully on 6th June 1900, the project as a whole was not without problems.

During the summer of 1899 work commenced on building the front wall of the 'New' brewery, but production was brought to a standstill for a time on the 20th June by heavy rain. Clarke noted 'partly idle all day. Heavy rains in brewing'. By the beginning of July the demolition began on the front of the old brewery and chimney. As the old brewery was removed new equipment was installed and over a five days period in July, Bloxham's men were engaged in shoring up and 'stuffing' the wort copper, the wort pump and other machinery.

By early 1900 the building work was completed and all the old plant had been removed, but the pace of the finishing off work progressed 'painfully slowly'. To make matters worse the quality of some the work appears to have been poor and Clarke vented his frustration in correspondence to William Bradford. The Waygood's lift for moving barrels down to the cellar had been installed, but it was not working properly and after a few loads it broke down. Clarke concluded that it had been set up incorrectly and that its installation was not vertical. He demanded that the engineer should return and 'have the defects made good'. There were more problems. The large hot liquor tank was leaking. Curative measures were taken and the bolts were tightened at the source of the trouble, but still it leaked. Further investigation revealed that the

The newly completed Copper House, spring 1899 (HNBC).

packing between the joints was not rubber, as had been used on another tank, but millboard. Eventually the problem was fixed but for more than three months it remained unlagged. Alban Clarke complained the job was 'hanging about too long'. The racking room floor was another cause for more concern, needing to be re-laid, because there had not been enough cement used in the original mix. Again Alban Clarke wrote pointedly to the architect, making it clear that 'we must not be charged for this work of relaying as it is caused entirely by the builder's error'. Brewing had continued without due incident for more than a year, but then on 2nd July 1901, the bottom of the Hop Back split through the middle of the centre plate, wasting the brew. Alban Clarke was not impressed and wrote testily to William Bradford.

> It is a bad joke and we cannot understand new work cracking up like this. There appears to be no support under the centre plate. We are writing to Buxton Thornley.

He was equally to the point in his letter to Buxton & Thornley.

We regret to inform you that the bottom of our new Hop Back split across the centre plate yesterday when full of wort, wasting a quantity. Can you account for this in anyway? On examination we do not find any support under the centre. Is this the cause? We are having a piece of iron riveted on the underside to go on with.

By the end of the year Alban Clarke's patience, had been sorely tested. He wrote to Bradford urging him to see through the completion of the brewery as soon as was possible. A request he repeated in January 1901, writing to urge the completion as the 'Directors are very anxious to get the work finished and [the] account before them'. Finally, in March 1901 at the meeting of the Directors, a formal resolution was passed to write to Messrs Bradford & Sons 'requesting them to complete the account for the building of the brewery as soon as possible', but it was not until

Shoring up John Harris's old brewery before building the new tower. George Groves, second from the left, in the group in front of the brewery. Are the two men to Groves' right William Bloxham, the builder and his foreman? (HNBC).

October that the final account arrived in Hook Norton. Bradford had estimated at the outset that the 'New Brewery' would cost £12,000, but the final total of £18,386/3/9 put the project over budget and with Bradford's commission the total was in excess of £19,000.

Alban Clarke's problems were not only with the equipment. Throughout the building he kept a diary. Keen to keep a close check on the budget he noted progress, the use of labour and rates of pay for specific jobs. As a result the relationship between the brewery, builders and suppliers was not always harmonious. Anything he felt that came outside the terms of the agreed contracts was noted and challenged. William Bloxham's day-work sheets in particular provided a continual source of contention and were scrutinised thoroughly. Any suspect entries were marked with red ink and annotated before being referred back to the architect. Dissatisfaction with Bloxham's charges began after only a few days work, Clarke wrote in his diary:

> WJB [the builders] to J.H. & Co re mortar mill from C.Norton. £1 charge. 7 horses 1 day/2 men and 1 boy. We think it would have taken ½ this from our own station.

The situation appears not to have improved, and again in May 1900, Clarke wrote to William Bradford, dissatisfied with the charges being made.

> We shall be obliged if you would arrange for a surveyor to make an appointment with us next week to investigate Mr Bloxham's day work charges as they are so very voluminous and evidently require the strictest investigation. We are not at all satisfied that the majority of the works … are legitimate charges.

Matters came to a head when William Bloxham made a claim for £45/16/1 for out of pocket expenses for work that fell outside the remit of his contract. Bloxham pleaded his case eloquently to both Bradford and Clarke, arguing that stone he was supplied with, to build the brewery, should have been dressed before delivery and that he had incurred extra costs in getting the stone into a useable condition. He had also had to bear a price rise for the iron work used in the building that was 'in excess of his schedule'. He felt he was 'fairly entitled to both claims', but his argument fell on deaf ears. Bradford and Clarke were in agreement that he was not, under the wording of his contract entitled to claim any recompense for the additional outlay.

It was not only Bloxham's charges that brought discontent. Buxton and Thornley's claim for £59/10/0 for a steam coil they said Alban Clarke had specifically requested, was a far more serious problem. The brewery having paid the final bill for Buxton & Thornley's work refused to recognise any further liability. Letters passed between both parties and the architect, but no solution was immediately forthcoming and to compound matters further, Mr Thornley refused to pay an outstanding bill for beer supplied to his home. The brewery's position was clear, 'unless we receive payment of our bill £6/8/6 within seven days we shall....hand the bill over to our solicitors'. With both companies prepared to take legal action the whole matter was set to be settled in court. Common sense, however, prevailed with a compromise drafted by William Bradford. The agreement involved Mr Thornley settling his outstanding bill, and as a matter of goodwill, the company in return, made a 'small payment' towards Buxton & Thornley's claim. The solution met with the satisfaction of both parties and the threat of legal proceedings was dropped.

The new brewery, essentially a much larger version of the old one, also worked on the semi gravitational principle. It was equipped with a 25HP Buxton & Thornley steam engine to drive the brewery machinery and Frank Beale became its first *driver*.[62] There were two mashtuns, one of 8 quarters, which had been refurbished and moved out of Harris's old brewery, and the other fitted new, which had a capacity of 20 quarters.[63] This not only provided a greater mashing capacity but also reduced the number of brewings necessary to achieve a larger output. It is clear from the analysis of the Brewing Books how the two mashtuns were used with production based on the working of the 20 quarter mashtun.

The copper from John Harris's 1872 brewery was moved and installed in the 'New' Brewery. It was used for brewing stout until 1907 (Jack Haney).

In 1899 there were 345 brewings using 2,354 quarters of malt. With the opening of the New Brewery in 1900, the number of annual brewings dropped to 225 while the quantity of malt used increased to 2,722 quarters. The annual quantities of malt mashed during the first decade of the new century never again reached this total. Quantities averaged 2,590 quarters a year until 1906, and then decreased by an average of 9% a year until the onset of the First World War. During the period between 1900 and 1914 the quantity of malt used in the mashtun fell by half and for the three years 1910 to 1912 there were annual reductions in the amounts of malt used in brewing of 14.2%, 14.4% and 18%.

From 1900 the use of the 20 quarter mashtun increased, with it being responsible for two thirds of all brewings (712), with particular peaks in brewing in 1902 (124) and 1904 (108). With no growth in demand after 1907, its use became less economical and John Harris's old, but refurbished mashtun began to bear the brunt of production. From 1908 the number of 20 quarter brewings decreased at a rate of twenty brewings

The 'New' Brewery c1901 (HNBC).

a year until 1912, before finally going out of production permanently in 1913, having completed a total of 1,005 of all brewings during a thirteen year period. The 8 quarter mashtun sustained 76% of all brewing until the outbreak of the First World War. The majority of these using 8 quarters of malt.

The mashtun in the foreground was moved to the 'New' brewery from Harris's 1880 brewery and refurbished. It was responsible for all mashing between 1913 and 1948. The original 20 quarter mashtun was replaced by the mashtun in the centre of the picture. The metal plates around its edge give some indication of the size of the original vessel. It has since been replaced by a new mashtun (see Chapter 5).

In the years before Alban Clarke's death in 1917, the working day at the brewery traditionally began at 6am. Some mornings he would check the punctuality of his employees and any man coming in late would be sent home until breakfast, losing two hours work and his wages for the period missed. A thirty minute break was taken at 8am for breakfast. Work then continued until 10.30am when the men took a mid-morning break, assembling in the engine room of the brewery, where a long table flanked by benches was arranged to receive a jar of 'allowance beer', which was served from a barrel kept in a room later used as a cold store for yeast. Prior to 1901 this allowance appears to have been about 7 pints a day for each man, but this was later cut by half. Recollections of the amounts of beer provided during this fifteen minute break vary from one to four pints and it appears that for a time the men were allowed to take their beer and consume it on the job where they were working. This privilege was abused by some and stopped. A lunch break was taken between 1 and 2pm, marked by the brewery's hooter. A further break for 'allowance beer' was taken in mid afternoon, with work finishing at 6pm, or 4pm on a Saturday.

Not all brewery employees finished work at 6pm. Frank Beale who lived next to the brewery, would as normal practice, and particularly so after Alban Clarke's death, return to the brewery just before going to bed to either turn off or alter the flow of water running through the fermenting squares. The 'New' brewery may have been modern and incorporated the latest brewing technology, but there was no electricity and in the winter when it was dark Frank Beale relied on a candle or oil lamp which he carried and hung wherever he was working. On very cold nights he would place a coke brazier in the cellar to keep the stores at an even temperature. Braziers were also positioned elsewhere in the brewery on winter nights to keep the pipes from freezing. Once he was old enough, Frank's son, Fred would accompany his father into the brewery to stoke up the braziers with coke. After a time Fred was sent on his own to carry out the evening tasks. He recalled what it was like to be in the brewery alone on a winter's night.

> If you went into the brewery the candle holders were kept just inside the front door. You had to light the candle …and carry it wherever you went. You just carried your light round with you and hung it wherever you were working. You can't imagine how it was possible to work in the brewery starting at half past five in the morning in the winter, perhaps with an oil lamp hung on the walls or candles. I can remember after I got big enough and after the first torches came, [they] were a real boon, Dad would send me in there with his torch to go and turn 'number so and so check, off'. I knew just which numbers the fermenting vats were. They were all squares in those days. I'll admit it was an eerie experience. I'd been in hundreds of times with him, but it's different when you go in on your own and there were crickets in the engine room in those days and there'd be a drop of water, you know, and in the brewery

everything is so still, just a drop of water dropping onto something, made a noise.[64]

By 1917 wartime restrictions had made oil and the candles used for lighting the brewery a scarce commodity and Percy Flick decided that with the exception of brewing days, the men's hours would be shortened and changed so they worked from 7am to 5pm and 1pm on a Saturday. Frank Beale thought this was 'wonderful', but Flick's motives were not based on the welfare of his employees, but on the 'considerable [financial] saving thereby effected'. The brewery continued to be lit by oil and candles for more than another decade. In the summer of 1928 the company was approached by the newly established 'Electric Light Company' which had been established in the village, with a view to installing electric light in the brewery, the offices, the Sun Inn and other public houses. In the prevailing economic conditions, it was felt that the installation of electric lights in the brewery would be a 'needless expense', but if publicans wanted electric light in their premises the company would finance and supply an estimate for the necessary wiring. The village generating station supplied 240 volt D.C. power until 1932 when it was taken over by the Shropshire, Worcestershire and Staffordshire Electric Power Company which had a contract to supply Sibford and the surrounding district at 8d per unit.

The First World War

The moral case for liquor control, voiced by the Temperance lobby, had by the beginning of the First World War lost favour and was replaced by the needs of 'national efficiency'. To this end, government controls were imposed on industry in general and, brewing in particular was subjected to stringent controls which deprived the Hook Norton Brewery of some of its traditional working practices and changed irrevocably a pattern of brewing that had been established over many years.[65] The preservation of food stocks required a reduction in the use of raw materials in the brewing process and in Hook Norton malting became a casualty of these restrictions, when the company failed to obtain a licence for anthracite in 1915. This brought to an end a century's old tradition of 'home-steeped' malt, although it was not until February 1917 that the Government issued a general order to prohibit the manufacture and sale of malt, except under licence from the Food Controller. The need for a new source of malt for the brewery was resolved when Percy Flick turned to an old school friend employed at Robson's in Pontefract. Agreement was reached and malt was sent by rail from Pontefract thereafter, to be collected from Hook Norton Station by horse and dray and carted to the brewery.[66] This arrangement continued until Robson's became part of Associated British Maltsters (ABM).

As the duty on beer and the cost of raw materials increased, national output fell dramatically although in Hook Norton the quantities of malt used in brewing during 1914 fell by only 6%. To further reduce the raw materials used in the production process, the Government successively lowered the specific gravity leading to weaker beer being produced. As a result, there were further annual decreases in the quantities of malt used in Hook Norton, which reached a nadir in 1918, with only 474 quarters being used. By the end of the war, the quantity of malt used had fallen to under half the 1914 total. In the pre-war months of 1914 the Brewery were producing seven beers, of which XXX and 8d appear to have been the most common brews, but by the end of the year, only XXX and Dark Stout of the original seven beers were still in production. The effects of these changes were felt immediately in the bars of the company's public houses. Percy Flick felt it necessary to write a letter to accompany a delivery to the Railway Hotel in Hook Norton to explain the situation.

> We are sending you today the special HNB beer as ordered, but it must be distinctly understood that we sell you this 54/- solely on condition that it is retailed at 3d per pint. We hope you will realise that it is our only wish to provide such beers that will enable you to maintain your trade and we feel sure the only way to do this is to send you the very best value possible in beer to retail at 3d and at the same time allow you your old rate of profit.

A further consequence of this fall in production was the large quantity of casks that were accumulating in the brewery yard which were surplus to requirements. It was decided, that if possible, these casks should be sold.

Although the company continued to produce a range of seven beers, in March 1915 a new set had replaced those brewed a year earlier, with M[ild], L[ight] M[ild] and T becoming the most common brews. In March 1916 P[ale] A[le] was re-introduced briefly but M[ild] and L[ight] M[ild] still dominated the output. By the end of the year only four beers were being produced and M[ild], L[ight] M[ild] and T were replaced by XXXpa blend, a new B[itter] and FXM. In the spring of 1917, XXXpa, and XXXm were added to the list of beers being produced, but output was concentrated almost solely on B[itter] during the following two years.

New customers were desperately needed and early in January 1917 Percy Flick spent an unsuccessful day in Birmingham trying to establish new business. The brewers, William Blencowe Co Ltd of Brackley were, however, in need of assistance, requiring another brewery to produce 250 barrels for them at specified gravities. Percy Flick took the opportunity and approached Mr Robert Longman, Managing Director at Blencowe's to tender for the work. On the 18th January he wrote to Alban Clarke at the Hook Norton Brewery, expressing an air of confidence after his disappointing day in Birmingham.

> Have been to see Mr Longman again this evening – will you please work out the cost of 1045° Bitter and Mild (150 brls) in 36's and 18's, and 1037° Mild in 36's and 18's (100 brls). I can, I fancy sell to him. I will be over tomorrow.

Agreement was reached and on 22nd January, Percy Flick received a letter from Brackley confirming the arrangements. The first brew of 55 barrels of Mild was to be 'put through' the Hook Norton plant three days later. Longman was very precise in his requirements. The brew was to reach a final attenuation of 14.6lbs, or as near as possible, it was not to be primed, finings were not to be added and no preservatives, save a handful of hops to each cask. A small bottle of Blencowe's Mild was sent to Hook Norton, so that the brew could be matched for colour. Racked into Blencowe's own casks, the brew was collected by Motor Tractor the following week. A further eight brews followed during February and March, increasing the total number of brews completed during the first quarter of the year by 16%.

The provisions of the Output of Beer (Restriction) Act 1916 clearly outlined regulations under which the supply of beer could be undertaken. Each brewer had a quarterly output fixed, based on the output of the corresponding quarter in the previous year, but reduced by 15%. Failure to comply with these regulations brought a fine of £100, plus £2 for every barrel brewed in excess of the quota, which for Blencowe's meant deducting the 250 barrels brewed in Hook Norton from their quota. Such arrangements agreed between brewers were not uncommon. In 1891, much of Courage's Anchor Brewery in Southwark was destroyed by fire. While the rebuilding was carried out, they bought £40,000 of 'London Beers' from Barclay Perkins to supply their outlets and for over thirty years they bought in, under contract, Pale Ales, first from Flowers and Sons Brewery in Stratford upon Avon and later, saving transport costs, from Fremlin Brothers of Maidstone.[67]

The brewing for Blencowe's was only a temporary solution to the problem, giving the Hook Norton Brewery work and the opportunity to brew their quarterly quota, until a more permanent solution was found. Ironically, that solution was provided by the same authority that had deprived the brewery of the private trade. The powers of the Central Control Board were far reaching and included not only the control of licensing hours, but the supply and specification of beer to be sold.

After Flick's fruitless trip to Birmingham in 1915, salvation for the company came in the form of trade with the Working Men's Clubs in Coventry. A consequence of the tighter controls implemented by the Central Control Board was there was a shortage of beer in heavy industrial areas. There was considerable unrest and in some areas, men went on strike. The Government investigated the matter and issued, in response to the problem, the Intoxicating Liquor (Output and Delivery) Order No 3 during October 1917. Under this order, the Food Controller allowed Brewers supplying 'necessitous munitions areas' to increase their output by a further 13.3%.[68]

Coventry was one of the 'munitions areas' covered by the Intoxicating Liquor (Output and Delivery) Order 1918 and as a result the Hook Norton Brewery was issued with two Special Licences, covering the second and third quarters of 1918, authorising the brewery to supply beer to clubs in the Coventry area.[69] Beer had been sent to Coventry since John Harris's time but it is less clear how the initial contacts were made with the city's Working Men's clubs. With the help of the war time regulations this new trade provided the brewery with a new, permanent market which is discussed in a later chapter in more detail. This new business was important, for the inter-war years were difficult for the company. While brewers like Courage embarked on a prosperous period of expansion and development, acquiring four breweries, rebuilding the Alton Brewery to expand its production capacity and increasing its total number of outlets to 886, the Hook Norton Brewery struggled.[70]

Problems and another War

The years after 1920 were a 'crisis time' for the Hook Norton Brewery. This is exemplified by the falling quantities of malt used in brewing. While national output of bulk barrels fell by a fifth in the period between the wars, the quantities of malt used in brewing in Hook Norton also fell, but more dramatically. When war was declared in 1914 the brewery was using 1,184 quarters of malt, by 1920 that had fallen to 776 quarters and in 1922 it had fallen to 559 quarters, reaching a nadir of 533 quarters in 1932. From this low point the fortunes of the company began to make a small and sustained recovery as economic conditions in the country improved. As in the country as a whole, the quantities of malt used steadily increased, although it was not until 1944 that the total quantity used in a year surpassed the 1914 figure. Unemployment in Coventry at the beginning of the 1930s produced three 'poor years' and was responsible for a decline in trade with the clubs. It was not until the middle of the decade that the brewery trade 'picked up' and production was increased.

From 1933 onwards, quantities of malt used steadily increased and by 1939 had returned to the amounts used in 1920. The quantities of malt used in each brewing, during the inter-war years, remained almost constant, at about 8 quarters. From 1914 to 1919, 4,668 quarters of malt were used in 585 brewings and between 1920 and 1939 there were 1,648 brewings using 13,140 quarters of malt, averaging about eight quarters per brew.[71]

These were difficult years and the Directors regularly reviewed the company's 'finance and sales statements'. With no replacement for the 'old style private trade' to provide extra capacity, the company struggled to increase its output. Brewing, however, continued as usual as the Directors continued to report a continuing decline in barrelage. January and February were particularly bad months with just one brew a week, but this was found to be uneconomical and it left the men with a lot of time on their hands. A more beneficial solution was to brew three times a fortnight, which was found to be both less depressing for the men and financially more viable.[72]

With reduced brewing, the quantities of malt bought from Pontefract were modest. In September 1922 an order for thirty quarters, made up of 10 quarter quantities of Pale Ale, Mild Ale and Californian malt was despatched to Hook Norton, but not all the malt came from Robson's. On the same date, an order for 24 quarters of malt was also despatched to Hook Norton by Messrs Gillstrap and Earp from Newark on Trent. From the correspondence it appears that Flick was not tying up capital by holding great quantities of malt in stock. As a result, orders were placed about a week or ten days before the malt was required for brewing.[73] During the General Strike in the spring of 1926, brewing in Hook Norton almost came to a halt because they were short of malt. There was an urgent need to re-stock and supplies were usually transported by rail to Hook Norton. With the railway workers out on strike in sympathy with the miners nothing could be moved by rail. With a ban being imposed on the movement of everything except foodstuffs there was the real prospect of the brewery having to cease production. Robson's, however, overcame the problem by hiring a lorry to transport the malt, placing a large placard on the front declaring that the load was 'Food Supplies'. Apparently, without incident the lorry arrived safely in Hook Norton, relieving the malt shortage.

The post-war period was particularly difficult for everyone living in Hook Norton. The brewery strove to re-build its beer sales, but when the entire workforce of the local ironstone quarry was laid off without warning in 1921, trade in the village slumped. Men had to walk in to Chipping Norton to sign on to receive a grocery ticket. Some of them chose to leave the village and went to work in Wrexham for the Brymbo Steel Company, sending money home to support their families in Hook Norton. Others left the village for good and settled in Coventry and the London area. With no alternative employment in Hook Norton, people 'hadn't the money to spend' and the situation 'caused a lot of distress'.[74]

It was during this period that Percy Hemmings joined the brewery as a seventeen year old. His situation gives some indication of the hardships experienced in 1924. Percy was only five years old when his father died. His mother returned to Hook Norton to bring up her sons. At fourteen Percy left school and went to work on a local pheasant farm, but after two years he was made redundant when the farmer's own son left school and was employed instead. For the next twelve months Percy 'dodgered about' between jobs, getting what little casual work he could find. If he didn't work there was no money, and there was very little work. There were no benefit payments to help support him and his widowed mother. A minimal amount of relief was forthcoming, but it did little to feed a growing youth. Percy's luck, however, changed when one day his mother met George Groves, the brewery company's secretary in the village High Street. As a result of their conversation Percy was told to report to the brewery stables on the following Monday. Others weren't so lucky. Percy retired forty eight years later at the age of

65 years, having worked in the brewery stables, bottling stores and after a period in the army during the Second World War, in the brewery itself under Bill Clarke.[75]

By 1939 output and profits had once again begun to rise. The previous two decades had seen the industry adjust to the production of weaker beers, paying increased excise duty, particularly on stronger beers. There was a growth in sales of bottled beers, an improvement in public houses and amalgamation as the larger brewers combined or acquired smaller businesses with the view of increasing the number of licensed properties to maintain the profitability of their businesses.[76]

Although there were restrictions, the war did not inhibit output, as it had done during the first conflict. The production of bulk barrels nationally, increased from 24,674,992 in 1939 to 31,332,852 in 1945. In Hook Norton the use of malt (including substitutes) increased from 776 quarters in 1939 to 1,204 quarters in 1945. This increase in malt used during brewing was reflected in the annual total of brewings. In 1939 there were 97 brewings, and these rose annually during the war years, peaking in 1945 with 152 brewings.

The largest increase was between 1940 and 1941, when usage rose by a quarter, for the remainder of the war, there were smaller increases, the largest of which was 8.1% in 1944 and the company were able to sell 'everything they could turn out'. The hot summer of 1941 led to record numbers of bulk barrels being brewed in May (883), June (811), July (963) and again in August (882), yet output could not keep pace with sales. This situation seems to have continued throughout the remainder of the year and by Christmas the brewery had completely sold out of draught and bottled beers even though they brewed 1,017 bulk barrels during December.

Amongst Bill Clarke's notes in the wartime brewing books is a breakdown of the costs incurred in producing a barrel of beer (at a gravity of 1034°) during 1941. The largest component of this total was the excise duty, which stood at £5/2/0d per barrel. The cost of raw materials he estimated to be 19 shillings, with coal at about 3 shillings, and finings, dry hops, shives a further 5 shillings. The average selling price of a barrel was £7/5/0d which produced a small profit (16 shillings) to cover all other overheads, but this he thought was 'rather too low' and he re-adjusted it to nearer £1.

Working within the wartime restrictions meant that limitations were again imposed on the use of materials; flaked barley and oats were used in the mashtun, and sugar was restricted so it was necessary to search out suppliers. Hops were also subject to restriction and in July 1941 the hop rate was further reduced by 5lbs to comply with the directive from the Ministry of Food to effect a 20% reduction. With labour being called up into the forces, some processes were suspended. When Percy Hemmings was called up for military service in July 1941 it became necessary to re-organise the staffing, with all the available labour being drafted into the brewery to maintain production. The immediate effect of the labour shortage was the cessation of drying the malt before brewing, a practice that had been employed since 1912.

Bottling also was limited to only small amounts of Guinness, which was rationed to the pubs. With brewing scheduled to happen three times a week, output was simplified to just one beer.[77]

Mechanical breakdowns were also a problem and with a shortage of spares it was necessary to cannibalise redundant equipment for parts. This was particularly true when John Harris's old 8 quarter mashtun began to show its age as parts began to fail. It had born the brunt of all beer production since 1913. There was a succession of problems involving the mashtun and brewing equipment. In July 1941 the mashtun rakes broke down and for a while mashing took place without the use of the rakes.

The same problem re-occurred in September, and later that month and again in December the plates at the bottom of the mashtun became disarranged and malt grains mixed with wort blocked the taps as the liquid was run into the copper. When the rouser failed in April 1942 brewing continued until the problem was fixed. A more serious problem occurred in April 1943 when the engine stopped during mashing and Bill Clarke noted in the brewing book:

A very bad mash. Could only get 75% at 7am, further 25% at 9am… Taps very thick", suggesting the plates had again been disarranged.

During the second half of 1943, the Agricultural Economics Research Institute at the University of Oxford carried out an investigation into the condition of rural life, which centred on the twenty four square miles covered by the 6 inch Ordnance Survey Map that included Hook Norton. Their report was published during 1944. Their findings reveal demand for beer was such that, with a full complement of men, production at Hook Norton could have been increased.

> There is a small brewery in one of the larger villages supplying the local public houses. In normal times about 20 men are employed, but if present demand is maintained the brewery could employ another 10 men and make half as much beer again.[78]

The end of the Second World War did not bring a return to normal brewing conditions. A world-wide food crisis in 1946 led to the government restricting supplies of barley for brewing. The industry was limited to producing only 85% of its standard barrelage of the previous year. This was a restriction applied to all brewers and later in the same year a 10% cut in average gravity was imposed along with a lowering of the minimum average gravity from 1032° to 1030°. Although this restriction was lifted a year later, brewers found it difficult to meet bulk demands and were unable to increase the gravity of their beer. Further cut backs occurred; a 25% cut in sugar consumption was imposed in 1948 and formed part of the government's curb on dollar spending, and a further decrease in output was introduced, reducing amounts to about 80% of the 1945 baseline.

The impact of these restrictions was felt in Hook Norton. The shortage of raw materials had the effect of rationing production and there were further reductions the following year.

Production was only about three quarters of that in 1945. During 1948 and 1949 there were small increases, only for the malt usage to again fall in 1950. To achieve the necessary restrictions on the use of raw materials, the government imposed a monthly barrel quota, limiting the quantity of beer that could be produced and through this mechanism was able to restrict the quantities of beer brewed. It fell to the local Excise Officer to monitor each month's output and if this was exceeded, the following month's quota was adjusted accordingly, ensuring that the total output allowed for the brewery was met. The consequence of these limitations was to inhibit production in Hook Norton and this caused shortages. It was not until the restrictions were lifted in 1951 that it was possible for the Hook Norton Brewery to resume the brewing of a bitter beer.

Notes

1   Woolley. R.M. The Development of the Hook Norton Brewery 1849-1913. M.Phil Thesis University of Wolverhampton. 2005. p.70.

2   Pearson. L. *British Breweries. An Architectural History.* 1999. p.25.

3   Bushnan. J.S. *Burton and its beer.* 1853. p.133.

4   S.A./23/91. 30/11/1754. Thomas Hill of Tern Hall at Atcham, Shropshire (now Attingham Hall) brewed 7 hogsheads 'in the season'. One was sent by road to the London house. Using a brewing season during the eighteenth century may have been normal practice for all brewers and not exclusively confined to the large London brewers.

5   Mathias. P. *The Brewing Industry in England 1700-1830,* 1959. p.19.

6   Bushnan. J.S. *Burton and its Beer.* 1853. p.132.

7   Reinarz. pp.307 & 314. Email 11/9/2002. Wagebooks…give detailed references…to workers 'gardening at home of C. Flower', or 'tending horses for Thwaites'. Workers usually worked at the homes of the owners or managers.

8   Mathias. P. 1959. p.55.

9   Oral Tradition. Conversation with W.A. Clarke. 1973.

10   Vaisey. J. The Brewing Industry 1886-1951, 1960. Ch1. A scientific approach to brewing became more prevalent during the second half of the nineteenth century.

11   Gourvish. T. and Wilson. R. *The British Brewing Industry 1830-1980.* 1994 p.639 Common Brewer: a Commercial or "wholesale" brewer. Their classification of a Common Brewer as someone who brews more than 1,000 barrels a year appears to be high as it excludes Common Brewers like John Harris who was brewing 500 barrels a year in 1855. See Glossary of Brewing Terms.

     Brewery Deeds. 'Confines of messuage malthouse cottages and premises dated 4th September 1852. Mr John Parish to Mr John Harris.....received ....from the within named John Harris the sum of £350.'

     Monckton. H.A. *A History of English Ale & Beer.* 1966. Appendix D. p.221. Column 2.

12   Eddershaw. D. *A Country Brewer Hook Norton 1849-1999.* Hook Norton Brewery Company Ltd. 1999. p.8.

13   Moritz. E.R. & Morris G.H. *A Text Book of the Science of Brewing.* 1891 pp.255. 400.

     Brewing Book. 22nd October 1872. 'Nice and bright hopped with ½lb brl'.

14   Pearson. L. 1999. p.172 Edward Holmes designed a new 7 storey brewery for George Wilkinson of Ashted Row, Birmingham in 1874.

15   Monckton. H.A. 1966 Appendix D. p.222. Column 1.

16   Oral Tradition: Conversation with Bert Heritage. 1973. See Chapter 5.

17   Gourvish and Wilson, 1994 p.30. Table 2.3 Per capital consumption of Beer in gallons. England and Wales.

18   Gourvish. T. & Wilson R. 1994. p.252.

Mathias. P. *The First Industrial Nation. An Economic History of Britain* 1700-1914. 1969. 449 Table 1: The population rose from 29.79 million in 1871 to 37.09 million in 1901. Over the same period the total number of licences fell from 112,884 to 102,848 and beerhouse licences fell from 42,590 to 29,064.

19   Moritz. E.R. & Morris. G.H. *A Text Book of the Science of Brewing.* 1891. p.169.

Monckton. *The History of English Ale & Beer.* 1966. pp.159-60, 172. By Act of Parliament in 1847 the use of sugars was sanctioned as an alternative to malt. Duty was levied at 21/8d a quarter or 22/6d on 180lb of sugar, calculated to be the equivalent of a quarter of malt.

20   Moritz. E.R. & Morris. G.H. 1891, pp.183-188.

21   Moritz. E.R. & Morris. G.H. 1891, pp.169/174-5.

22   Moritz. E.R. & Morris. G.H. 1891, pp.170/179-181.

23   The Oxford Shorter Dictionary describes 'whiting' as a preparation of finely powdered chalk, p.2421. 'Chalk' is described as 'an opaque soft white earthy limestone, consisting of carbonate of lime with some impurities.' p.288.

'Whiting' was used in the preparation of whitewash.

24   Moritz. E.R. & Morris. G.H. 1891. p.174.

SBTRO: F. Kendall and Son. Letter 30th November 1900. (DR197/203). The letter appears to be sent to all customers to re-assure them that Kendall products were arsenic free.

25   Banbury Guardian, November 29th 1900. 'Arsenic in Beer'.

26   Gourvish. & Wilson. 1994, p.296.

27   Banbury Guardian, January 1st 1901, Notice the Hook Norton Brewery. Hunt Edmunds Brewery (Banbury) and the Messers Blencowe (Brackley) placed similar notices in the Banbury Guardian announcing their beer was free of arsenic contamination. 13/10/1900.

28   SBTRO: Report to Manchester Brewers' Central Association. 15/12/1900. (DR197/203).

29   SBTRO: Beer. A Bill To amend the Law relating to the Manufacture and Sale of Beer 19.2.1901 (DR197/203).

30 Gourvish. T. & Wilson. R. 1994. p.296. fn90.

31 Daily Mail, September 12th 1905, p.6.

32 Sigsworth. E.M. 1964/65. p.544.

33 Sigsworth. E M. 1964/65. pp.544-545.

34 SBTRO: Briant. L. Report. Undated. Probably 1900.(DR197/203).

35 HNBC Archive: F. Kendall & Son: Analytical Report 718. October 31st 1901.

36 Moritz. E.R. & Morris. G.H. 1891. pp1-12. identify 'Waters containing large proportions of gypsum' as being excellent '...waters for pale ale brewing... [giving] Burton beer its original great pre-eminence...'
Gourvish T. & Wilson. R. 1994. pp.50, 83. '...until the successful application of gypsum [calcium sulphate] in the 1870's none of the experiments was successful' [in replicating Burton Water].

37 Brewing Book 1896 Brewings 244 & 245. 30/31st December 1896. The cost of hardening given as 3/4d.

38 Dingle. A.E. *Drink and Working-Class Living Standards in Britain.* 1870-1914, 1972, p.620.

39 Vaizey. J. *The Brewing industry 1886-1951.* 1960. p.xii.

40 Gourvish. T. & Wilson. R. 1994. p.25.

41 McKenna. J. *Birmingham Breweries.* Brewin Books 2005. p.62.

42 Oral tradition. Fred Beale 10.8.1982. Talking about his father, Frank Beale; brewery employee.
Oral Tradition. Conversation with Bill Clarke 1974. The practice of drying malt the day before use persisted until the outbreak of WW2, when a shortage of labour made it impractical. The brewery now uses a temperature controlled malt storeroom.

43 Gourvish. T. & Wilson. R. 1994, p.294.

44 Pearson. L. 1999, pp.4, 43, 72-75.

45 Stapleton. B. Thomas. J. *GALES: A study in Brewing, Business and Family History.* 2000. pp.42-43.

46 Reinarz. J. 1998. p9.
Pearson. L. 1999 pp163, 177, 200-1, 205. Barnard A. John Wackrill enlarged the Shropshire Brewery in Wellington (Shropshire)and added a maltings in 1883. See Woolley. R.M. *John Wackrill the brewer Wellington forgot.* pp.1-19. BHS Journal No:152 Spring 2013.

47 Pearson. L. 1999, pp.61-66.

48 Pearson. L. 1999, p.66.

49 Trinder. B. *Victorian Banbury*, 1982, p.34.

50 Built for R.W. Flick in 1890. He was the father of Percy William Flick, Managing Director of the Hook Norton Brewery 1912-1951.

Pearson. L. 1999, p.174. No mention is made of any building at Hunt Edmunds Brewery or the work done for John Harris by Pontifex and Kinder.

51 Trinder. B. *Victorian Banbury*. Phillimore. 1982. p2.

52 Pearson. L. 1999, pp.66, 184.

Scammell. G. *Breweries and Maltings: Their arrangement and Construction*. 1871. pp.87-88.

Census Return 1871. John Harris described himself as a 'Brewer, Maltster and Farmer of 22 acres employing a traveller, clerk, Brewer, 9 men and a boy.' When he bought the property in 1852 he farmed 52 acres of land.

53 Bradford. W. *Notes on Maltings and Breweries*. 1889. Chapter 2. Systems.2.2 p.25.

54 Pearson. L. 1999. pp.69,174.

55 Letters to John Harris from Arthur Kinder, 8th, 10th, 15th May 1880. Kinder suggested that Harris meet him at the Red Lion, unless Harris met him at the station. www.jaist.ac.p. Calendar May 1880. The builder was Alfred Groves of Milton under Wychwood, his firm later built the present Offices and enlarged the stables.

56 High Court of Justices-Chancery Lane 1898 HN02301 – Estate of John Harris 1.10.1895.

57 Oral Tradition: Conversation with Fred Beale 10.8.1982. His father was one of the brewing staff who worked nights during the final years of the nineteenth century. HNBC Archive: Personal diary kept by Alban Clarke. 8/5/1897. Brewing till 12 midnight.

58 HNBC Archive: The Diary of Alban Clarke. Entry 17/4/1898 'Mr Bradford here – final look through plant list. Instructions for him to commence getting tenders in at once'.

59 The Diary of Alban Clarke. Entry 2/2/1897 *'George White here. 10.30-11.30* arranged about Office fittings'. Entry: 2/2/1897: 'Berrington here about office seating'. Entry: 26/5/1897 'Laying down cord carpet in Office'. Entry: 7/6/1897. 'moving safes into new Office'. Entry 28/9/1897: '…moving old books into new offices'.

60 Pearson. L. 1999. p.154.

61 Oral Tradition: Conversations with Fred Beale. July 1973 and 10/8/1982.

62 HNBC Archive: Messrs Buxton & Thornley. Account for works executed from 20/6/1898 to 30/3/1901. "…for Horizontal High Pressure Steam Engine £175.0.0".

63 Oral Tradition: Conversation with Bill Clarke. 8/3/1981.

64 Conversations with Fred Beale. May and July 1973. 10/8/1982 Frank Beale retired to bed between 9.30pm and 10pm. The Beale's cottage was at the head of Brewery Lane, next to the present Visitor's Centre. It was condemned and demolished. The site is now the entrance to the present Company car park. He referred to the process as "turning off the checks".

65 Oral Tradition: W.A. Clarke 1974.

Lord Devonport, quoted in *"The Restricted Barrelage and Victory"* Brewers' Gazette. London. March 1st 1917.

66 Brewers' Gazette. *"In Parliament"* 1917.

OCMTRC: Documented evidence of malting can be dated back to the early eighteenth century. Malt production was centred on approved producers. Robson's of Pontefract became Hook Norton's suppliers of malt.

Shadwell. A. *Drink in 1914-1922 A Lesson in Control*. Longmans, Green & Co. 1923. p.83.

67 *Letter from Brackley District Library 2/2/1983.*

Hardinge. G.N. *Courages Brewery 1787-1932*. Courages. 1932. p.19.

68 Letter from Brewer's Society. 16/2/1983 Brewer's Gazette 25/10/1917.

69 Customs & Excise Form: Restriction on Brewing April 1918.

70 Hardinge. G.N. 1932. p.19.

71 Oral Tradition: Conversation with Bill Clarke 1973.

Sayers. R.S. *"A History of Economic Change in England. 1880-1939."* OUP. 1967 Oral Tradition: Conversation with Bill Clarke 1973.

72 Oral Tradition: Conversation with Fred Beale. 1973. Reporting a conversation between his father and George Groves, the Company Secretary.

73 Oral Tradition. Conversation with Bill Clarke. 1981. He recalled that after the 1st War that gravities 'fell so much that [the brewery] didn't need the bulk [purchases] of barley used before the war.'

74 Oral Tradition: Conversations with Fred Beale and Sid Heritage 1973.

75 Oral Tradition: Conversations with Harold Wyton and Ernie Marshall 1973 and with Percy Hemmings. 1982. Percy Hemmings had a brother who went to live in Coventry.

76 Vaizey. J. 1960. pp.7-8.

77 Monckton. H.A. 1966. p.222.

78 Agricultural Research Institute, Oxford. *Country Planning*. OUP. 1944. p.88.

Chapter 3
Putting the Beer on the Road

The dray wagon leaving the brewery.

Establishing a customer base

In the eighteenth century a brewer's economical marketing area was limited to the area in which he could effectively deliver beer by horse and dray; a distance of about five miles. Rural brewers were further disadvantaged by the scattered nature of the population in which they traded.[1] These problems faced John Harris when he began brewing commercially a century later. During the first years of production, Harris's fledgling business had only two employees and no organised transport system to deliver the beer. Given the manpower available to fulfil all the roles necessary to successfully run the business, including the farm, it seems likely that Harris's trading area was initially restricted to the immediate village and neighbouring villages.

For the bulk of his business Harris must have relied upon private individuals, in and around Hook Norton and although there are no documented records of Harris's customers at this time, there is circum-stantial evidence suggesting that two clergymen, Joseph Heathcote Brooks and Henry Rendall, both incumbents at Great Rollright, may have been customers during the early years.[2]

Beer may have been sold on a wholesale basis to beer houses and other established licensed properties, but any such trade would have been limited by these potential customers brewing their own beer or receiving supplies from other brewers.[3] In 1852 the village had three carriers, going to Banbury three times a week, and also to Chipping Norton on a Wednesday. They may have been used to carry Harris's beer further afield. Before the railway links to both towns were fully established, one of the carriers, Edward Summerton, went to Heyford Station every Saturday.[4] During the first decade business grew sufficiently for Harris to engage Richard West as brewer's clerk, but it was not until the arrival of Richard Howse in about 1863 that there was someone specifically responsible for obtaining orders and delivering the beer.

Howse's role coincided with the beginning of a period of sustained growth in sales of Hook Norton beer and was crucial to the early success of the business. With his horse and trap he acted as a salesman; visiting local towns and villages to secure orders from established customers as

1901, at the age of 40 he was paid 19 shillings a week to look after the horses. His colleague was Richard Cross, the father of drayman William Cross. Richard worked at the brewery from 1900 until 1911 and was paid 18 shillings a week when he started. This rose to 19 shillings the following year and from 1902, to 20 shillings and remained unchanged until he left the brewery's employment following an accident in 1911.[15]

At the outbreak of war, in 1914, John Hall was paid 17 shillings a week and his colleagues, George Hall, Ernest Pinfold and Harry Alcock 16 shillings a week. The following year both the Halls received 20 shillings a week, while Pinfold and Alcock were paid 18/6d a week, but from 1916, they were both away serving in the forces. Although there were further wage increases during the war for both John and George Hall, it was not until 1919 that all four draymen were paid the at the same rate of 40 shillings a week, which rose to a peak of 45 shillings a week during 1921. From 1923, however, both George Hall and Harry Alcock received 40 shillings a week, while Ernest Pinfold and John Hall took home 38 shillings. These weekly rates remained unchanged for the rest of the decade, after which the use of dray wagons was phased out.

The uncompromising local geography meant that steep hills had to be negotiated on routes out of the village. To assist the drayman to negotiate his load up these hills a 'trace' horse was coupled to the dray wagon. Once the hill had been traversed, a boy would return the 'trace' horse to the brewery. The number of horses used for a journey depended on the size of the load or, in snowy winter conditions, the state of the roads. In such circumstances the load might be adjusted for safety and only a part order might be delivered to a licensee. Alternatively the customer might be asked to meet the drayman at a mutually convenient place and time, so that the order could be transferred to the customer's own vehicle, so alleviating the need for the drayman to negotiate icy hilly roads with a heavy load. Particularly heavy loads were usually pulled by a pair of horses otherwise a single horse worked the journey.[16] Out on the road, the drayman was responsible for his horse and saw to all its needs.

The prompt collection and return of empty casks to the brewery was essential to the efficient running of the business. The drayman played an important part in ensuring that this happened. Having delivered an order, he was expected to collect any empty casks from customers and return them to the brewery for cleaning and re-use. This brought benefits for the company by ensuring the prompt collection and re-use of casks. The drayman was paid for every empty barrel he returned and by this means was able to supplement his fixed weekly wage.[17] A second benefit gained by this efficient working of the collection system was 'the fact that [in 1903] the Company has not required any new casks for 9 months', even though trade was increasing. A similar system of remuneration operated for the collection of empty bottles. It is not surprising that with several companies competing for custom within the same area that some 'foreigners' were collected by mistake. When some of Messrs Hitchman's bottles were collected mistakenly by a Hook Norton employee and then re-used for Hook Norton beer, Hitchman's complained and Percy Flick wrote diplomatically to reassure the Chipping Norton firm that this was an isolated incident.

> We regret to hear that we are using some of your bottles and renewed instructions have been given, both to our carters and bottlers not to pick up or use any. We have endeavoured to be most particular in this matter, but it is as you will readily understand very hard to prevent "foreign" bottles from getting on to the place. In future, as we come across any of yours, we have given instructions for them to be put on one side, and when there is any quantity returned to your Brewery. We hope to do this generally and trust our friends will see their way to reciprocate.

New casks were not coopered on site but bought in as required from commercial coopers. The brewery did, however, employ a cooper to look after the maintenance of the brewery's stock. When Bill Clarke was young the brewery retained two coopers and later a cooper and a blacksmith. One cooper was George Matthews. He came from a coopering family in Chipping Norton. Matthews senior and his five sons were all involved in the trade, but it is the brothers George and Bert who are remembered in Hook Norton, being the brewery coopers for a period spanning more than sixty years.

George Matthews, centre, and other workers cleaning and preparing casks for use (HNBC).

It is not clear when George Matthews was first engaged by the company as a cooper, but his name appears in the Wage Books from 1895, at a time when Alban Clarke and John Henry Harris took over the management of the business from John Harris's trustees. George's pay varied. The first entry by his name records him being paid 3/4d a day for four days work, but the following year his weekly wage was £1. Unlike other employees George Matthews was paid at two rates, one 'time' appears to be a weekly wage but this was augmented with 'piece work'. Ten of the thirteen years he worked at the brewery he was paid in this manner. In 1905 his 'time' payment was 22 shillings and 'piece work' 17 shillings. The following year he was paid 21 shillings for both types of work but in 1907 his piece work rate was higher than the 'time' weekly payment. In 1901 George was 35 years old and described himself as being a cooper at the brewery, a position he maintained until his death in the autumn of 1908.[18]

At the time of his brother's death Bert Matthews was completing a contract in Liskard. For some years he had travelled the length and breadth of the country doing contract work wherever a business needed a cooper. This might mean making as many as a thousand casks for a customer. With the news of his brother's death, Bert, the youngest of the brothers, decided it was time to settle down and fill the vacancy at the Hook Norton Brewery. The first entry for Bert in the Wages Book, however, is not until 1912, but unlike his brother he was paid a weekly rate which rose from 30 shillings in 1912 to 53/6d a week in 1930.

When Bert and his family first moved back to Oxfordshire they had no accommodation in the village so they stayed with his parents in Chipping Norton. Bert would leave home at 6am every morning and walk to work, in all weathers. Even after they had moved into a cottage

Tunnel leading to the cellars (Jack Haney).

in Hook Norton, the family would walk to Chipping Norton twice a week to visit Bert's parents. For the children a return trip on the train was a treat, but Bert always chose to walk and would be home with the kettle on by the time his wife and two sons arrived home.

The cooper was one of the cellarmen and in Hook Norton most of Bert Matthews work involved the repair of casks, but he supplemented this by doing private work; making bowls, washing up tubs used by pubs, wine casks and 'scalding tubs' for butchers. Bert Matthews worked at the brewery for more than fifty years and only stopped when it became too much for him.[19]

At the beginning of the twentieth century the brewery kept between thirty and forty horses at any one time. Most were 'Light draught horses', for use on the dray wagons, while a small number of Cobs were retained for 'outride' work with the traps. A new horse did not begin work until it was 3 years old and, after it had been broken in, it spent two or three years doing light jobs before being put into service on the drays. In 1903, the brewery had more horses than could be stabled at the new brewery, and accommodation had to be found elsewhere. The question of stabling was critical. Horses returned from a day's work were turned out into a field adjoining the brewery stables whatever the weather. The field had no shelter and the matter of 'erecting a shed with stabling' was considered by the Directors. The matter was left to John Henry Harris and Alban Clarke to deal with but the outcome of their deliberations is unclear as no further mention is made of the shed. Other horses were kept at John Henry Harris's farm, or stabled at Scotland End House.[20]

A list dated 1901, gives some indication of the costs incurred in providing horsefeed. Forty quarters of oats were purchased from a local farmer at 22 shillings a quarter and from another farmer, sixty quarters cost 23 shillings a quarter. Three tons of straw cost £4/10/0, four tons of hay £12 and twenty quarters of beans £38. In total, this list itemises 46 tons of 'Horsekeep' at a cost £217/1/3. The amount spent replacing horses, however, varied from year to year, but a total of £1,117 was spent on new horses during the last six year of the nineteenth century, which represented about a quarter of that spent on horsefeed.

Workers at the brewery c1901 (HNBC).
Back row: Spatcher, Percy Buggins, Philip Randle, George Beck, T Cox, Will Coleman
(cellarman), T Harris, G Messer; Middle row: J Gibbins (assistant brewer), H Busby,
H Haynes (stoker), Frank Beale (engine driver), George Matthews (cooper), W Beck,
George Hall (maltman), Fred Beale (maltman); Front row: Will Hall, G Horn,
F Beale, Charlie Buggins, E Savage, E Embra, Joe Pinfold.

In November 1903 Alban Clarke presented his Annual Report to the Directors, in which he reviewed the Brewery's stock of horses and their working costs.

> With regard to the Brewery horses, we have sold six during the twelve months, two have died and nine have been purchased. The numbers now stand at 35. Eight of these are at four of the Agencies, others are at home. The same numbers placed stood at this time last year. Cost of the horses was about £144 less, which works out at 13 shillings as opposed to 15 shillings working cost per horse. Even this figure is not as low as it should be considering the facilities for buying in the best market which the Company possesses. We have now adopted the plan of rolling the oats system, which we have every reason to think will prove advantageous and economical.

The brewery kept about a dozen dray wagons, some with four wheels others with two. Repairs on the vehicles were carried out by the local wheelwright or blacksmiths. In 1901 James Robins, the village wheelwright, was paid £4/14/6 for repairing carts and wagons and £2/8/6 for repairs to brewery carts, while the two blacksmiths were paid for a range of jobs completed. William Weston was paid £11/7/3 for shoeing and 6/3d for repairs to vans, and Thomas Borsberry [21] £7/19/4d for repair to harness.[22] In 1903, the company entered into a new venture by 'employing a wheelwright and sign writer on the premises and fitting up a smith's shop with a view to cutting costs'. The previous year repairs to the dray wagons alone had cost £140. Under the new arrangements all repairs to the "vans and vehicles" and other "sundry" work on the premises came to a total of £172/7/5. How long this arrangement lasted is not known, but villagers recall repair and maintenance work being carried out on the brewery vehicles by Austin Hall, a self-employed wheelwright who turned to steam threshing and pump making.[23]

During the last years of the nineteenth century there was a modest investment in rolling stock, the largest amount spent being £107/1/0 in 1899. A further £53/13/0 went on new harness. In contrast, only £14/4/10 was spent on new harness in 1898. The total expenditure on new equipment between 1899 and 1901 was twice as much (£669) as that for the previous three years and corresponded with the expansion in production prior to the building of the new brewery and the incorporation of the company.

In its first decade the Hook Norton Brewery Company, spent over two thousand pounds on transporting costs in all but one year, and whilst the first years of business were moderately successful, from 1907 trading became increasingly more difficult. In the years immediately after the 1910 Finance Act, when the brewery struggled and economies were made, the total annual amount spent on transporting beer fell, but the cost of horsefeed was consistently the largest single item in maintaining the horse drawn fleet. Part of the problem appears to have been the lack of a clearly defined policy regarding who should place orders for hay, and as a consequence, the stables were overstocked and there was a lack of money in the bank. The full extent of this problem is not documented, but it was not until Percy Flick became Managing Director that the problem was brought under control when he took sole responsibility for the purchase of hay.

During his first decade as Managing Director, Flick halved amounts spent on 'Horsekeep, Carriage and Travelling' yet these costs still represented a fifth of the company's total expenditure. In the early 1920s there was an increase in transport costs, reflecting the high costs of raw materials, but this expenditure began to stabilize with the move towards motor transport in 1928 and a reduction in the number of horses employed.[24]

With the outbreak of the Second World War the final horse drays were withdrawn and sold off, although David Clarke recalled a horse and dray being used around the village after the war.

> I do remember, as a small boy, we used to keep [a horse] for delivering on Saturday mornings round the village and the pubs. At that time there was a lot of local trade delivering to people's houses. I seem to remember I used to be allowed to go round on the dray on a Saturday morning in the village. It must have been late 40s or very early 50s.[25]

The day of the horse drawn dray seemed to have passed, but in 1985 the brewery re-introduced a working horse drawn dray to deliver to local pubs within five miles of the brewery. Worked by a pair of shires the dray served the village pubs in Hook Norton and the White Swan at Wigginton. In 2011 Consul retired from service aged 27 years to be replaced by Albert. Now, he, along with Major and Nelson are responsible for deliveries.[26] Originally, when not involved with deliveries, the dray attended fêtes, pub openings and occasionally a Horse Show but this has been scaled back and the horses can now be seen regularly in the village and at the brewery.

The Steam Wagon

The Steam Wagon in the Brewery yard (HNBC).

In the early years of the twentieth century breweries began to invest in steam wagons. Bentley's Yorkshire Brewery in Leeds operated two and Gales Brewery at Horndean had used a traction engine with trucks for deliveries. By 1903 they had invested in a steam motor wagon, but this was replaced in 1908 by their first petrol-engine lorry.[27]

The decision by the Hook Norton Brewery to invest in a steam wagon appears to have been made as much for the welfare of the horses engaged on long journeys, as it was for possible financial savings. At the Directors Meeting in November 1903, Alban Clarke drew attention to 'The enormous amount of wear and tear of the horses in doing very long journeys, such as Witney, Byfield, Bicester and Brize Norton'. These he considered as 'Much too great for any horse to accomplish in one day without putting an unfair strain on them'. Even the 'very best horses' he considered, could not sustain such journeys 'for any length of time'. Having expressed his concerns, Clarke suggested that the Board should consider whether 'An improvement and saving [could] be effected by the employment of a steam wagon for long journeys'. After some discussion of the matter it was left for further consideration by Alban Clarke and John Henry Harris.

Clarke sought advice from Edmunds & Kench Ltd in Banbury who had recently acquired a steam wagon. Mr Kench was enthusiastic about the performance of their wagon and was of the opinion 'It does the work of six horses, and if it could be kept going within a radius of 7 or 8 miles, it would do the work of ten'. He thought a steam wagon would be best suited for moving heavy loads between Hook Norton and Banbury, instead of using two horses on the journey.[28] The decision to purchase a steam wagon was taken, and in May 1904 the brewery took delivery of a Mann's Patent Steam Wagon, at a cost of £530. An additional £10 was spent on 'Double Steerage' and a 'second footplate' and some iron bars for the motor shed were purchased from Hoods in Banbury for 5/6d.

Operating the vehicle required a driver to be trained. Clarke's initial choice, however, apparently failed to meet the required standards and the duty fell to a succession of regular draymen to take the vehicle to Witney during the first few months, before John Hall became the regular driver.

The Steam Wagon, or 'Motor Dray' as it is referred to in the brewery documents, went into service on the 20th May 1904, completing 123 journeys between its initial journey and the end of the year. At the end of its first year in service Clarke costed the savings made by using the vehicle.

He concluded that it would pay for itself within the first three years, saving 'six horses at 12 shillings a week', labour costs (£75) and a reduction of £150 on the railway account. He estimated a total saving of £442 could be made, while the running costs amounted to £230, of which the largest amounts were wages (£73) and fuel (£71). In the following two years 205 journeys were completed in each year but thereafter the annual total number of journeys began to decline. In 1907 there were 160 journeys, the following year 149 and in its final year only 75. The reduction in the number of journeys reflects the difficult trading conditions experienced by Hook Norton and the industry in general during the first decade of the twentieth century.

During six years in service the motor dray was used on the route to Witney and a dozen draymen drove the vehicle during that period, making a total of 922 journeys. The majority of these were made by John Hall, who completed a total of 827 journeys. Of the other draymen, only four completed more than ten journeys and of these William Hall drove the most, twenty five over a five year period. It is not clear whether the driver travelled alone, but contemporary correspondence suggests that two men 'crewed' the vehicle. Mann's wagon was designed to be operated by one man, with the firehole door by the driver's feet and with the coal supply easily to hand. The brewery records only show payments to a driver and a second man on the vehicle may have been to help with off loading casks.[29]

Motor Dray Journeys 1904 – 1909

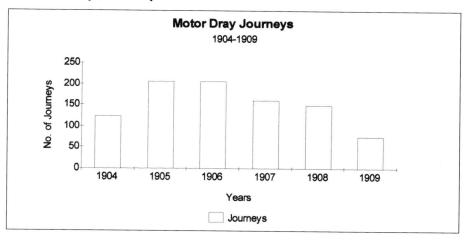

Source: HNBC Archive: Motor Dray Journeys 1904-1909.

In a world that was used to travelling at the speed of a horse, the steam wagon provided a new and noisy perspective on commercial transport. There are only two recorded complaints about the driving of the vehicle and its impact on the rural communities that it passed through en route to Witney. Although its approaching presence could be heard 'miles away', W.J. Howse appears to have been caught unawares while cycling in Ramsden during May 1904.[30] The steam wagon was reported to have been travelling at speed along a narrow stretch of road and Howse had to throw himself and his cycle into the hedge 'to save being run over'. That fortnight George French completed nine journeys with the steam wagon and would appear to have been the driver involved in the incident. It may be coincidence, but having completed the fortnight, he did not drive the wagon again.

A year later in July 1905, G.F. Braggins was driving a horse-drawn Phaeton when he met the steam wagon. The 'smoke and noise of gearing' frightened his mare, and she shied up onto the pathway and he nearly lost control. He complained to Alban Clarke,

> Your drivers were most culpable and indifferent to the risk they put on me and had I had anyone with me I sh'd have turned back and given them a very forcible remonstrance against their abominable carelessness of which I hope there will not be any recurrence. If I see Mr Harris on Thursday evening I will tell him the particulars as your firm might easily be put to a deal of trouble by want of caution on part of your drivers.

Two drivers, John Hall (8) and D. Hopkins (1) drove the nine journeys completed during the fortnight in question, but it is not possible to identify which of them was involved in the incident.

Like other brewery workers, the steam draymen were paid fortnightly, effectively working a 'ten day' week and for each journey the driver was paid a shilling bonus. A round trip to Witney of about 30 miles took a full day and by analysing the number of journeys completed each month, it is possible to build up a picture of demand and the working pattern of the wagon. During the six years in operation, the wagon only operated for the full ten working days of the fortnight on eleven occasions. The more usual working pattern was to complete eight or nine journeys. There were exceptions however. Very occasionally eleven or twelve journeys would be completed within the fortnight, with the extra journeys being made at the weekend. It was unusual though for one driver to work the full ten-day period. Although John Hall drove 90% of all journeys, he only worked a ten-day period twice and twelve days once. The more usual practice was for the working period to be shared by two drivers, with John Hall driving most of the journeys within the period. After the wagon was withdrawn from service, John Hall returned to working with the horse drays and was still in the employment of the company in 1930.

Winter weather does not appear to have restricted the use of the motor dray. Operating during the four months from November to February in each of the years from 1904 to 1909, the wagon completed sixty journeys in the first two winters, forty five and forty one journeys in the following two winters and only twenty six in the final winter.

There were working periods when the motor dray made no journeys. During the spring of 1908 there were two periods when no journeys were made and during the first six weeks of the same year only three journeys were made, but for both periods John Hall was recorded as being "absent", perhaps through illness. In the autumn of 1909 the motor dray worked only one fortnight in each of the months September, October and November, completing only sixteen journeys in the three months. By December journeys had ceased.

The capacity of the vehicle is unknown but from the sole surviving photograph, it is possible to estimate that the vehicle might have carried about thirty barrels. On this assumption, a fully loaded wagon might then have transported between 270 and 360 barrels during the fortnight, supplying the agencies and freehouses in the Witney area. Between 1905 and 1908 the motor dray averaged between thirteen and eighteen journeys each month between May and December. The haymaking and harvesting months were the busiest, with June (17), July (18) and August (16) the busiest months. October (16) and November (15) were also busy, with deliveries for the Christmas period.

The second fortnight in July consistently appears to have been the busiest period of the year. Between 1904 and 1909 the motor dray completed a total of sixty one journeys during that fortnight. In contrast, the quietest fortnight of the year started in the last week of January. In the six years it operated, only ten journeys were run during this fortnight and these were between 1905 and 1907. In both of the following years no journeys were made at all. In 1908 when John Hall was logged as being 'absent', one journey was made by a colleague during the previous fortnight. A year later journeys did not resume until the beginning of March due to extensive repairs.

From the Ledger entries it is difficult to identify any regular maintenance pattern although entries in the 'Goods Purchased' books for years 1904 to 1908 record the acquisition of spares and expenditure on repairs. The fitter was required to replace a main axle bracket and connecting rod in January 1907 and worked on the wagon again twice during the Spring of 1908, including extensive repairs costing more than £50.

Most entries are for items less than £2, but a number exceed this figure. Items relating to the wheels were amongst the most expensive; in November 1906 'new tyre sections' for the driving wheel cost £3/15/0, a 'road wheel' was sent to Leeds for repair in August 1908 at a cost of £5/12/6, and a new set of tyres for the driving wheels was acquired in June 1907 at a cost of £4 and another set was bought in September 1908 costing £2/19/10. More expensive though was a 'main driving wheel pinion' which cost £10/12/0. Many of the items listed refer to the replacement of equipment used in the boiler or in the production of steam.

In 1906 it cost £5/4/8 to re-tube the boiler, and on several occasions in 1907 'grate bars' were replaced. The 'steam pipe' needed repairing in December 1907 and was replaced with a new one in January 1908. Other items replaced included parts for the pump, cylinder covers, a '1HP piston body and rings' and 'complete connecting rod' which cost £3/18/0. Paying the fitter to effect repairs was also an expensive item. In January 1907 he was paid £7/16/9 and in March 1908, £5/1/6, but by far the largest expenditure on repair came in May 1908 listed under the general title 'Repairs to Steam Wagon', cost £51/12/0. The total expenditure on parts and labour for 1908 was £143/11/2 of which thirteen items costing in excess of £2 accounted for £108/4/9.

During early May 1909 the vehicle suffered a major breakdown. It was on a journey and about twenty miles from Hook Norton when the piston rod and cylinder cover both broke. A new low pressure rod and cylinder cover was ordered, the brewery requesting that the parts be sent at Mann's earliest convenience by 'fast train'. Deliveries resumed but only five journeys were possible during the fortnight. The list of 'Motor Dray Journeys' records a further sixty journeys made between May and the middle of November; these came to an end during the fortnight ending 12th November 1909, but under what circumstances is not clear. With no money available for an immediate repair, due to the company's difficult financial situation, the vehicle remained idle.

The possibility of a replacement was ruled out by the directors during August 1910 and with the repercussions of the Finance Bill severely impacting on the company's financial situation the decision to 'dispose of the steam wagon at the earliest possible opportunity' was taken. Yet eleven months later, the steam wagon was still at the brewery. In November 1911, almost two years to the day since the steam wagon's last journey, the directors decided to write off a number of accounts as depreciation to the total value of £1,212/19/5, including the steam wagon, valued at £62/10/0, and horses and drays, valued at £131/1/0.

In 1904 Steam Wagons were at the forefront of the development of goods carrying vehicles and the brewery's decision to purchase a vehicle demonstrates a willingness to employ the new technology.[31] The motor dray appears to have been a reliable vehicle and it was only in its final year of operation that major mechanical problems seem to have occurred. The withdrawal of the steam wagon from service in 1909 was brought about more by financial events beyond the control of the brewery, than a loss of faith in mechanised transport, as there is evidence to suggest that the purchase of a new steam wagon was being considered. Other vehicular transport was also dispensed with at this time and the Directors resolved that all journeys should in future be made by either rail or horse.[32]

The Railway

The brewery did not rely solely on its horse drawn fleet of drays to deliver beer; markets beyond the distances normally worked by horses were supplied by rail. Although the railway did not come to Hook Norton until 1887, both Banbury (1850) and Chipping Norton (1855) had stations and from notes made in the brewing books it is clear that by 1874 John Harris was sending beer to Coventry, Buckingham, Shipston on Stour and Woodstock. Some of these destinations were beyond the limits of a day's work for a horse and must have gone by rail.[33] Some local customers received orders by rail and beer was sent to Charlbury and Brackley. Beer was sent long distances by rail through Chipping Norton station during the 1880s. Consignments to West Dean near Chichester, were being routed via Reading and Guildford to Singleton in Sussex and other orders went via London and then transferred to Sussex by one of Messrs Pickford's horse-drawn wagons, but it was the use of the railway to supply more distant customers that allowed the brewery to expand its markets across the Midlands during the last decade of the nineteenth century. The brewery established a thriving market in the West Midlands. Hook Norton beer was sent to Birmingham and Black Country towns from West Bromwich to Wolverhampton, as well as outlets in Leamington, Kenilworth, Cheltenham, Gloucester and Oxford, all of which were supplied by rail. Not all consignments, however, arrived on time and there were regular complaints directed to the station master at Hook Norton about the late or non delivery of orders; much correspondence between the brewery and the Great Western Railway was concerned with the collection and return of empty casks. The problem was summed up in a letter to the Station Master at Hook Norton, Mr Beechey, in April 1895.

> We wish to call your attention to the neglect of the Railway Company in collecting our empty casks in Birmingham. We wrote to the Goods Manager at Hockley on March 15th enclosing a list of addresses of our customers whose empties required calling for. Not receiving the empties in the course of

a fortnight we again wrote. We giving them [the Goods Manager] to attend to the matter at once. We wrote a third time and we have not even received a reply to either of our letters. In the meantime our customers are complaining that the empties have not been called. We should be glad if you would take the matter up for us as this state of things is a great interference with our business.

The root of this problem was based on a misunderstanding. The brewery believed that the railway company had a duty to collect empties when they delivered a new order. This appears not to have been the case and the situation was resolved by the brewery requesting, through the local station master, that casks of named customers be collected 'as per the other side' (from the customer) and the cost of collection charged to the brewery's account.

The non collection of empty casks was an annoyance to the customer and a great inconvenience to the brewery as the casks could not be re-introduced into the production cycle. Equally annoying for the brewery were deliveries that were damaged. In December 1896 the brewery ordered some 'spirit store vats', specially coopered in Bristol. When they were unpacked three were damaged. A letter was sent to Mr Beechey at Hook Norton station, complaining about the 'gross carelessness of the railway service', claiming for 15 shillings damages. The extent of the problem of damaged casks is not clear, but this was not an isolated incident. In February 1900 a kilderkin was returned from Birmingham 'in a smashed condition' with the staves on one side completely broken.

Much of the brewery's railway trade after 1917 was concentrated on supplying beer to Working Men's Clubs in Coventry and Birmingham and it became necessary for the company to increase its stock of good quality barrels and hogsheads to cope with the wear and tear on the casks in meeting the demand created by this trade. One of those clubs supplied by rail was the Cotteridge Social Club on the Pershore Road in Birmingham, which first took Hook Norton beer, during the summer of 1917.[34] The brewery's dealings with this Club during 1921, are typical of the experiences of others situated beyond the limits of the dray wagon deliveries, receiving their beer and spirits by rail.

During March the brewery received an order for ten barrels of beer from the Cotteridge Club. Arrangements were made by George Groves, for the consignment to be sent to Lifford Station,[35] where the order was to be collected by the Birmingham Agents of Messrs Pickfords Ltd, who were to deliver and cellar the beer. Five days later another consignment of five barrels of ale was put on 'the rails', and again delivery and cellarage was to be provided by Pickfords. Not all deliveries arrived in Cotteridge in perfect condition. A consignment of beer sent during May arrived in a damaged state and the Social Club reported that one of the casks had been damaged and at least 10 gallons of beer was lost. George Groves's response however, offered little comfort to the Social Club Secretary as the damage had not been reported to the Railway Company at the time of delivery and as a consequence they were not entitled to any allowance for the lost beer. Nevertheless, Groves pursued the matter, writing to the Stationmaster in Hook Norton to lodge a claim for compensation for the ten gallons of beer that had been lost.

The summer of 1921 was extremely hot which caused problems with the oak casks sent by rail. As they stood on the platform, the sun's heat dried out the staves and leakages were reported by customers. The company responded by requesting that casks leaving Hook Norton station be covered to protect them from the sun.[36] Beer was not the only commodity sent by rail. At the end of July a consignment of goods, including a two gallon jar of brandy, was dispatched to Cotteridge. A fortnight later it had not been delivered. With his usual efficiency, George Groves requested that the village stationmaster, now Mr Morris, investigate the delay. A few days later Morris reported that a jar of Brandy had been traced to Cardiff, but this, it turned out was not the one originally destined for Birmingham and a replacement jar was immediately despatched to Lifford Station to fulfil the order. In the seven years that Hook Norton beer was sent to Cotteridge the trade was worth more than £5,000 to the brewery, with the annual trade growing from £297 in 1917 to a peak of £1,568 in 1922. Although the correspondence between the brewery and the Cotteridge Social Club records their business transactions in 1921, the end of year total for this trade is inexplicably not recorded.

There was a change in brewery policy in 1925, with the hiring of a lorry from Banbury to transport beer to Coventry. Reliance on the railway with the inherent problems of damage and lost goods seem to have driven this change to road transport, but it wasn't until 1928 that the brewery acquired its own lorry. Even though the brewery had its own lorry, Coventry deliveries were still made by a hired vehicle.[37]

Lorries had been used to transport beer from the first decade of the century and by the 1920s larger breweries used them regularly for deliveries. The Northampton Brewery for instance delivered beer to Banbury, including supplies for Hook Norton houses, on a weekly basis and as has been already related, a lorry was used to transport malt to the brewery during the General Strike.[38] Even with the growing use of lorries, it was the state of the roads and the maintenance of the dray wagons that focussed the minds of the Directors on the need for the company to acquire a lorry. At a Directors' meeting in July 1927 it was agreed that the company might be 'compelled to adopt motor traction owing to the state of the roads' and that to save money, the repairs to dray wagons be 'limited to what was absolutely necessary'. In November of the following year it was proposed the company purchase a 30cwt Morris lorry, which was bought just before Christmas from County Garages at a cost of £331/13/9d.[39] As a consequence it was decided to end the brewery's reliance on horse drawn drays. Horses were sold and some wagons found their way onto farms, others stood idle at the brewery. When war was declared in 1939, there was just one dray left in service. When the drayman was 'called up' the horse and any remaining wagons were sold off to make way for the army, who had requisitioned the brewery stables. For the duration of the war, with the brewery short staffed, the beer was delivered by hired lorry from Chipping Norton which took deliveries to Coventry once a week. It was not until 1951 that the Company again had its own lorry.[40]

Notes

1. Mathias. P. *The Brewing Industry in England 1700-1830.* 1959 p.xxii.
   Mathias. P. *Industrial Revolution in Brewing 1700-1830.* Explorations in Entrepreneurial History Vol 5. 1952/3 p.xxii.
2. There is a story emanating from Germany, that Joseph Heathcote Brooks applied for and got permission to build 'an English Brewery' at Senhals. He was assisted by a John Harris, but as yet, there is no proof that this was John Harris of Hook Norton.
3. The Bell Inn Hook Norton brewed its own beer.
   Deeds of Wheatsheaf Inn: The Wheatsheaf was supplied by Hopcroft and Norris.
4. Lascelles & Co Directory and Gazetteer of Oxfordshire 1853. p.189. The railway came to Banbury in 1850 and through services to Birmingham were possible from 1852. The railway reached Chipping Norton in 1855.
5. Census Returns of 1861, 1871 and 1881.
6. The 5 mile radius is taken as an average of the four to six miles suggested by Mathias.
7. Dingle. A.E. *Drink and the Working Class Living Standards in Britain.* Economic History Review. Vol XXV No 4. 1972 p.610. Quotes Professor Levi's estimate that 56% of the population drank alcohol. Levi's estimate is dated 1871.
8. Victoria County History: *"Oxfordshire".* Vol 2. 1987. p.216 There were 14,967 living within a five mile radius of Hook Norton in 1891.
9. Jenkins. J.G. *The English Farm Wagon – Origins and Structures.* David and Charles. 1972. p.182-187.
   Arnold. J. *The Farm Waggons of England and Wales.* John Baker. 1969. plate 8.
10. Packer. F. Photograph. Hitchman's wagons standing out side the Company Office. West Street, Chipping Norton. c1920.
11. Oral Tradition: Harold Wyton, Bill Clarke, Bert Heritage, Kate French, Nan Cross and others. 1973-76.
12. Oral Tradition: Nan Cross. 1983.
13. Oral Tradition: Conversations with Harold Wyton and Fred Beale. July 1973.
14. Oral Tradition: Nan Cross. 1983.
15. In 1911 a barrel fell on his leg and he was unable to work again, although he lived to be over ninety.
16. Oral Tradition: Conversation with Harold Wyton. 1973. It is possible that this was one the jobs Harold did as a boy before the First World War.
17. Oral Tradition: Conversations with Kate French and Bert Heritage. 1973.

18 Census Return 1901. George Robert Matthews. Age 35 Cooper at Brewery. GRO: Deaths. Banbury District Volume 3a p.493.

19 Oral tradition. Conversations with Leslie Matthews and Harold Wyton. 1973.

20 Oral Tradition: Conversations with Bill Clarke, Harold Wyton, Leslie Matthews and Kate French. 1973-1976.

21 Oral Tradition: Conversation with Mrs Borsberry, widow of Alf Borsberry, village Blacksmith. The harness was probably repaired by Thomas Borsberry, Alf's uncle, who had a saddlery and harness business opposite the churchyard. Other Borsberrys also ran a drapers and shoemaking businesses.

22 HNBC Archive: To James Robins, Carpenter etc. List of Work carried out on vehicles. Christmas 1902. There was at least one covered wagon at the brewery in November 1902, which had been sent for repair.

23 Oral Tradition: Bill Clarke and Mrs Veale. 1973 Austin Hall 1853-1930. His father Thomas Hall 1815-1870 was also a Wheelwright and pump maker.

24 Companies House, Cardiff Report of Directors: 1900-1913 and 1900-1941.

25 HNLHG Oral History Project: Interview with David Clarke 8/4/1998.

26 www.hooknortonbrewery.co.uk. The Shire horses working for the brewery. 31/3/2008 Consul died 29th September 2012.

27 Correspondence with Derek Rayner. C.Eng. M.I. Mech.E. President of Leeds & District Traction Engine Club, author of *Steam Wagons* Shire Books. 2003. 11/7/2003.
Stapleton B. & Thomas J.H. *Gales: A study in Brewing, business & family history.* 2000, p.72.

28 Eddershaw D. *A Country Brewery 1849-1999.* Hook Norton Brewery Co Ltd. 1999. p.87-89.

29 Correspondence with Derek Rayner. 8.10.2003.

30 Oral Tradition: Conversation with Leslie Matthews. 1973. '...had an old steam wagon which you could hear miles away.'

31 Correspondence with Derek Rayner C.Eng. M.I. Mech. E 11/7/2003.

32 The round trip from Hook Norton to Witney is about 30 miles. It is not known whether any of the 917 journeys were to destinations other than Witney.

33 Oral Tradition: Conversation with Harold Wyton. 1973. Horses worked journeys up to 15 miles from the brewery.
Nan Cross. 3/6/1983. Her father William, apparently took beer to Coventry with a horse and dray. No independent evidence has been found to collaborate this story.

34 The brewery started supplying the Stainton WM Club on 2/5/1917 and the Earlsdon WM Club in Coventry on 4/7/1917.

35 http://www.railaroundbirmingham.co.uk/Stations/lifford.php and http://www.miac.org.uk/gloucesterline.htm.
Lifford is an area of south Birmingham between Cotteridge and Stirchley. The station was the third to carry the name and was part of the Birmingham – Gloucester Railway, known locally as the Camp Hill line. The station was opened in 1885 and closed as temporary 'wartime economy measure' in 1941, but was never reopened. Letter Books show that orders to the Cotteridge Social Club were between 5 and 10 barrels.

36 Oral Tradition: Conversation with Ernie Marshall. 8/8/1975. He recalled that in 1921 unemployed ironstone workers slept on grassy banks because it was so hot. James Bunting of Fordwells also remembered that summer and said he didn't go to bed for three months.

37 Oral Tradition: Conversations with Bill Clarke and Harold Wyton. 1973. The decline in the use of the railway for transporting beer is not well documented and is the subject of current research.

38 Stapleton B. & Thomas J.H. *Gales: A study in Brewing, business & family history*. Ashgate. 2000, p.72.
Oral Tradition: Conversation with Fred Beale. 1973.

39 Oral Tradition: Conversation with Bill Clarke. 1973.
January 1st 1933 The 30cwt Morris was traded in for a new Bedford 2 ton lorry and four years later this was exchanged for a new Bedford lorry.

40 Oral Tradition: Conversation with Bill Clarke and Harold Wyton 1973.
Oral Tradition: Conversation with George Dumbleton. 1974. Apparently John Henry Harris had two double shafted dray wagons on his farm which were converted to single shafts. After his death the old brewery wagons were sold off at a sale of his effects. Ernest Wyton who later rented Harris's farm also had one.
HNBC Archive: Report of Directors: 1951 Companies House, Cardiff. Cost of lorry given as £637/11/0.
HNLHG Oral History Project: Interview with David Clarke 8/4/1998. He recalled a lorry being hired from Mr Johnson of Chipping Norton, probably during the immediate post war years.
HNLHG Oral History Project: Interview with Mrs Doris Cadd. 7/3/2006. She recalled the last horse kept at the brewery was called Prince.

Chapter 4
Selling Hook Norton Beer

The Pear Tree Inn, a Hook Norton house since 1869.

Early trade

Maltsters were a traditional part of the fabric of village life and it is probable that the trade was established in Hook Norton long before Thomas Hyatt became the village maltster early in the eighteenth century.[1] There appears to have generally been only one maltster in Hook Norton, although during 1834 there were two working in the village. One of these, William White, a maltster and brewer, appears to have been involved in supplying beer for some years and was still in business in 1847, by which time he was combining farming with brewing. The arrival of John Harris, however, seems to have put him out of business as his name disappears from the records.[2] The only other documented brewer was James Robinson, the licensee at 'The Bell' who described himself as a 'victualler and brewer' and there may have been some sort of reciprocal agreement between him and John Harris, with Harris buying yeast from 'The Bell' in 1858 and Robinson's malt being supplied by Harris's maltings.[3]

As village maltster Harris probably sold malt to the other village pubs, as well as local farmers and villagers, but once he began to brew commercially, the pubs became potential outlets for his beer. The 'Wheatsheaf', 'Red Lion' and the 'Griffin Inn' at Swerford all formed part of the business interests of Alfred Hopcroft, a Banbury brewer and their needs would have been supplied from his own brewery.[4] More promising customers for Harris were the 'The Gate' and 'The Sun Inn'. Neither attracted any interest from rival brewers until late in the century, when Lardner's Brewery of Little Compton had tenure of 'The Sun' for some years.

If some licensed properties in Hook Norton were brewing their own beer or being supplied from a rival brewery in 1849, the village beerhouses needed supplies. In 1852 there were two beer retailers operating in the village.[5] Neither was identified by a name or sign and there is no record of whether they took Harris's beer, but the property now known as 'The Peartree'[6] with its close proximity to the brewery, would seem to be his most likely customer, particularly as it became the brewery's first acquisition in 1869. Interestingly, the Pear Tree is not

The Griffin Inn Swerford 1950s.

identified by name in either Census Returns or Trade Directories until
the beginning of the twentieth century. The location of the second
beerhouse is unknown, but it may have been the small property in Down
End, which by 1902 was part of the Hook Norton Brewery Company's
tied house estate.[7]

A third beer house, identified by name in the 1881 Census was 'The
Blackbird'. Little is known of 'The Blackbird', except that it was being
run by William Somerton and his wife Elizabeth. William was a 'Dealer
in Poultry', while his wife 'attend[ed] the beer-house', reflecting the
common tradition of people providing a means of supplementing their
earnings with a second income.[8] In Hook Norton, farming was a
common source of the second income for village innkeepers, typified by
Thomas Prickett, the licensee of the 'Fox and Hounds'. Being a farmer of
some substance, he employed three men and two boys to work his 160
acres in 1871.[9] The fate of The Blackbird, like other licensed premises,
was recorded in verse by George Dumbleton (1901-1996) in his poem
Hooky (1970):

The former Beer House in Down End, sold in 1948.

"The Blackbird and the Wheatsheaf gone
They both have closed their doors
The beerhouse too has gone the same
They thrived when folks were poor."

Another traditional source of brewing was private or home brewing. Evidence of domestic brewing can be found in old Wills, where brewing equipment is specifically identified in the bequests of the deceased.[10] It was customary for the farmer's wife to be responsible for overseeing the brewing of beer for use on the farm, particularly at harvest time, as George Ewart Evans has described.[11] We can only speculate about the size of the domestic brewing in the Hook Norton area, but with other local villages supporting their own maltsters it would appear to have been substantial.

The emphasis of Harris's business changed when he declared himself to be a commercial or 'Common Brewer' in 1852. Beer was now his commodity and through its sale we can trace the early development of his business. Harris's Stock Book of 1855 provides the first evidence of his monthly and yearly sales of each type of beer he brewed. Sales peaked in both 1859 and 1866, and mark significant points in the development of the business. The small increase of 329 barrels sold between 1856[12] and 1859 reflects Harris's first tentative steps towards the widening of his market beyond the immediate Hook Norton area. In the following two years sales flattened out, but from 1861 began again to increase, rising from 660 barrels to 1212 barrels by 1866 as the impact Richard Howse's journeys beyond Hook Norton began to yield results.

The Growth of John Harris's Business 1855 to 1876

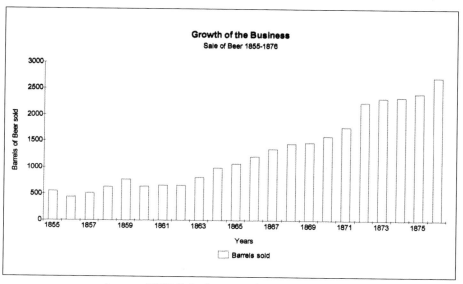

Source: HNBC Archive: Stock Book 1855-1876.

This increase in sales continued and between 1861 and 1876 there were annual increases in all but six years which were all in excess of one hundred barrels a year; for example, in 1872 and 1876 there were increases of 479 barrels and 300 barrels respectively. Over the whole period sales rose by more than 300% and laid the foundation for the success of the business.[13] This success was not an isolated event. For nationally, over the same period, output grew from 20,443,000 barrels brewed in 1863 to 32,279,000 in 1876 and this is reflected in the increase in demand for beer, which rose from 31.2 gallons per head to a peak of 42.2 gallons in 1876.[14] It was a period of growth and prosperity for all brewers, fuelled by a growing and better-off urbanised population and a time associated with heavy drinking, particularly amongst working class men.[15] These conditions presented a ready market for beer and not confined to just urban Britain, as Harris's growth in sales confirms.[16]

This trend of rising sales continued. A thousand more barrels were sold between 1877 and 1884, but there were years when sales fell, notably in 1877, 1879 and 1881 corresponding with a national fall in consumption. In 1884 Harris sold 3,581 barrels, more than he had sold in any other year, but during the three years prior to his death in 1887, sales fell by about 15% and this decline did not correspond with any fall in the annual consumption per head, which remained almost constant, averaging 32.5 gallons a person.[17]

The purchase of four public houses between 1869 and 1878 marked a broadening of Harris's business and trading area, but at a time when in London, most public houses were tied to brewery businesses, trade in rural Oxfordshire concentrated on supplying customers at home. The nature of this trade, known as the 'Private Trade' provided the core of Harris's business.

The Private Trade

In the eighteenth and early nineteenth centuries most of the beer produced was sold locally through the traditional outlets; inns, taverns, ale houses and after the Beerhouse Act, through beer shops and later off-licences. Often these premises were privately owned and if the licensee did not brew on the premises, supplies were bought in from local brewers. To supply private individuals and free houses, brewers developed systems by which they were able to obtain orders and extend their markets to areas distant from the brewery. This trade, known as the private trade, was operated by travellers whose job it was to represent the interests of the brewery employing them, and obtain orders. The nineteenth century writer, C. Howard Tripp, identified four categories of travellers operating in the late nineteenth century.[18] The 'local traveller', was a man living near to the brewery and using it as his base. He would be expected to call upon customers within his 'journey',[19] including the tied houses, and obtain orders. He might be paid a salary between 30/- and £2 a week. In addition he could claim out of pocket expenses and was perhaps paid a commission. A lack of documented evidence makes it difficult to pinpoint when travellers became an essential part of a brewer's business, but certainly in Shrewsbury during the second decade of the nineteenth century travellers were employed to solicit business.

In April 1813 Sir John Heathcote & Co, brewers in the town appointed Robert Poole as their 'travelling clerk', replacing James Skidmore, suggesting that a traveller had been part of their operation for some time. At the rival firm of Thomas Hawley & Co, Thomas Cooke, one of the partners, also acted as the firm's 'travelling clerk'.[20]

The 'district traveller', living at some distance from the brewery would work an area with a radius of forty or fifty miles, visiting towns and villages within this area and having to communicate with the brewery regularly with new orders. The 'branch agent' and 'district traveller' undertook more responsibility. In addition to travelling in the district, he would also have responsibility for the management of tied houses in the district and have several members of staff working under him. Finally the 'agent' working on commission, was usually a grocer or wine and spirit merchant, who might be able to generate a large private trade through his business.[21] Bad debts accrued by a negligent agent were the biggest worry for the brewer, but a network of agencies became an integral part of the business structure for many brewing ventures.[22] In some cases, grocers preferred to be 'buying agents', but R.W. Hayward of Oliver Street in Birmingham, was an exception. Hayward was a coal merchant with several yards in the city and wrote to Hook Norton in 1896 to enquire if he could 'take a buying agency for [their] beers'. The buying agent purchased his stock from the brewer at a discount, allowing small discounts to customers, but having to pay all expenses and bear the losses caused by bad debts themselves.

Like many other brewers, a combination of methods was employed in Hook Norton to supply the private trade. In the absence of documentary evidence the beginnings of the business must be a matter of speculation, but as has already been suggested, John Harris himself acted as traveller establishing outlets for his beer within the local area in the first instance. It was not until he was able to employ a full time local traveller that his business benefited and Richard Howse played an important part in developing the company's private trade.[23] He operated from the brewery office, and went with a pony and trap and a boy around the villages canvassing for orders, not only for beer sold in 5 or 9 gallon casks, but also for malt, hops and wines and spirits. He would visit 'free-houses', public houses unattached to a specific brewery and take orders.[24] The traveller was as an extension of the brewery office, collecting payments on orders and carrying messages between customers and the brewery. The collection of bad debts was an additional part of the traveller's remit, often following up a letter from the brewery, demanding payment to the traveller on an appointed date. In May 1895 George Groves wrote to such a customer as follows:

> We are very surprised you paid Mr Howse only ten shillings yesterday, especially as you did not keep your promise to send up some cash during the fortnight. Under the circumstances we must decline to supply you with any more beer until the account is reduced.

A traveller was not only responsible for obtaining orders and handling payments. As the brewery's representative he might on occasions be called upon to represent the management. In 1901 a new tenant was appointed in Stow on the Wold and Mr Brotheridge, the brewery's traveller for that area, was required to accompany the valuer from Banbury to Stow on the Wold. While the property was being valued, Brotheridge discussed with the new tenant, Mr Hunt, the arrangements for possession of the property. On his return to Hook Norton, Brotheridge reported to the Directors that Hunt had accepted the post, if they agreed to a valuation of the property of £48, at 5% interest. The following week he returned to Stow on the Wold and let the house to Hunt on the agreed terms.

Much more is known about the local traveller at the turn of the twentieth century, because of the documentary evidence held in the Hook Norton Brewery Archive. At the beginning of the century, the newly incorporated company employed three 'local' travellers, Messrs Brotheridge , Wilkes and Stratford. Each had his own 'journey', which he worked throughout the year. The largest 'journey' was to the west of Hook Norton and worked by Mr Brotheridge. Each town or village acted as a centre from which he would work to collect orders from other nearby settlements. Brotheridge's journey in 1905 stretched from Burford, Witney and Eynsham in the south, to Chipping Campden in the north and Hornton and Shenington to the north-east. The eastern boundary ran from Eynsham, through Woodstock and Enstone to Shutford. A year later the area to the north west of Little Compton, including Moreton in Marsh and Chipping Campden, was removed from the journey, as sales had decreased.

Mr W.A.Wilkes worked the second 'journey' to the east of Hook Norton, running from Lower Brailes and Cropredy in the north to Middle Barton and Souldern in the south. To the east it included the villages of Ayhno, Kings Sutton and Middleton Cheney. Wilkes's journey included Banbury with business being obtained in both the town and the cattle market. The smallest of the three journeys was worked by Mr F. Stratford. In 1905 it covered two clusters of villages. One to the north east of Hook Norton included the villages of Deddington, Adderbury, Bloxham and the Sibfords and the second to the south east of Chipping Norton centred around Shipton under Wychwood, Chadlington and Charlbury. In the following year, the clusters came together with the addition of the intervening villages of Steeple Aston, the Bartons, Wigginton and Swerford.

Traveller's journeys 1905-07

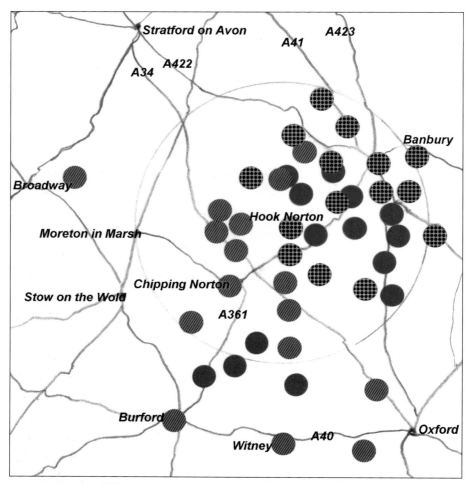

Source: HNBC Archive: Comparison of Travellers Sales 1905-1907.
KEY: Stripes = Brotheridge; Plain = Wilkes; Polka dot = Stratford.

In 1908, as part of his review of trading figures, Alban Clarke compared the sales performance of the three travellers. He looked at their individual free sales for the financial years ending 30th September 1905 and 1906 and the calendar years ending 31st January 1906 and 1907. Why the periods under examination were changed from financial year to the calendar year is not explained, but there is an overlap in the figures for 1906, providing two end of year totals, one in September and the other in December. These figures, however, are transitional points between the beginning of Clarke's survey in 30th September 1905 and its conclusion in December 1907.

Two of the travellers obtained 'free trade' business in both country towns and villages. Mr Brotheridge's journey took him to six country towns to the west of Hook Norton, of which Chipping Norton consistently generated the largest share of his total business, although his annual business in the town fell from £630 in 1905 to £543 in 1907. A similar trend occurred in the other towns he visited. Witney, Burford, and Woodstock, between them contributed almost half of total business done, but again trade from these towns also declined. In Chipping Campden he only collected £8/4/2 during 1905 and this fell to £3/15/0 the following year and Campden was dropped from his journey at the end of 1907. Brotheridge's trade generated more money than either of the other journeys, but during the period of Alban Clarke's scrutiny of the business, his trade fell by £81 in 1906 and £84 at the end of 1907.

Wilkes's business at the Banbury cattle market was one of the few venues where trade increased. In 1906 this went up by £39 and again, more modestly the following year, by £16. Of the other places on his 'journey' only Brailes produced a better return, trade increasing by £46 in 1906. There were a few small increases from other villages, but only of a few pounds, the general trend was for business to drop, most noticeably at Mollington (£61), Bourton and Wardington (£57), Middleton Cheney (£39) and in Banbury town where trade fell by £27. In stark contrast to the brewery's poor 'tied house' trade in Banbury, discussed later in the chapter, Wilkes's 'free trade' showed a small overall increase of £4/13/7 during the period of Clarke's analysis.

Most of the business came from the villages where all three travellers operated, but there was a general decline in this trade as well. In 1906 Messrs Brotheridge and Wilkes respectively recorded falls in business of £2 and £7 although Mr Stratford's trade fell by nearly £139. The following year, fortunes were reversed with Mr Brotheridge's trade falling by £198 and Mr Wilkes's by £245, whereas Mr Stratford increased his business by £226.

These figures, however, mask the effect of changes in the journeys, as some villages were worked by one traveller in 1906 and transferred to another in 1907. The village of Swerford for instance, was worked by Wilkes in 1906, but the following year Stratford did the visits. Other villages were moved from one journey to another. Whichford and Ascott, were worked by Mr Wilkes in 1905, but were put onto Mr Brotheridge's journey for the following two years. Similarly in 1907 Little Tew was added to Mr Brotheridge's journey having the previous year been worked by Mr Wilkes. Overall there was a net decrease of £275/12/9 in the sales of the three travellers but in both years the 'free trade' contribution to the annual total drinks sales was 29%. When added to the 'tied house' sales, the combined sales accounted for only 54% of drinks sales.

With traveller's returns diminishing it was decided at a Board meeting in October 1909, to review their sales 'about once a month'. Initially, at least, the traveller's figures were viewed as 'satisfactory' but by 1914, their returns were giving cause for concern. First, Mr Stratford (1914), and later Mr Wilkes (1917) were offered alternative positions by Percy Flick until 'normal times' returned. Both men declined and their journeys were phased out.[25]

The Stables. Mr Stratford's trap stands against the stable wall (HNBC).

John Harris must have had a large customer base to support the growth of his company. In Hampshire the records of Gales Brewery suggest that the company supplied nearly '200 customers privately' between 1878 and 1888,[26] but Alban Clarke's comparison of the performance of his three travellers gives no indication of how many actual customers they had. A 'Returns' book for 1900 gives the names and place of abode of 250 individual customers, but whether this was the total number of private trade customers is unclear. This information provides evidence of the distances the brewery sent beer at that time. Some customers lived in the local area, within the 5 mile radius of the brewery, which would probably have been the extent of John Harris's initial contacts.

A second group of customers lived within 15 miles of Hook Norton and were served by an agent. A third group lived further away in Birmingham, Leamington, Oxford, and as far away as Kent. Their beer travelled by rail.

The Private Trade became a casualty of the First World War with the canvassing for trade being prohibited by the Central Control Board. The measure was designed to limit the availability of beer, by stopping the trading of beer at people's houses and as a result the trade in bottled beer declined dramatically. The Hook Norton Brewery was not the only brewer affected by the prohibition on canvassing for trade. Brains Brewery in Cardiff placed an advertisement in the local paper explaining how beer delivered to the door could still be obtained.

> Brain & Co Ltd, regret that for some reason unknown to themselves, the taking of orders and receiving payment for most kinds of Beer and Spirits at private houses has to be discontinued.
>
> This means that to order and have delivered to your house any of the various brands of Brain's Beers that they have hitherto had the pleasure of supplying to you, they must be ordered and paid for on licensed premises, before your instructions as to delivery can be carried out.[27]

Brain's Light Bitter, however, was a 'non-intoxicating beer', which did not come under the Control Board's restrictions because of its low alcohol content. This was available to Brain's customers and could be ordered and paid for in the way most convenient to the customer.[28]

In Hook Norton there was no alternative brew and Percy Flick's response was to stop brewing stout for bottling and further decrease the amounts of beer brewed for bottling. The loss of the 'private' trade on which the company had built its business left it with surplus capacity, placing a heavy reliance on the public house trade as its principal source of income although individual businesses, like George Cross and his successors at 21 West Street, Chipping Norton continued trading with the company until just before the Second World War.[29]

With the First World War nearing its end, Percy Flick outlined 'his future policy to trading', taking into account the changed trading circumstances. His intention was to 'conserve whatever wholesale trade was possible and only as a last resort attempt to reconstruct the old style private trade' because of the high costs of delivery and large amounts of capital locked up in book debts.

While the company were pursuing other business options, the licensee of the Great Western Arms in Aynho saw an opportunity to extend his trade in the village by becoming an agent for the company as well as the landlord of the public house. He wrote to the brewery to explain his plans. The response from the brewery was cool as George Groves explained the legal implications.

> With regard to the question of agency, as you know we are not in love with this business as it generally involves attempts on the evasion of the law. We believe if you act as a beer dealer you would have to take out a beer dealer's license and carry on such a business from another premises as distinct from your present licensed premises and we do not think you would be able to even receive an order for anything over 4½ gallons on your house licence premises, either verbally or by post. We have reason to believe that much stricter outlook is being kept

for evasion of the law and [we] should be very sorry to see either you or ourselves in trouble.

The Aynho agency idea appears to have gone no further, but the brewery did employ Frank Veale, on Flick's initiative, as a traveller in 1923 so that 'he might earn an adequate salary'. In December that year, his employment was extended for a further three months 'to see if such visits yielded [benefits] for the company'. Veale's appointment was not a serious attempt to resurrect the private trade. It seems to have been a short-term arrangement made as much in response to a humanitarian need, as to the business benefits it might accrue. There was no revival of the private trade; the company's trading policy thereafter concentrated on sales through the tied houses and clubs.

Tied Properties

By the late 1860s the enthusiasm for the 'free licensing' of the Beerhouse Act had faded and the national mood was for more control to be introduced. Under new legislation the Justices were empowered to issue licences for the sale of beer at both *on* and *off* premises. This included beerhouses.[30] With the re-introduction of licensing control in July 1869, the cost of public house licences increased and became more valuable. Prospective licensees found it difficult to raise the money, so they turned to the brewers for loans which were secured by a tie on the supplies of beer. Brewers nationally recognized, with the number of outlets diminishing, that it was prudent to acquire public houses otherwise they would lose custom and eventually face losses.[31] Gales Brewery in Horndean, a small brewer with an output of about 10,000 barrels a year,[32] typified the move towards acquiring properties by adding nine new licensed premises between 1864 and 1869, to their tied estate. Demand, however outstripped Gales production and it became necessary to lease brewing premises in Portsmouth at £41 per annum, suggesting Gales also had outlets in Portsmouth and were supplying a more densely populated area.[33] Hunt Edmunds & Co Ltd in Banbury was another brewery that had not invested in 'tied houses'. In 1874 they had just one, the Unicorn in the Market Place. Over the following twelve years the company invested heavily in property and bought out two rival breweries in Banbury, acquired sixty four public houses and established stores in local towns.[34]

In contrast, John Harris's entry into the tied house market had been more modest, beginning with the acquisition of the Pear Tree beerhouse in Hook Norton, which he bought for £210 in April 1869. In the following decade he purchased three more properties, situated in Woodstock (1872), Bloxham (1878) and Deddington (1878). These provided an opportunity to expand trade further; particularly the purchases in Woodstock and Deddington, both of which were more than the notional five miles from the brewery. Sales figures for both 1872 and 1878 reflect Harris's business acumen and there were increases in sales of 479 and 325 barrels respectively, representing increases of 27% and 12.6% on the respective previous years.

The Sun and Red Lion pubs.

An examination of the deeds[35] of ten Hook Norton properties reveal three periods of acquisition during the last twenty five years of the nineteenth century. Under the management of the trustees, following Harris's death in 1887, a second period of acquisition took place with four properties being bought between 1888 and 1894 including both The Gate Inn (1888) and The Sun Inn (1891). The third period came during the last four years of the nineteenth century when a total of ten new properties were acquired, with five being purchased in 1899 alone. This phase of buying was completed in 1901 with the purchase of the Black Horse in Leamington Spa and the White Swan Inn, in Stratford upon Avon.

The circumstances surrounding the acquisition of the White Swan were not straightforward. At the end of May 1901, George Groves wrote to Gilbert, the company's Stratford agent and thanked him for 'having obtained the offer of the White Swan lease' but the directors 'could not entertain [its] purchase at the present'. The brewery had, however, already signed the 'terms of sale' for the lease of White Swan Inn with Miss Mary Elizabeth Walker on 25th May, four days prior to Groves sending his letter. The company placed a £50 deposit on the property as a part payment of the full amount of £610. The balance of this 'purchase money' was to be paid in full on completion day, 24th June 1901, when the property would be available with vacant possession. Yet the new lease was to run for 15 years from 29th September 1901. Four days after the completion, the transaction was confirmed at the meeting of the directors. The brewery took control of the Inn, but Miss Walker and her brother-in-law remained on the premises 'for the convenience of the Company'. It is not clear whether they were acting as licensees and working out the last few months of their lease, or just assisting Mr Chappell, the new tenant, before they vacated the premises. Whatever the intentions of the Board, Mr Hand, Miss Walker's brother-in-law, was clearly not impressed with the way they had been treated and wrote to William Toy at the beginning of September to 'give… notice to fulfil [their] contract dated 25th May 1901 forthwith'. Some work needed doing on the property and after making extensive additions to the White Swan Hotel, the company declared '[we possess] a fine property although the full benefit will not be derived for a year or two. Still everything points to a growing trade. Our tenant Mr Chappell is gradually building up a fair business'.

This optimistic view was shared by the Banbury Guardian. In 1902 the paper carried an article celebrating the Hook Norton Brewery Company's incorporation and the completion of the new brewery. The newspaper commented that 'the brewery has 28 hotels and public houses and beerhouses attached to it, while in addition…[it also has] 25 agencies attached, one of which is the very successful Banbury branch recently opened at the Coach and Horses.'[36]

This optimism did not endure, trade became increasingly more difficult, and in 1905 Alban Clarke began an analysis of the performance of the company's twenty eight 'tied' properties. This analysis ran concurrently with his investigation into the business of the travellers covering the same period of time. The outcome of the 'tied trade' analysis revealed that only nine of the properties increased their trade, during the period and that there was an overall net decrease in trade of £608/9/2d. This net decrease in trade coincided with the general trend in the industry at the time, but masked the source of the problem.

By grouping the properties by location and examining more closely Clarke's figures for the individual performances of each house over the two years, an insight into the nature of the company's business becomes clearer. The properties can be grouped into four separate categories. Firstly, there were the public houses situated in Banbury, Leamington Spa and Stratford upon Avon. These were the company's 'flagship' properties. All three towns were served by major road, rail and canal routes and had more specialised shops providing customers with a greater choice. Here it might be expected that the changing attitudes to beer, supported by the temperance message would have had a deleterious impact. Other properties were in smaller country towns, like Chipping Norton and Stow on the Wold where communication routes were less developed. They were served by major roads, but lacked either a major rail connection or canal provision. In these towns shops were more likely to be 'general' stores, selling a wide range of products, rather than the more specialised shops found in the larger towns.[37] Finally, there were those properties found in the villages, which formed two distinct groups; the public houses and beerhouses.

Between them, the ten properties situated in the towns, accounted for 86.2% of the decrease in 'tied' house trade during the period. The largest proportion of that decrease came in the larger towns. In the country towns the decrease was less dramatic, being only a third of that experienced in the more urbanised areas. The 'Black Horse' in Leamington was the only one of the four public houses situated in the large towns to increase its trade, but only by £11. In Stratford upon Avon trade fell by £45, while in Banbury, the trade of the company's two houses fell dramatically by £356. The village pubs also experienced a drop in revenue, but the combined total fall in revenue for both public houses and beer houses accounted for only £82 of the total. Further examination of these trade figures, illustrates a slight shift in the nature of the trade. At the end of September 1905, the 'town' properties contributed fractionally more (50.6%) of the total 'tied' house revenue for that year, although the single largest contribution came from 'village' public houses (41.2%). A year later, the balance had changed with the 'village' properties contributing a combined total of 52.6%, against the 47.4% coming from the 'town' properties making up the year's total 'tied' house revenue.

The village and country town properties, between them contributed almost three quarters of the revenue in both 1905 and 1906. Even so, at the end of his review of public house trade, Alban Clarke was left with the stark fact that at twenty of the twenty nine properties, trade had fallen and the company suffered a net decrease in trade of £608/9/2.

In the villages the alternative leisure facilities were very much more limited. Research carried out by the Agricultural Research Institute at the University of Oxford in 1943 found that 'the public house was still the centre of social activity in every village'. The only alternatives to the public house were social activities organised by different groups of people coming together out of common interest. These conclusions mirror Flora Thompson's description of the village pub in *Lark Rise* [38] some sixty or so years earlier.

> There the adult male population gathered every evening, to
> sip its half-pints, drop by drop, to make them last and to

discuss local events….none of them got drunk; they had not money enough, even with beer, and good beer, at two pence a pint….. for it had its own social centre, warmer, more human and altogether preferable, in the tap room of the 'Wagon and Horses'.

To spend their evenings there [the pub] was, indeed, as the men argued, a saving, for with no man in the house, the fire at home could be let die down and the rest of the family could go to bed when the room got cold.

The nature of the village pubs Clarke analysed would have been very similar to Flora Thompson's descriptions and the loss in revenue suffered in the villages during the period was still £176 less than the losses experienced by the larger urban properties. Changing attitudes towards beer had yet to impinge on country life. The public house and beer were still at the centre of social life in the villages and as a consequence sales did not fall significantly, although sales of beer over the bar contributed only about a quarter of the total drink sales in both years.[39]

The reasons for the Hook Norton Brewery's difficulties in Banbury become apparent when the structure of the town's retail beer trade is examined. While the population of the parish of Banbury was rising, that of the town was in decline. In the thirty years between 1871 and 1901 the population of Banbury town fell by 17.7% while in the neighbouring township of Neithrop the population rose by 15.3%.[40] In 1880 there were eleven agencies, representing six different brewers operating in Banbury.[41] A decade later there were 36 public houses, 39 beer retailers, 8 brewers and 6 agencies in the parish.[42] By 1907 the population of Banbury (including Neithrop) was in excess of 12,000 people and the town supported a total of seventy outlets retailing beer, made up of 36 inns, hotels and public houses and 34 'beer retailers', probably corner shops with 'off' licences, selling bottled beer. Of this total, there were only two Hook Norton public houses in the town, the 'Reindeer' and the 'Coach and Horses'. These two houses represented only 2.9% of all Banbury's beer trading outlets or 5.5% of the public houses in the town. The Hook Norton Brewery's tied houses were in the town, not Neithrop, and it is not, therefore, surprising that with a declining population base, falling demand and fierce competition, their share of the custom in Banbury was small. If the nineteenth century claim that 56% of the population drank alcohol is correct, then in Banbury town there would have been 1,900 drinkers and with only 5.5% of the public house trade, the Hook Norton Brewery might have attracted about 100 customers, but as their properties were losing custom this seems unlikely.

In an effort to improve the financial position of the company, a number of uneconomic pubs were sold off. The sale of the "Reindeer Inn", in Banbury, intended to raise £4,000, was an embarrassing failure, dragging on for two years. A buyer was eventually found for the pub's wooden panelling in "The Globe Room", which sold for £1000, but this sale drew disapprovingly negative comment from both the Banbury Guardian and shareholders.[43]

The pub trade had been in decline, since the turn of the century. In 1905-6 public houses contributed only a quarter of the total drinks revenue and by the end of the decade the situation had not improved, but as the private trade declined, the tied trade came to represent a greater percentage of the total drinks sale.

At a Board Meeting in January 1910, the Directors reported that the 'trade at houses continued to decrease' and by the end of the year it had reached its nadir. In the years immediately prior to war, the public house trade slowly began to revive, seeing small annual increases in the annual income from the tied trade which continued throughout the war, in spite of Government restrictions. The largest of these annual increases in the public house trade was a rise of 103% in 1911.[44]

Within months of War being declared in 1914, the Government had more than trebled the duty on beer, to 23/- a barrel. The directors of the Hook Norton Brewery acknowledged the over-riding need was to 'preserve the trade even after reduced profits' and adjusted the cost of a barrel so that publicans could continue to sell beer and stout at 3d a pint. The impact of Government restrictions hit the company sales hard. At the regular meetings of the Directors the 'sales and finance statements' were considered. Early in 1915 the figures for the three months ending 31st December 1914 were viewed as satisfactory as there had been an increase of £60 in beer sales, but by June, the figures for January 1915 had fallen by 100 barrels compared with the previous year and sales continued to fall. In November 1915 they were described as showing 'a considerable falling off compared with 1914'. It was not just the sale of beer that declined. Bottled beer and stout also suffered and sales fell by 50%, so it was decided to stop brewing bottling stout with immediate effect and to cut back further the bottling of beer. Percy Flick admitted he saw 'no hope of being able to arrest' this decline because of a falling customer base caused by the 'continual withdrawal of men from the district for service in France, or as munitions workers'. It was not only potential customers that were being called up; staff from the brewery were also involved, as was the tenant of the Queen's Own public house in Woodstock, who left his wife to run the pub. Things seem to have got too much for her and she packed up and left the house which remained closed until a new tenant could be found.

The licence of the Blue Pig in Southam became redundant during 1915. The house was closed and the company claimed compensation from the Warwickshire County Licensing authority under the 1904 Act. The Authority's offer of £575 was deemed insufficient and Flick referred the matter to the Inland Revenue as arbiters. At a Board Meeting on 11th July 1916 he reported the Revenue had awarded the brewery £660 in compensation. This was to be divided between the brewery as owners, receiving £611 and Mr Hopkins, the tenant, who was paid £49. The Blue Pig was auctioned during the following month as an unlicensed house for £290, the business being handled by Percy Flick's firm, Flick and Lock in Banbury.[45]

With the war over further financial problems loomed. Cash was short and profits were 'shortening owing solely to the rising costs of [raw] materials'. It was probably no coincidence that the company sold four licensed properties, of which the most significant was the White Swan in Stratford. An offer of £4,500 had been received from Messrs Flower and

Sons for both the White Swan and the Elephant and Castle in Rowington. The directors were mindful to accept this offer, but stipulated that the agent's commission should not exceed 2%. Public houses were the currency of the business and if a property was unprofitable it was sold off or the lease was not renewed. The Chilson beerhouse was one such property which was doing 'very little trade' in 1921. The cost of delivering two or three kilderkins of beer was as much as delivering a full load elsewhere so it was decided not to renew the lease and let the property go. Notice was given to the tenant and the tenants of two adjoining cottages, with instructions for them to leave any outstanding rent with Mr Cox, at the beerhouse.

In the immediate post war years trading remained difficult and beer sales were not sustained, but Percy Flick strongly advocated the company 'should endeavour by any means, [to maintain] its expenditure to retain sales' even though this could involve using the company's investments in National War Bonds to acquire new and 'advantageous' licensed properties.

Between April 1919 and February 1929 the Board considered the purchase of thirteen new licensed properties and only once did they decline to take action. The Board deferred to Percy Flick's expertise as a property valuer and estate agent and authorised him to conduct transactions on their behalf, leaving it to his discretion whether or not the property was purchased. It was usual for the Board meeting to set him a bidding limit which was probably influenced by Flick's valuation of the property. Typical of this was the Board meeting in November 1922, called to discuss purchase of the Tower, at Edge Hill. The 'matter [of the purchase] was left at the discretion of the Managing Director [Flick]', but a bidding limit of £3,300 was set. When those houses of Messrs Blencowe's, situated in the district, became available in September 1925, a special meeting was called to discuss the matter. It was agreed that Percy Flick should attend the auction at the Grand Hotel in Birmingham on October 13th.

At the next meeting he reported that he had purchased five public houses, at a total cost of £3,975.

Agencies

The Hook Norton Brewery's network of agencies formed the outer edge of its trading area, being established during the last quarter of the nineteenth century, but it was the Burton brewers who had led the way earlier in the century with the creation of 'agencies' as a way of commercially developing distant markets. In 1888, for instance, there were three different wine and spirit merchants in Banbury acting as agents for three different Burton beers.[46] Brewers were reluctant to pay a large retaining fee for the sole agency, or be too charitable with the discount offered. The agent's personality and behaviour in acquiring business, as a representative of his employer, was also important. Any injudicious comment or approach could damage his business. It was he who secured the orders and was the brewery's representative in the area, responsible for promoting their beer. Agents working for larger breweries became responsible not only for the procuring of orders, but also the management of staff working from the agency, which might include travellers, storemen and draymen.[47] C. Howard Tripp recommended that when appointing an agent, brewers should look for someone who was smart, 'of good education, had temperate habits and above all, affable in manner, as well as [being] strictly conscientious and straightforward'.[48]

It was deemed a further asset if the agent 'could bring connections', trade contacts he had made previously. When in 1899 T. Boulton and Son of the Shire Oak Brewery wanted a traveller to sell their beer in Walsall, the advertisement in the local paper specifically stated 'preference given to one commanding a small connection' but an applicant who overstated his connections was given little time to prove his worth. A.J. Ebsworth, claiming to have 'command [of] a large trade' was appointed as Flower & Sons London agent in 1868, but within a month he was reprimanded for failing to increase the company's pale ale sales. After only five months, he was dismissed, having been found to have no connections at all.[49]

To guarantee the company against possible losses incurred through the malpractices of an agent, the Hook Norton Brewery appear to have taken out a guarantee for a specified sum of money against the name of specified employees with "The Law Guarantee and Trust Society Limited". Two examples of the Society's application form survive in the Hook Norton archive, a hand written copy, dated February 1897, specifying a Mr Rowles and the second, a completed un-named typed carbon copy, dated 1903. The form consisted of ten questions about the firm and employee, so as to establish the name and nature of the business, the character of the employee to be guaranteed and whether he was employed by the company. Further questions ask for information about the nature of his job and responsibilities, particularly when handling money.

The final questions dealt with weekly wages and expenses and enquired about his credit worthiness. How frequently these forms were used is difficult to ascertain,[50] but details on the 1903 form, suggests it may relate to the company's agent in Stratford upon Avon, Mr Gilbert. His previous employment and job description tally with the information on the guarantee form and perhaps crucially, this form was found amongst papers relating to his working in Stratford during the spring of 1903.

Gilbert had previously worked for the Shipston on Stour Brewery as an agent and had been given a good reference when he joined Harris's Brewery in 1898 and became the company's ale stores manager and traveller for the Stratford area, based in Arden Street.[51] As part of the job, Gilbert collected cash from his customers and this could have been as much as £100, which he paid directly to the brewery every week with a statement of money received. For this he was paid 35/- a week and received £1 for expenses and 5% on the net cash which came as a cheque from the brewery. Everything seemed to be going well. The company appeared to have had no complaints about his work. Then in August 1901 complaints were made about the manner in which he looked after the beer and when a year later, a cheque paid by Gilbert to the brewery, was refused, his position appears, thereafter to have been under scrutiny. The events that followed illustrate the procedure used by the company to dismiss an employee.

Gilbert's actions as the company's representative in Stratford upon Avon failed to meet the essential qualities of an agent, advocated by Tripp, namely to be "conscientious and straightforward" and although his dismissal was based on three complaints, they reflect a failure to meet Tripp's criteria.

First, was the neglect of one of the company's horses. Gilbert had been to Rowington and returning to Stratford, the horse fell, badly injuring its knees. The horse could not continue the journey and was stabled at an Inn in Pinley where Gilbert was of the opinion the animal would be well looked after. There was, however, a delay of four days before Gilbert informed Alban Clarke of the incident. There was a further delay before he sent a telegram on April 7th, advising Clarke that a vet had diagnosed the animal with lock jaw and when instructions were sent, telling him to have the animal destroyed, he was absent from his Office. The telegram was then delivered to the company's landlord at 'The White Swan Hotel', Mr Chappell, and it was left to him to effect Clarke's instructions. Chappell went to Pinley, and engaged the services of a local farmer and his men to destroy the animal. As a result of his actions, Gilbert was given 3 months notice to quit, receiving a verbal notice on the 30th March and written confirmation the following day. Gilbert acknowledged this and the option for him to resign, but further investigations into the running of his agency revealed more irregularities. He had, contrary to instructions, been selling to other brewers licensed houses and to a customer of known bad debt. His books were not kept up to date and he had failed to notify the brewery when customers changed their addresses. With this evidence Alban Clarke visited Chipping Norton to seek legal advice from William Toy. It was Toy's opinion that Gilbert should be discharged with immediate effect. So Clarke travelled to Stratford and paid Gilbert off, paying him £18/10/0 for the period between his last salary and the 17th April. To this he added £4/5/0, in lieu of notice, for the seventeen days up to the 4th May, although it appears Gilbert wanted to be paid up to 30th June.[52]

That was not quite the end of the matter. In June 1905, William Toy received a letter from J.R. Phillips, a solicitor acting for Mr Gilbert, arguing that his dismissal was unreasonable and contesting that Gilbert was entitled commission on sales he had made to the value of £18/4/3. Phillips concluded that he hoped matters could be concluded amicably without having to go to litigation. William Toy confronted this challenge and invited Mr Phillips to 'commence an action', as the company would dispute Gilbert's claim and bring an action against him 'for damage done to [their] horse'. The two solicitors agreed, however, that copies of the relevant accounts would be supplied to determine whether Mr Gilbert was entitled to the commission on sales he had made, in an attempt to settle the matter amicably.

Brewers did not, however, rely solely on agencies. A common pattern of distribution evolved through the use of both agencies and stores to fulfil their trading objectives. Stores differed from agencies in so much that they were run by the brewery, either from their own premises or a rented property and in Banbury, the Hook Norton Brewery operated a store behind the "Coach and Horses" during the first decade of the twentieth century. Some of the larger breweries, however, used neither, instead relying on travellers working from the brewery to supply the tied houses and develop the free and private trade in their area. Such practices were found in the largest conurbations and with a high population density were often extremely profitable.[53]

When the Hook Norton Brewery was incorporated in 1900, the company boasted 25 agencies.[54] The network stretched from Birmingham and Solihull in the north to Oxford in the south and included the towns of Bicester, Brackley, Daventry, Leamington and Stratford upon Avon and the village of Quenington. Only five of the agencies, Banbury, Chipping Norton, Stow on the Wold, Shipston on Stour and Kineton were within ten miles of the brewery.[55] Deliveries of stocks were made by horse and dray up to a distance of about fifteen miles from the brewery, beyond that, beer was sent by rail. New agents, like Mr H. Golding of Byfield, took advantage of the business opportunity and by 1900 was running two of the company's nineteen agencies. The occupation of the agents varied. Six of them, like Golding, combined the agency with their trade as grocers or running a general stores, three ran brewery stores and the remainder appear to have operated solely as agents for the company but may, like H.A. Cox of Stechford in Birmingham, have been wine and spirit merchants.

Hook Norton Brewery Agencies 1900

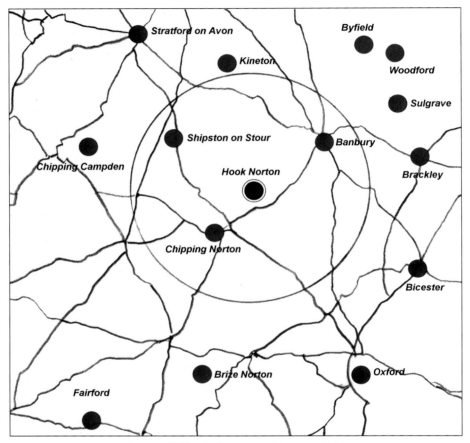

Source: HNBC Archive: List of Agencies 1900.

A picture of how this trade operated can be constructed from the Minutes of Directors' meetings, company letters and Alban Clarke's notes. In March 1892 Clarke reviewed the operation of the Quenington agency, run by a Mr J. Arnold, with a view to lowering the operating costs, which swallowed up a fifth of the revenue. Having analysed the business done by the agency, Clarke suggested an alteration to Arnold's working practice by reducing his travelling expenses. In 1891 Arnold's trade was £404/3/3d of which he was allowed 10% net on money paid to the brewery. During the year he spent 26 days travelling on business and may have worked as a 'district traveller', as well as agent. For his travelling, Arnold claimed £24/13/4 in expenses. It was these expenses that Clarke aimed to reduce, in his revised plan for working the Agency. It was assumed that the annual trade for the agency would be £400 a year. Clarke proposed that the percentage allowed to Arnold should be increased to 12½% on 'nett cash remitted to the brewery', which would increase his annual earnings to £50. In return the number of journeys would be reduced from twenty six to nine. By this measure, travelling expenditure would be reduced by 75%, the company gained 2% on the trade and Arnold would spend 17 more days working at the agency.

Suggested change in working practices at Quenington

1891		New Proposal: March 1892	
Arnold's delivery account + extras for new customers and collecting cash	10%	Arnold's 12½% for collecting orders and cash and delivering to customers	12½%
Travelling Expenses and 26 days absence	6%	Travelling Expenses. Say 9 Journeys @ 15/-	1½%
Discounts	3%	Discounts	3%
Store Licence + Rent of Store	2½%	Store Licence + Rent of Store	2½%
Total	**21½%**		**19½%**

Source: HNBC Archive: A.A. Clarke's Notes: Agencies March 1892. Quenington.

While Arnold was set to receive 12½% during 1892, other agents operated on different allowances, negotiated to suit their situation. In Solihull, the agent Mr Ledbrook received 17½% on the invoiced prices, but this was to offset the fact that he received no store rent, could not allow discount on orders, and was responsible for delivering to the customer and collecting cash from them. In Birmingham, John Banks received 15% on the invoiced price, but he could allow small discounts on orders. He was also responsible for collecting cash from the customers. The improvement in the business during the final decade of the nineteenth century led to an expansion of the agency network. The conditions of engagement for agents were set out in this letter to a prospective new selling agent in Cheltenham in 1894,

> …We can offer you 20% on all cash paid to you on your account. Out of this you would have to allow any small discounts where necessary to business … Our terms would be that you pay into us all collected cash at the end of each month, less 20% due to you and send us an account of any extra carriage charges dispersed, which amounts shall be remitted to you.

The first decade of the new century saw the number of agencies cut by half because of the general decline in trade and measures to reduce expenditure on agencies were introduced. Agencies in Witney, Oxford and Stratford upon Avon were closed during 1910, although the trade of the Stratford agency was run from the White Swan Hotel for a while. Although no agent operated for the full decade, Messrs Godfrey and Walton in Sulgrave traded for seven of those years. There were further changes before the outbreak of war. A meeting of the Directors in 1912 resolved that all remaining agencies be put on a new working basis when there was a change of management.

Allowances were to be capped at no more than 20% and for buying agents 25%. By 1913 Arnold's profits at Quenington were deemed unsatisfactory by the Board and it was suggested he take over the business of the agency as a 'buying agent'. Arnold declined to change his working arrangements, so the agency was closed at the end of January 1914 and the business offered to a brewery in Stroud with 'the good will and book debts of the Agency'.

Ordering Beer

The point of contact for the publican ordering supplies was George Groves, at the company office. Here, for more than half a century, Groves oversaw the day to day business of trade. Much of his work revolved around the supply and payments for beer and this reflected in a set of letters which cover the period from 1920 to 1923.

George Groves with the Office staff (HNBC).
Back row: Frederick Stratford (out ride). Middle row: Drake, Walker and Allen. Front row: Frank Veale, Harold Wyton, F. Robbins and George Groves, Company Secretary.

When duty on beer was raised first by £3/10/0 per barrel in April 1919 and then to £5 the following year, the brewery responded by writing to all their tenants (and the Coventry Clubs) offering beer brewed before the budget at the old prices. A few days later Groves indignantly wrote to the Northampton Brewery Company to query why the cost of 2 kils of stout supplied to the tenant in Woodstock had been charged at the new price, even though the order had been placed three days before the budget and ten days before the price rise was supposed to take effect.[56] It was not until June 1920 that Hook Norton Brewery tenants needed to re-order beer under the new prices imposed due to the rise in duty. Letters were sent to tenants informing them that the new prices were, per barrel, 134/- for PAB and 96/- for Bitter with the beers retailing at 7d and 5d per half pint respectively. Some tenants enquired whether more favourable terms were available, but Groves always replied with the same argument explaining the company's position.

> We regret it is impossible for us to vary these terms as the increased duty, coupled with the high price of making malts, plus 1919 hops, leaves our margin of profit very restricted. We use nothing but the very finest materials and find it is better to rely on the quality of our ales rather than the discount to keep up sales.

Orders were despatched with an invoice which itemised the price at which particular beers were to be sold. In January 1921 an order sent to the Red Lion Hotel in Banbury was incorrectly invoiced by the clerk. Discovering the error Groves wrote to clarify the position, explaining that the correct price for half a pint was 5½d in the public bar and not 6d and that the price of a pint was 9d in the public bar and 11d elsewhere.

When payment for an order was received a receipt was enclosed with an acknowledging note thanking the tenant for payment, but if the tenant was a bad payer or their settlement was short of the amount owed,

Groves took a firm line. The tenant of the Queen's Own in Woodstock sent a cheque for £33/0/6d as payment for an order, but this was £25/3/0 short of the full total. Groves's letter, with receipt for the cheque received, was to the point, asking for the outstanding amount to be paid within a week. The licensee of the George Hotel in Shipston on Stour was another to receive a rasping letter from Groves over a longstanding debt.[57]

Trade in the twenty years following the First World War reflected the economic difficulties of the times. In the immediate post-war years, there was much unemployment in Hook Norton, as elsewhere, with 10% of the country's population without work.[58] The income from all the Hook Norton Brewery's public houses slumped, and by 1922 the yearly total had fallen by almost £2,000 compared with two years earlier. The economic condition of the country did not improve and during the following four years the yearly income rose and fell by small increments, eventually reaching £10,234 in 1926 and remained at this level for the next three years, varying by only a few hundred pounds. The records list fourteen properties at this time earning a total of £84,372 for the decade.

For the Hook Norton Brewery there were three poor years between 1930 and 1932, which was attributed to unemployment in Coventry, but after 1935, output and the sale of beer 'picked up'. The annual trade totals for the decade beginning 1931 for the company's twenty one licensed properties reflect this assessment. These fell from £9,887 to £8,019 and only in 1933 was there a minute improvement, a matter of just £34. By 1935, however, there were incremental increases in the annual totals as they rose from £9,038 to £15,004 and by the end of the decade the total trade of the twenty one houses was £100,407.

Two Wars and the Club Trade

The loss of the private trade left the Company with surplus capacity, placing a heavy reliance on the public house trade as its principal source of income.[59] In an attempt to find markets for this surplus capacity, Percy Flick visited Birmingham in 1915. The visit was fruitless and although a number of temporary arrangements helped to keep the business going, salvation came in the form of trade with the Working Men's Clubs in Coventry. The brewery had been sending beer to Coventry for many years as part of the private trade. The city was one of the 'munitions areas' covered by the Intoxicating Liquor (Output and Delivery) Order 1918, but it is not clear when or how Flick came to make the initial contacts with the clubs. Former company secretary, Harold Wyton was of the opinion that Percy Flick had 'a bit of luck' keeping the brewery at full production by supplying these clubs. It has been generally assumed that Flick's 'bit of luck' had been in obtaining the two special licenses, covering the second and third quarters of 1918, authorising the brewery to supply beer to clubs in the Coventry area.[60] The company trade ledgers, however, tell a different story. Flick's 'bit of luck' may have been his ability to secure orders before the clubs came under the jurisdiction of government orders. On 2nd May 1917, the brewery began delivering to the Stanton Working Men's Club in Coventry. A week later the first deliveries were made to the Westbury Working Men's Club. The effect of the Intoxicating Liquor (Output and Delivery) Order, rather than establishing the club trade, consolidated the brewery's position in Coventry by authorising them to supply these clubs. Although the arrangement with the Stanton Working Men's Clubs lasted only three months, a further five clubs from the area began taking beer from Hook Norton during 1918. In addition, the District Workers Union and the Selly Oak Conservative Club, both in Birmingham, were supplied with Hook Norton beer, although this trade fell outside the jurisdiction of the Intoxicating Liquor (Output and Delivery) Orders. In all, twelve clubs were being supplied by the Hook Norton Brewery during 1918, of which the trade of nine in the Coventry area was controlled by the conditions of the Intoxicating Liquor Orders.

Once the War was over it became apparent that the number of on-licensed premises had fallen; large brewers like Ind Coope and Allsopp and Whitbread, saw clubs as a marketing opportunity and built up a considerable trade supplying 1,590 and 3,920 clubs respectively by 1948.[61] In comparison Hook Norton's involvement in the club trade was minute, but having established trade in the Coventry area, the brewery had with the help of the war time regulations established itself in a new, if small, permanent market. This was important, for the inter-war years were difficult for the company. While brewers like Courage embarked on a prosperous period of expansion and development, acquiring four breweries, rebuilding the Alton Brewery to increase its production capacity and increasing its total number of outlets to 886, the Hook Norton Brewery struggled.[62] The impact of the loss of the private trade and the failure to increase sales presented a gloomy future. Only the hope that more trade could be done with the clubs, even at the risk of greater expenditure provided any sign for optimism.

In October 1921 the Board of Directors met to review the previous three months trading figures. The news was gloomy. There had been a considerable fall in the sale of beer compared with the same months in the previous year, which was attributed to falling sales in Coventry. William Toy expressed his regret at hearing these figures and ventured that this was in part due to the company policy of curtailing travelling expenses. He strongly advocated 'that the company endeavour by any means of maintaining its expenditure to retain the [Coventry] trade'. His comments brought a consensus to the meeting and it was agreed that it had been, 'one step in the wrong direction and that the company could not expect to retain the trade unless it was prepared to act in an equally generous way to its customers as other brewers did'.

This resolution was soon put to the test. In the days just before Christmas 1921 the company held its Annual General Meeting and under discussion was the suggested loan, in the form of a mortgage, to one of the Coventry clubs. The meeting was told that 'there must be some element of risk to advancing money on a club premises' but it was agreed that 'in view of the business done with the club it formed a fair trade risk'. The argument in favour of the loan was accepted and carried unanimously and the sum of £3,000 was advanced to the club at a rate of 4.5%. There were further requests for financial help during the following decade from clubs wanting either to relocate or to rebuild their existing property. These requests all seem to have been dealt with sympathetically, but in one case the directors, on the advice of Percy Flick, deferred any loan until the club could provide the necessary security.

It appears that part of the company's strategy in maintaining the Coventry trade was to entertain parties from the clubs at the brewery and as Managing Director, Percy Flick played a central role as the host. Flick also made visits to Coventry, supporting their entertainment programmes by providing clubs with medals and prizes. The investment of Flick's time in supporting the Coventry clubs proved financially beneficial to the company, while his entertainment costs accounted for less than 2%, the revenue from the clubs provided a large part of the company's annual income.[63]

There was, however, no rapid expansion of the club trade during the years between the wars, with the total number of all club outlets remaining under ten. A survey taken at five yearly intervals between 1922 and 1942 shows that the number of clubs in the Coventry area, supplied by the brewery at each five year point, fluctuated and was never more than six.

In 1917, the five Coventry clubs accounted for most of the brewery's business contributing £1,114. By 1922 that share had risen to £7,991 although only four clubs were being supplied. Trade to the Coventry clubs fell in 1927 to £7,611, but this still amounted to three quarters of the total club trade. The downward trend was again reflected in 1932, with some unemployment in Coventry, but although the trade in the city had decreased it still contributed most of the brewery's club trade. From 1935 the 'business picked up' and by 1937 there were six Coventry clubs earning £8,067, but it was not until the beginning of the Second World War that Percy Flick saw the real growth in club trade he had identified twenty years earlier as being so important.

Business generated by the clubs was not confined exclusively to the Coventry area, nor to just Working Men's Clubs. One of the first clubs to take Hook Norton beer was the Cotteridge Social Club in Birmingham and two other Birmingham clubs followed, taking beer from Oxfordshire for a short while. The failure of the brewery to exploit this market may be due to difficulties experienced in delivering beer and competition from Birmingham brewers. In the years between the wars, several clubs in Banbury and Rugby were also supplied with Hook Norton beer and in 1931 and 1932, beer was sent to the Ninian Stuart Club in Treherbert, South Wales. No convenient description fits the group of fifteen other clubs that made up this trade. Divided into five general categories they represented political, sports, public services, press/country club interests and the British Legion, but they provided only a small percentage of the total business secured by the brewery. In the period between 1917 and 1942 the club trade contributed 50.1% of the brewery's total income.

The brewery's ability to 'sell everything they could turn out' during the Second World War was reflected in the trade done with the Coventry clubs. During both 1939 and 1940, the clubs contributed 96% and 94% respectively to the club trade total and in 1941 the entire club trade revenue came from Coventry. From 1942 to the end of the decade, the Coventry contribution to the club trade total never fell beneath 80%, which saw yearly increases in the total revenue throughout the decade, peaking in 1949 at £57,883. The backbone of the Coventry trade during this period however, was the business done by just four clubs, the Earlsdon (Albany), Coventry Amalgamated Engineers, Vauxhall and Binley Colliery Working Men's clubs, which between them contributed 75.2% of the total club trade done with Hook Norton.

A consequence of the Second World War was the establishment of a temporary trade with thirty nine military units stationed in the Hook Norton area for training. The presence of British and American military units stationed in the area between 1939 and 1948 provided the brewery with a transient business, supplying the Officers', Sergeants' or Corporals' Mess and the NAAFIs with beer. 1942 was the busiest year, with twenty four units stationed in the area doing business with the brewery, while in 1944 and 1946 there were only seven units, including the US Army, stationed at North Aston during 1944. Some units appear to have made only one transaction, while others, operating for the duration, bought in substantial amounts of beer. The NAAFI at

Chipping Warden (£6,839) and RAF Shenington (£5,796), accounted for most of this trade.

Business with the military units grew from 1941 until the end of the War, by 65%, reaching £4,588 in 1945. Between 1941 and 1948, when the last unit left the area, the Allied Forces were responsible for £18,026 worth of trade. Yet compared with the nineteen clubs who were trading with the brewery at this time, the military trade seems almost insignificant, with the clubs providing £365,698 worth of business. The largest percentage increases in trade during the Second World War were seen in 1942, for both the club trade (106.5%) and tied trade (25.4%) and in 1944 for the tied trade (28.2%). The club trade, after the large increase in 1942, continued to make annual, but less spectacular increases until 1949. The immediate post war years were marked by the return of government restrictions with increases in the duty on beer being imposed in four out of the six budgets between 1945 and 1950. The impact of these increases is reflected in the performance of the pub trade between 1945 and 1950. Between 1940 and 1945 the annual totals from the tied house trade rose from £16,605 to £27,813, but the post war restrictions imposed by the Attlee government saw the pub trade fall from £27,813 in 1945 to £17,658 at the end of the decade and only in 1948 was there a small increase of £407.

Notes

1   OCMTRC: Thomas Hyatt was the village maltster in 1729. This is the earliest documented reference to a maltster in Hook Norton. Humphry Harris (1741) and W. Harris (1762) followed Hyatt as maltsters in Hook Norton during the eighteenth century.

2   Robson's Commercial Directory. c1834.

    Post Office Directory. 1847. p.2195.

3   Gardener's Directory. *History Gazetteer and Directory of the County of Oxford.* 1852. p.851.

    HNBC Archive: Brewing Book 28/7/1858 Yeast from Bell Inn, HN. Work well.

4   Deeds of the 'The Wheatsheaf'. Courtesy of Mr R. Collin. May 1984 The house was formerly known as the 'Fleur de Lys or (Lis)'.

5   They were referred to in the Census Returns and Trade Directories as 'beershop', 'beerhouse' or 'beer retailer'. Whichever term was used to describe the property, they fulfilled the same function.

6   The 1907 spelling (Kelly's Trade Directory). Thereafter the name is given as two words.

7   Deeds of 'The Pear Tree' 13th February 1899, Deeds of the 'Beerhouse' 4th October 1902.

    Oral Tradition. W.A. Clarke Folder 1972-74.

8   Harrison. B. and Trinder. B. *Drink and Sobriety in an Early Victorian Town: Banbury 1830-1860,* 1969. p2.

9   Census Returns: 1871, 1881.

10   Seventeenth Century Wills of John Haull (1631), William Hall (1640), William Prue (1686).

11   Evans. G.E. *Ask the Fellow who cuts the hay.* Faber. 1972. pp.60-65.

12   It is not clear whether the 548 barrels sold in 1855 represents the peak of sales in the immediate Hook Norton area.

13   HNBC Archive: Stock Book 1855-1876. In 1860 646 brls sold, 1861 660 brls sold, 1862 661 brls sold.

14   Gourvish. T. and Wilson. R. *The British Brewing Industry 1830-1980.* CUP, 1994, pp.600-602. Table 1.

    Monckton. H.A. *A History of English Ale & Beer.* Bodley Head. 1966 pp.221-2. Appendix D.

15   Gourvish. T. and Wilson. R. 1994. p.38.

    Fletcher. T.W. *The Great Depression of English Agriculture 1873-1896.* Economic History Review. Vol XIII No 3 April 1961. p.418.

16 Agricultural Economics Institute, Oxford. *Country Planning*. OUP 1944 p.88. There is evidence that the public House still remained the social centre of villages.

17 Gourvish. T. and Wilson. R. 1994, pp.600-602. Table 1. Per capita expenditure peaked in 1876 at £3.16/person.

18 Tripp published a book entitled *'Brewery Management'* in 1892, being a collection of these articles.

19 The 'journey' was the route followed by the traveller.

20 Salopian Journal. 14/4/1813 and 18/6/1819.

21 C.H. Tripp. *Brewery Management*. 1892. pp.73-76.

22 Gourvish. T. & Wilson. R. 1994. p.162.

23 Banbury Guardian: 5/11/1896. 'Employees of John Harris & Co presented Richard Howse with a valuable arm chair of antique design on retiring from the Company after 33 years.' He joined Harris in 1863.

24 Oral Tradition: Conversation with Harold Wyton. Folder 1972-1974.

25 Mr Brotheridge left the Company's employment in 1908 after financial irregularities were found in his accounting.

26 Stapleton. B. & Thomas J.H. *Gales: A study in Brewing, business & family history*. Ashgate 2000. p.48.

27 South Wales Echo. *Notice* 10/5/1916. Supplied to Central Control Board by the Chief Constable of Cardiff.

28 South Wales Echo. *New Cardiff Ale*. 1/5/1916 Brain's Light Beer contained less than 3% 'proof spirit'.

29 Shadwell. A. *Drink in 1914-1922. A Lesson in Control*. Longmans, Green & Co. 1923 p.42. Canvassing, along with Treating, Credit and "The Long Pull" were prohibited and classified as 'Minor Restrictions'.
   Ledger 1933-1942. Godfrey and Walton traded with the Company until 1929.

30 Jennings. P. *The Public House in Bradford 1770-1970,* 1995. p.157.
   Clark. P. *The English Alehouse A Social History 1200-1830*. 1983. p.338.

31 Monkton. H.A. 1966 pp.167-8.

32 Stapleton and Thomas, 2000. p.5. Gales Brewery closed in February 2006.

33 Stapleton and Thomas, 2000. p.41.

34 Hunt, Edmunds & Co. Ltd 1896-1946. 1946. p.7.

35 Deeds of the Hook Norton Brewery Company. Examined in 1976.

36 Banbury Guardian. 20/3/1902.

37   Trinder. B. *Victorian Banbury.* Phillimore 1982. p.162.

38   Thompson. F. *Lark Rise.* Folio Society. London 1979. p63 Originally published by OUP 1939.

39   Agricultural Economic Research Institute.Oxford. *Country Planning.* OUP. 1944. pp.228-231.

40   Victoria County History: '*Oxfordshire'.* Vol 2. 1987. p.216.

41   Gourvish. T. & Wilson. R. 1994. p.161.

42   Kelly's Trade Directory. 1891. pp.582-587. Includes Neithrop, but excluding Grimsbury.

     Kelly's Trade Directory 1907. pp.38-43.

43   The Globe Room panels were returned to the Reindeer in the early 1980s.

44   Between 1912 and 1918 the Company established a small trade selling yeast to thirteen other breweries in the Midlands, including Boulter's Shire Oak Brewery and the Highgate Brewery both in Walsall, the Holt Brewery in Birmingham and Dunnell's in Banbury. The revenue was small, a total of only £165.40.

45   Eddershaw. D. *A Country Brewery:Hook Norton 1849-1999.* Hook Norton Brewery Co Ltd .1999. p.66-68.

46   Banbury Guardian April to June 1888.

47   Gourvish & Wilson. 1994. pp.152, 156.

48   C.H. Tripp. 1892. p.67.

49   Plummer. C.W. *Economic History of the Highgate Brewery Co Ltd.* B.Phil 1981, p.101 Advert published in the Walsall Advertiser 23/9/1899.

     Reinarz. J.A. *Social History of a Midland Business: Flower and Sons Brewery 1870-1914.* 1998. p.172.

50   The Law Guarantee and Trust Society Limited form. 1897 and 1903.

51   Kelly's Directory. 1892. "Wm John Gilbert. Agent for the Shipston Brewery."

     Correspondence with R. Bearman 7/8/2006. "W.J. Gilbert is a brewery agent in Arden Street."

52   C.H. Tripp. 1892. p.67.

53   Gourvish. T. & Wilson. R. 1994. p.159.

54   Banbury Guardian. 23/3/1902.

55   Agencies also situated elsewhere in the Birmingham conurbation.

56   Gourvish. T. & Wilson. R. 1994. p.318.

57   HNBC Archive: Letters. 11/6/1920, 7/8/1920, 28/1/1921.

HNBC Archive: Letter to Mr W. Davis. The George Hotel, Shipston on Stour. 11/3/1921.

HNBC Archive: Letter to Mrs Peach. Queen's Own Woodstock. 16/5/1923.

58 Sayers. R.S. *A History of Economic change in England. 1880-1939*. 1978. p.51

59 Oral Tradition: Conversations with W.A. Clarke and Harold Wyton. Folder 1972-4.

60 Special License 1350 1/4/1918 for 50 Standard Barrels.

Special License 4821 1/7/1918 for 40 Standard Barrels.

61 Gourvish. T. & Wilson. R. 1994. p.413. Nationally, Clubs were seen as a serious competitor to the licensed public house. For the decrease in on-licenses see Chart 10.2. p.413.

62 Hardinge. G.N. Courages 1787-1932. Courage. 1932. p.19.

63 HNLHG: Oral Tradition Project: Mrs Doris Cadd recalled seeing Percy Flick welcoming visitors from the Coventry Clubs at the brewery, 7/3/2006.

Oral Tradition: W.A. Clarke Folder 1972-4.

Chapter 5
New Dawn –
A Postscript

The Hook Norton Brewery 2011 (Elena Woolley).

New Dawn

The post war years did not lead to a period of immediate recovery and brought great hardships to the whole country. All industries, including brewing, were required to bear their share of austerity, which included an embargo on the repair of damaged breweries and demolished public houses. Priority needed to be given to the rebuilding of private houses and factories upon which the economic revival of the country depended.

For the brewing industry the severity of the post war years was more acute than during the war itself with the industry struggling against the gloomy backdrop of further restrictions and falling output. The government considered beer to be 'a moral armament' and made every effort to enable supplies to be maintained, but with shortages of both malting barley and sugar this could only be achieved by reducing the strength of the beer. In May 1946 a world wide food crisis caused the government to limit each individual brewery to 85% of its standard barrelage output. Three months later average gravity was cut by ten percent and the minimum average gravity was cut to 1030°. Although the measures were later relaxed many brewers could not increase their gravities as they were hard pressed to maintain their bulk output. Fuel cuts and coal rationing during 1947 did not help the situation and from January 1948, as part of a cut in dollar spending, a twenty five percent cut in sugar consumption was ordered.

Output was cut from 85% to 82% and in January 1949 this was further cut to 78%. These restrictions were accompanied by high taxation, which continued to dog the industry. Increases in duty in November 1947 and April 1948 added 2d to the retail price of beer which did nothing to improve the supply or quality of the beer. Inevitably there were shortages, and public houses restricted the number of hours they could sell beer and when the weekly quota ran out the publican was obliged to close his doors. From 1949 the situation eased, duty was reduced, an enforced price reduction of 1d a pint was introduced, but further reductions in duty had little impact. By 1950, bulk barrelage was restricted to three-quarters of the 1945 figure, and remained at this level until the middle of the decade.[1]

Between 1958 and 1973 a total of 12,800 of the nation's larger brewing businesses disappeared through mergers and acquisitions at a rate of 856 a year. This national phenomenon became known as 'merger mania'. Led by the activities of the Canadian entrepreneur E.P. Taylor and Charles Clore of Sears Holdings, the structure of British brewing was changed dramatically. A total of one hundred and sixty four brewery mergers were completed between 1958 and 1972; seventy five of these were completed between 1959 and 1961 and the number of breweries used for production fell from 479 in 1954 to 162 in 1973.[2]

This process of acquisitions and mergers had started during the war and reduced the number of brewery companies from 840 in 1939 to 680 by 1945. Small companies sold up and larger brewers captured an increasingly larger share of the market, but the structure of the industry remained very much the same. By 1955 there were forty seven companies of national or large regional status with capital exceeding £4 million. These included Watney Combe Reid, Ind Coope and Allsopp, Courage and Barclay and Guinness. There was a second group, which included regional brewers with capital of £1-2 million pounds, yet the largest surviving group, consisting of 40% of the total, were the 144 small brewers, like Hook Norton and Donnington near Stow on the Wold, serving their local markets, producing between ten and twenty thousand barrels a year. Their small number of tied houses, maybe up to fifty, contrasted markedly with the larger companies with tied estate of more than a thousand houses and producing in excess of a million barrels a year.[3]

Smaller companies, like Hook Norton, were able to resist the surge of 'merger mania' as it engulfed the industry. Being a private limited company, with no stock market listing, the Hook Norton Brewery Company were immune from unwelcome approaches, but it has also been suggested that its geographical location coupled with the nature of the company's business was not sufficiently attractive to alert any hostile interest, yet Hook Norton had its own problems.[4]

Having avoided the attentions of the large brewers, the firm itself was in some turmoil during 1950, as a conflict of interests within the Clarke family threatened its future. The difficult times through which the company had struggled had not yielded huge dividends and with the future looking far from secure, Bill Clarke's two sisters Nancy and Frances Mary (Molly) made a determined and persistent effort to realise the full value of their holding in the company, urging Bill to sell the business. Bill was more optimistic about the future and was reluctant to sell. This placed him in the unenviable position of having to look elsewhere for financial investment, as he was unable to buy out his sisters. The investment came from the Gilchrist family, who were brewers, and whose family owned the independent Burtonwood Brewery in Warrington. This was a private investment and involved them not just

Brewery Advertisement in the Chipping Norton Official Town Guide c1960s.

buying the shares of Nancy and Molly Clarke, but also the majority of Bill's as well.[5] At a meeting of the Board in November 1950 a motion was passed agreeing the deal, with Mrs Mary Gilchrist being co-opted as soon as she had a controlling interest in the company. The one dissenting voice at this meeting was that of Percy Flick, whose views on the matter went unrecorded.[6]

The transfer of shares from the Clarke family to the Gilchrists took place on the afternoon of 20th December 1950 at a meeting chaired by Bill Clarke at Lincoln's Inn, in London. During the meeting the Clarke sisters tendered their resignations from the Board and their shares, as well as most of Bill Clarke's, were transferred to three members of the Gilchrist family, Mrs Mary Gilchrist, Mr Ian Gilchrist and Mr Norman Gilchrist.[7] Now majority shareholders in the company, they were appointed directors, filling the positions vacated by the Clarke sisters. It was not, however, until after Christmas that the new Board met formally for the first time to discuss business.

Early in January 1951 a meeting of the new board was convened at the brewery. It marked the beginning of a new dawn for the company. After a period of thirty eight years in which he had overseen the management of the business, Percy Flick tendered his resignation, relinquishing the trio of positions he held of Chairman, Managing Director and Company Secretary. These were now taken by members of the Gilchrist family with Mary Gilchrist becoming the new Managing Director and Chairman and Bill Clarke being appointed Managing Brewer. The meeting noted the zeal with which Percy Flick had carried out his responsibilities and as an expression of the company's 'esteem and appreciation' he was invited to 'accept a suitable expression of the company's regard and good wishes.'

Village gossip suggested that Flick did not care about the business because of his apparent unwillingness to spend money and as such 'let the pubs go to rack and ruin', but these suggestions cannot be sustained. The pages of the minutes of Directors' Meetings speak clearly, showing a man well aware of the needs of the company who did not shirk from making difficult and unpopular decisions. His single-mindedness saw the brewery through difficult years, ensuring that the company had a future.[8]

With a new Board of Directors changes were inevitable. The Gilchrist family became directly involved in the business and brought a new vitality to the running of the company. Freed of Government restrictions in 1951, the firm looked to the future and the first major decision was the plan to convert John Harris's 'old' malthouse into a bottling and bottle washing plant for a new bottled bitter to be called 'Jackpot'. During the summer that year, the brewing of 'Best Bitter' was re-introduced and by July, Bill Clarke reported that 'sales of bitter exceeded expectations'.

Hook Norton Brewery bottle labels: Jackpot and Hook Ale introduced in the 1950s.

Establishing the new bottling facility took place over a period of about eighteen months with new equipment being added regularly to the facility. During the spring of 1952 a sterilising filter was obtained and fitted and a 'great improvement was noticed in the beer'. By the end of the year the need for a new bottling plant was identified and Norman Gilchrist was commissioned to investigate the availability of such equipment. Early in 1953, first a chilling and carbonating plant was acquired from Messrs Montague Sharpe and by August a new bottle filter had also been installed.

The early post war years saw changes. The public house still remained the principal retail outlet for beer sales, but a growing trend towards drinking at home was developing and with it, the growing demand for bottled beers. This did not pass Hook Norton by, and in early 1961 the Board were considering the need to upgrade the brewery's bottling facilities. An improved method of handling cases of bottles in the stores and a mechanical labeller were identified as necessary. These were installed and working by May that year as well as a pasteurising unit, bought for £420 from Messrs Harman of Uxbridge brewery. As the decade progressed, further refinements were made to the bottling plant, a tank was installed for handling bulk deliveries of Guinness (discussed later in the chapter), a new 24 head bottling machine was installed during September 1967, purchased from Messrs Pontifex at a cost of £1,950, which came into service the following month. Such was the demand for bottled beer it became apparent that the bottle washing

The Bottling Plant (Jack Haney).

machine needed replacing as the existing equipment had 'not sufficient output [to cope with] the increased bottle trade'. It was decided to purchase a Dawson Junior with automatic discharge which was the largest machine that could be housed in the old malthouse.[9]

The acquisition of lorries was identified as a necessity. In August 1951 Ian Gilchrist reported that he knew of a Bedford lorry for sale. The vehicle met the brewery's needs and was purchased. A second lorry was acquired, an Albion 'Chieftain'. After twelve years service the original Bedford needed replacing. It was Ian Gilchrist again who took responsibility in 1962 for obtaining details of possible replacements. There were three possibilities, a Bedford Diesel, another Albion 'Chieftain', similar to the one already in service and an Albion 'Claymore' with an aluminium alloy platform. Although the 'Claymore' needed some modification to its bodywork, it was agreed that it suited the company's requirements and was purchased. When, some six years later it became apparent that one of the Bedford lorries should be sold for scrap, it was Ian Gilchrist again who provided details of the alternatives available. The following year when the discussion again focussed on acquiring a new lorry, the responsibility had passed to David Clarke and it was he who took on the responsibility of the company's transport needs.

The Hook Norton Brewery Company has been incorporated for more than a hundred years. For more than sixty years the management of the business has been the successful partnership between the Clarke and Gilchrist families. Continuity has been a feature of this association with each succeeding generation seamlessly taking on the responsibilities of running the company. When Richard Gilchrist became non- executive chairman in 2005, he was the third generation of his family to hold the position and be actively involved in the running of the business. His tenure of the post was cut short by his untimely death in January 2009 in a tragic riding accident, while following the Cheshire hunt. He had been a director of the company since 1977 and had taken an active role in the running of the business, being committed to ensuring the survival of the company as an independent family brewer.

Richard Gilchrist's tragic death necessitated changes to the board of directors. During the spring of 2009 the decision was taken to appoint Charles Williams, who joined his wife as a director. It was also agreed that a new non-executive chairman should be appointed from outside the business to succeed Richard Gilchrist, echoing events of a hundred years earlier when Percy Flick had been engaged by the company. During the summer of 2009 Jonathan Paveley was appointed as the new chairman, bringing with him industry experience at both Greene King and Punch Taverns.[10] The re-shaping of the Board was completed with the arrival of Nigel Churton, who joined his stepmother Alice as a director. There was a further change, the role of the managing director was split between James Clarke, who took responsibility for beer production and the pubs and Adrian Staley, coming from the St Austell brewery; appointed to look after the commercial side of the business.[11]

Post War Trade

An early decision of the new Board in 1951 was the re-introduction of bitter beer. Production commenced during the summer and by July, Bill Clarke reported to the satisfaction of the Board, that 'sales of bitter [had] exceeded expectations'.

Despite this success it was not, however, an auspicious time for launching a new beer. The brewing industry faced difficult times in the years following the War and consumption of beer fell from its 1945 peak. Sales suffered nationally, a trend mirrored in Hook Norton. When the Gilchrists joined the Board in 1951, the number of annual brewings had fallen to ninety two and this downward trend continued reaching its nadir in 1957, when only seventy one brewings were completed. Sales of cask beer were poor, particularly to the Coventry clubs.

With food being de-rationed, the standard of living improved, and previously scarce foodstuffs became available again from the early 1950s. People began once again to spend on clothes and luxury items. Leisure activities became more focussed on the family, the home and the television set, but these changes did nothing to increase beer production.

Tastes were changing as more people began to drink wine rather than beer at their local public house.

At one of the first Board meetings presided over by Mary Gilchrist, she suggested that the company should consider appointing a traveller for the Coventry area in an effort to extend trade. Initially no action was taken, but in August 1952 the matter was again discussed and it was decided to advertise for a traveller to work the Coventry, Nuneaton and Bedworth areas. The following month an appointment was made. The expected benefits of his appointment failed to materialise and there was no real improvement in trade. After a period of about fifteen months the traveller was given notice that his services were no longer required and his position was left in abeyance. It was not until September 1956 that the company decided to try again and appoint a new traveller to work in the Coventry area and by November a large number of applications had been received. A short list of two was agreed and the candidates were interviewed and a new traveller was appointed. The post carried a salary of £500 and a commission of 3 shillings a barrel and 2 shillings a dozen bottles on existing club trade and 5 shillings a barrel on any new trade. A car would also be provided.

The club trade in the Coventry area was fiercely competitive and three months into the job he had made very little impact; a few new accounts were opened but the intended increase in trade did not materialise. It was of little surprise that in the spring of 1958 the Board decided to dispense with his services as he, like his predecessor had failed to acquire the new trade the company desired. Even though the company had failed to secure a larger slice of the club trade, the idea of a traveller in the Coventry area was not abandoned. In May 1958 Mr A.J. Brown was appointed traveller on a part time for a trial period of 6 months. He was to be paid a salary of £100 and with the same amount available for expenses. A month later he requested an increase in his expenses and the company responded by offering him a maximum of £5 a week extra for calling on clubs. The outcome of this trial period is uncertain as no further mention of Mr Brown and his dealings in Coventry is recorded in the documentation.

Trade with the clubs in the Coventry area varied from year to year. In June 1955 sales for the previous month had increased by 14 barrels and the Board were generally happy with the free trade sales, but by August 1958 a worrying trend had been identified. During the previous nine months there was a falling off in trade, particularly among clubs that were some of the brewery's long standing customers. Two months later there was still no improvement and it was only through the business with Bell Green and Willenhall clubs that any increase had been achieved. The Board hoped that with the combination of the completion of a new extension at the Willenhall Club and Mr Brown's efforts that further increases in trade would be realised.

While finding new business in Coventry proved difficult, the company's existing customers were seeking financial help to develop their premises. Thirty years earlier the Board under Percy Flick's stewardship had acknowledged that the company needed to be as generous with their customers as other brewers were and this principle was endorsed by the Board as they dealt with requests from the clubs for financial help to allow the development and modernisation of their properties during the post war years. Requests were treated sympathetically and whenever possible mutually suitable arrangements were reached. Some loans were guaranteed with security on the club's premises; in one case the company guaranteed a loan made by the club's bank and on another occasion the loan was tied into a trade agreement by which the club agreed to increase its trade by three or four barrels a week and to repay at least £1,000 a year. At another club the loan was made on the condition that they only sold Hook Norton Mild for the duration of the loan as it was feared that Ansells would 'command all the club's trade'. Loans varied from £500 to £8,000 and were repaid at rates of interest varying from 4½% to 6% and in some cases these were reduced if the weekly trade increased substantially.

Through the early 'sixties' trade was deemed to be satisfactory, and in 1961 the Brewery was supplying twenty three clubs, thirteen in the Coventry area, producing £60,000 of income, although fifty percent of this trade was being generated by just one club. When in May 1967 trade was reviewed for the first eight months of the brewing year, 320 fewer barrels had been sold and although bottled beer sales had shown a small increase, it was sales of Mild beer in the Coventry area that accounted for 75% of the fall in trade. In such a competitive market it was agreed that to encourage trade, clubs should be paid a small bonus based on the quantity of bottled beer sold in a year.

An important component of the Coventry business was the sales of bottled Guinness. While the sales of Mild had fallen, demand for Guinness increased. The increase in sales highlighted the need for a tank in the bottling store, allowing the company to take bulk deliveries from the Guinness Brewery at Park Royal. Meetings with representatives of Messrs Guinness were held with the view to establishing whether they would be prepared to give 'any assistance' towards the installation of a tank. Initially Guinness seemed cool on the idea, asking for 'various ancillary equipment' with the implication of increasing the cost of installation, but finally, in January 1964 agreement was reached and the acquisition of a bulk tank became a priority.

Early in the search for this new tank, the brewery were offered a glass lined vessel for £150, but its provenance could not be guaranteed and the offer was declined. Responsibility for finding the new bulk tank was taken by Ian Gilchrist, who had led the negotiations with Messrs Guinness. Using his contacts at the Burtonwood Brewery he sought advice and procured a tank with sufficient capacity to meet Messrs Guinness's minimum delivery of 14 barrels. The new tank arrived and was installed during June 1964, ready for the first delivery, planned for the first week in July. To reduce the cost of installation the Board decided a 'rousing attachment' was not necessary if the beer could be delivered between 7.30am and 8am, so bottling could to take place the same day.

With a general shift towards drinking at home, bottled beer accounted for about a fifth of the brewery's production. A major part of the bottling output was Guinness for the Coventry clubs and when Guinness decided to introduce a foil cap on the bottle in 1987, the company felt they could not justify the investment in the necessary machinery. The decision to stop bottling Guinness meant that the brewery lost half its bottling volume and the decision was taken to withdraw from bottling, contracting this out to other brewers. Jackpot survived for a while, the final batch being bottled at Donnington in 1992. Trading conditions with the Coventry clubs changed. Much of the business had been supplying Hook Norton Mild and Guinness to these clubs, but as industry in the city changed so did the palate of the beer drinkers and the Hook Norton Brewery ceased trading with the clubs in 2000.[12]

Trade figures were regularly reviewed and disappointment was expressed in particular with the poor sales of draught beer through the tied properties. In the autumn of 1954 these 'caused deep concern' and tied house sales had again dropped in the period up to the following June. When three months later the Board met at the end of the brewing year the overall trend showed a decline in sales, but Bill Clarke was able to point out that the losses had been incurred early in the year and figures from June 1955 showed an 'overall improvement'. The business of two tied houses where sales had dropped by about fifty barrels was discussed and they exemplify the importance of the role played by the tenants. The first, the Red Lion in Chipping Norton, had the previous year exceeded all previous sales due to the efforts of the tenant and his wife and they had drawn trade away from other licenced premises in the area. They had now moved on and the trade had slipped back to its previous level of two years earlier as the transient trade returned 'to other houses'. Sales at the second property The Black Horse Inn in Leamington Spa were also poor and the tenants were asked to explain the disappointing returns. By the end of the year there was no improvement in the situation and they were given notice to quit.

It was not all gloom. In March 1956 the Board again reviewed the trade figures. Sales of draught were still declining, falling by 8 barrels but bottled beer sales had increased by 18 barrels. Progress was maintained. During 1957 sales of draught beer were 'up most weeks'. These trade figures marked the turning point in the company's performance. The improvement was maintained through to the end of the decade and into the 'sixties', peaking in 1965 with the sale of 10,141 barrels. This up turn in trade coincided with the national trend which saw a renewed interest in beer consumption which rose by 60% over a period of two decades, and was part of a general rise in the consumption of alcohol, as people with more disposable income spent it on leisure activities and alcoholic drinks. It was, however, the growing impact of the sales of lager and keg beers across the country that began to cut into production in Hook Norton and output again began to fall after the 1965 peak.

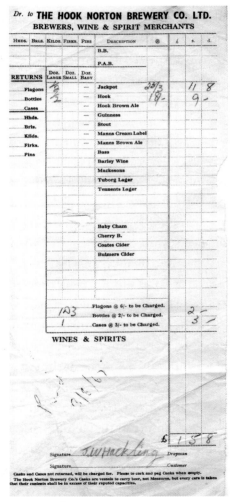

Delivery note 581967, 1967.

Spear-heading the renewed interest in beer was lager, which before 1960 had only been available as an expensive bottled import, and keg. The growing popularity of lager brewed under licence in Britain and available on draught appealed to a wider social spectrum than the traditional beers and attracted the more affluent younger drinkers of both sexes. Ind Coope led the way with their Skol brand in 1959 and sales increased from 2% in 1964 to 50% by 1989.

Keg, a brewery conditioned, carbonated beer proved to be a significant development in the revival of draught beer and was pioneered on a small scale by Watneys during the 1930s. It wasn't, however, until the successful introduction of Flower's Keg in 1954 that the product began to make an impact. With the launch of Red Barrel by Watney Mann later in the decade and Double Diamond early in the following decade, sales of Keg gained an increasing share of the market at the expense of draught mild, brown ale and bottled stout. The popularity of Keg reversed the trend towards bottled beer which was further enhanced by its suitability for canning. The sale of canned beer through supermarkets for consumption at home played an important part in the growth in demand for beer.[13]

As part of the sales push of keg and lager, the larger brewers made advances to smaller brewers, like Hook Norton, with overtures offering trading agreements in return for selling their beers. Hook Norton was courted by several of the larger players offering a variety of packages in return for the right to sell lager or keg beers in Hook Norton houses. In December 1956 the company had had communications with Messrs H. & G. Simmonds regarding the marketing of their beer in Hook Norton pubs, but this came to nothing. The first serious approach came from Messrs Watney Mann in June 1963, with an offer to allow Hook Norton to sell their draught and bottled beer in one of Watney Mann's houses in the area, 'on an equal basis', in return for Red Barrel being made available in Hook Norton pubs. Bill Clarke was asked to pursue the matter. Three months later a new proposal was received from Watney Mann, offering the lease of one of their houses 'doing the same appropriate barrelage' in return for Red Barrel being made available in some Hook Norton pubs.

After considerable discussion the Board concluded there would not be any benefit for the company and the proposal was rejected. It was three years before the next suitor arrived. The offer to put Ruddles keg in Hook Norton houses was purely financial, the company receiving £2 for every barrel sold. Ruddles would supply a traveller and supply a mechanic to install the necessary equipment but the Hook Norton Directors were far from impressed and saw 'very small benefit to the company, if any, financially' and so declined to follow up the offer. During April 1966 Bill Clarke met a representative from Messrs Whitbread and they discussed the possibility of selling Tankard bitter in Hook Norton houses 'where the trade warranted'. In return, the brewery could sell Hooky beer in one or two of local Whitbread houses. This proposal had more potential and the Directors asked Bill to obtain more information, but it was nearly two and half years before the Whitbread proposal began to come to fruition.

Their offer had been amended. Whitbread were now prepared to offer the Hook Norton Brewery three of their houses on lease at peppercorn rent over a period of twenty one years, in exchange for a trading agreement allowing Tankard or Heineken lager in fifteen Hooky pubs.

The Hook Norton Brewery were interested. They had been offered the New Inn, Whichford; The Gate, Brailes and The Plough, Stretton on Fosse. All three properties were visited and whilst the first two were 'acceptable' it was felt that 'The Plough' was in poor condition and the directors asked if Whitbread could offer another property instead. They responded with the Churchill Arms, Paxford. Although the trade at this house was poor at that time, the directors decided to look into the matter further.

It was not till May 1969 that a draft agreement from Messrs Whitbread was initialled. Further discussions had led to an improved proposal with Hook Norton taking over four Whitbread houses; the Wellington, Moreton in Marsh; the Churchill, Paxford; the Gate Inn, Brailes and the New Inn, Whichford, on a lease for 21 years. In return Whitbread Tankard or Gold label would be available in 12 or 15 of the

Hook Norton houses and Heineken lager where 'there was any demand'. The agreement was to begin on 2nd June 1969.

While sales of keg and lager dominated the draught beer market, not everybody enthused about them and serious beer drinkers began to bemoan the lack of choice at the bar. During the 'sixties' a number of fledgling groups voiced their concerns about the availability of a range of beers, most notably the Society for the Preservation of Beer (SPBW). None of these groups, however, were able to sustain their campaigns and disappeared. The emergence of CAMRA, the Campaign for Real Ale, in 1971, succeeded where others had failed because it caught the mood of the time. Beer drinkers wanted a change from the heavily advertised keg and lager beers produced by the larger brewers and embraced the campaigns ideals with enthusiasm.

The campaign to revive British beer grew from an idea spawned by four friends, Michael Hardman, Bill Mellor, Graham Lees and Jim Makin during a holiday in Ireland in 1971. The campaign had one over-riding aim, the survival of cask ale, and this dominated their actions, inspiring both passion and dedication to the cause. At first progress was gradual, but by 1973 the campaign had attracted 5,000 members. CAMRA held its first major demonstration in Stone to protest against the closure of Joule's Brewery. More than six hundred members turned out gaining wide media coverage. Membership continued to grow and by February 1974 there were 9,000 members and the first local branches were formed by activists. In the following two years major advances were made. The first national Beer Festival was staged at Covent Garden and membership reached 30,000. A major campaigning success was achieved in 1976 when Ind Coope launched Burton Ale in a thousand pubs simultaneously. CAMRA were hailed as the 'most successful consumer group in Europe', yet for all the campaign's success, a 1975 MORI poll conducted for the Brewers Society, showed that only 12% of those interviewed had heard of the organisation. Through its campaign CAMRA re-introduced the virtues of mild and bitter beers to the middle class, ironically at a time when working class drinkers were turning to the 'up market' keg and lager beers. Through the growing popularity of cask conditioned beers, particularly amongst the middle class drinkers, the marketing strategy of the 'Big Six' changed and by 1980 they were selling over eighty different brands of real ale.[14]

In 1973 with falling demand, the number of annual brewings in Hook Norton reached a new low point. The directors had seriously considered selling a keg beer under their own name as early as 1967, but had decided to defer any decision.[15] Some equipment had been purchased in readiness, but it may have been some of the enthusiasm shown by CAMRA members for Hook Norton beer that helped to sway the decision against producing keg commercially. The fortunes of the brewery began to change, slowly at first; starting from a low of just under 7,000 barrels a year in 1973, sales had doubled by 1978. A decade later the company were selling over 20,000 barrels a year.

By 1974 the campaign to promote 'Real Ale' was beginning to make an impact and beer related stories began to appear in the media; the BBC were first to feature the Hook Norton Brewery. During the summer of 1974 filming took place at the brewery and a ten minute film was shown on BBC2 later that summer as part of a series entitled the 'Industrial Grand Tour'.[16] The formation of local CAMRA branches in Oxfordshire also drew the attention of the local newspapers and the subsequent coverage not only promoted the activities of CAMRA, but also associated the organisation directly with the Hook Norton Brewery.

In the interim, between the BBC's filming at the brewery and the broadcast of the programme, the Oxford branch of CAMRA organised an evening visit to the brewery, taking with them a reporter from the Oxford Times. It was a mixed group of about forty people, including members of the legal profession, teachers and a councillor. After a tour of the brewery, the visit concluded with an opportunity for the party members to sample the beer. With membership of CAMRA growing nationally at a rate of about a 1,000 members each month, new branches were regularly being created and in December 1974 the inaugural meeting of the North Oxfordshire branch was held at The Reindeer Inn in Banbury. News of this attracted the interest of the local paper. Under the banner 'Drinking a toast to real ale' the Banbury Guardian report outlined CAMRA's aims and achievements and the group's intention to hold alternate monthly meetings in a Hook Norton pub where they could enjoy a pint of 'very high quality ale'.

The revived interest in 'Real Ale' spread beyond the enthusiasm of the local CAMRA branches and the company was inundated daily with mail enquiring about the brewery. In response to this ever growing interest 'open' weekends were introduced. In 1974 the dates were only advertised locally, yet visitors came from far and near and had to queue. The following year the opening dates were only advertised in trade magazines, but over a thousand visitors passed through the brewery on the first of these open weekends. The second of these was arranged to coincide with the village's 'Open Days' in early June and this again proved to be a major attraction as visitors queued once more waiting for a tour of the brewery.[17]

Bottle label to mark the Queen's Silver Jubilee, 1977.

From these early beginnings, brewery tours have become an important part of the business. People now visit the brewery for many reasons. Some come for the architecture, others for the history or just out of general interest, but most are interested in the beer. As demand for brewery tours grew new facilities to accommodate visitors became a necessity. The £250,000 conversion of John Harris's 1865 malthouse during 1999 provided those facilities. This was officially opened by the Princess Royal on September 10th 1999. Her visit lasted 90 minutes and included a tour of the brewing facilities before the official opening of the new centre.[18] Tours of the brewery are now booked in advance allowing visitors to see the brewery at work. The tour concludes back in the Visitor Centre with a visit to the brewery museum and an opportunity to taste a little of each beer and experience their individual flavours.[19]

Visitor's Centre Notice (Elena Woolley).

Initially the tours were conducted by Bill Clarke and his son David, assisted by Fred Beale, but after Beale's death in 1991, Barbara and Howard Hicks were invited to take over the role of brewery tour guides. During their first year they completed about twenty tours, which at that time were restricted to the trade and local organisations. After more than twenty years as brewery tour guides, Barbara and Howard retired in the spring of 2012, having been part of a team of six responsible for looking after visitors' tours, as the brewery's heritage work became an integral part of the business.

As a requirement of the successful lottery heritage grant in 2014 towards the cost of renovating the redundant brewhouse chimney, the company are improving the signage around the brewery site so that visitors can more easily access and understand the history of the brewery. A number of initiatives are being explored. Six acres of ridge and furrow grassland adjacent to the brewery site has been acquired, primarily for the Shire horses and it is hoped to develop it to provide natural habitats for wildlife. A pond has been dug, a wet area is proposed and it is intended to plant trees that reflect woods traditionally used in construction. The public will have access to the field and it is hoped that it will become part of their visit to the brewery.

The Buxton Thornley steam engine, which powered the brewery for more than 100 years, is now 'retired' but visitors to the brewery on the first Saturday of the month, and bank holiday Mondays, have the opportunity to see it in operation. It is run for an hour from midday. Those on the morning tour see the engine working at the end of their tour. Those going on the afternoon tour see it before the tour begins. In addition to their appearance on 'steam engine days', the horses and dray can be seen in the village, weather permitting, during the late morning on Wednesdays, Thursdays and Fridays and at other times they can be found in the stables, or about the brewery yard.

The Visitor Centre has been open for 15 years and it is intended that facilities will be extended by bringing the redundant part of the 1864 Malthouse into use. With an increasing demand from visitors to learn more about the process of brewing beers, it is planned that an improved sampling area with a small kitchen will be provided, so that further work on beer and food matching can be undertaken. Already a number of corporate events have been staged in the Visitor Centre and by enlarging these facilities this aspect of the business can be expanded.

As James Clarke points out, 'We have a lot of access to heritage. This is not an old mill converted into flats to save the building, this brewery is about heritage. People come here and see it working, but we want to do more than that. We want our visitors to come here to stay longer. It's all about visitor engagement and providing them with access to the history.'

Into a new age

The process of replacing ageing equipment has been an on-going requisite of the business. The post-war period has seen the replacement of worn out equipment and the installation of new, larger vessels to cope with the increased demand for Hook Norton beer. The story of the old 8 quarter mashtun from John Harris's brewery, renovated and installed in the new brewery has already been related in an earlier chapter. Worn out, it began to fail during the war years and a replacement was urgently needed. In 1948 the redundant 20 quarter mashtun was scrapped and replaced by a new 10 quarter cast iron vessel which remained in production for more than half a century. As demand increased it became necessary in recent years to mash 'a bit thick', using about two tons of malt and a lot of sugar to produce 75 barrels. By 2002 a new mashtun was needed. One became available, coming from Ruddles Brewery, which had the right dimensions to fit the floor aperture where the old 20 quarter mashtun had once stood. The intention was to replace Harris's old 8 quarter mashtun which had been idle since it was de-commissioned, with the 1948 10 quarter vessel. When this was being dismantled the cast iron case was found to have hair line cracks. A new stainless steel case was commissioned and installed and equipped with the working machinery from the 1948 vessel. Installing the new mashtun from Ruddles presented problems; being too large to be fitted in one piece it had to be cut in half around its girth, with the top being installed first.

This new mashtun brought benefits; importantly, mashing no longer had to 'be a bit thick' and could be carried out at the correct consistency and it was no longer necessary to shovel out the spent grains at the end of the process as the equipment came fitted with automatic grain discharge and cleaning. For the first time in almost a hundred years, the brewery had the flexibility of two working mashtuns allowing production to be tailored to demand.

Steam to power the Buxton Thornley engine, was originally generated by two coal fired furnaces. By 1957 these old furnaces were in need of modernisation as they were uneconomical to operate. New furnaces were supplied by the Turbine and Equipment Company and by the middle of the following year they were in operation. Coal for this process was delivered to the brewery yard and had to be barrowed to the boiler house for use. The smoke from the brewery chimney caused some consternation in Scotland End, particularly on Monday mornings when the day's washing was hung out to dry. By the mid 1960s the company were having problems acquiring the 'right kind of coal' and the decision was made to convert to an oil fired system.[20]

The old and the new: coal and oil fired furnaces (Jack Haney).

Another factor in the decision to turn to oil fired heating was the condition of the original copper. By 1960 it was in need of repair and the company were advised that its working life could be extended if it was converted to steam boiling. More recently the installation of a new, larger copper acquired from Flowers of Cheltenham, has further enhanced the production capacity. To place the new copper in situ, the roof of the copper house had to be removed and the equipment lifted into position by crane. The size of the Victorian copper house provided sufficient space for the new vessel to be installed without interfering with production.

The new copper.

The flat cooler, at the top of the brewery, was initially made of cast iron, but with the constant expansion and contraction as the hot wort passed through, the vessel began to crack and leak and was constantly being repaired and it was replaced in 1954 by a copper vessel. This new cooler remained in service until 2004 when it was withdrawn from use. This was partly due to the requirements of new legislation, but also to meet the standards set by supermarket chains requiring the brewing process to be undertaken in enclosed vessels. On the floor beneath the flat cooler, a vertical fridge stood, which further cooled the wort prior to fermentation. By the turn of the present century it also showed signs of wear. Made from brass and copper with soldered joints; it began to leak.

In April 1994 it was replaced by a plate heat exchanger. Now, with the flat cooler no longer in use, all the cooling before fermentation is done through this heat exchanger.

Cooling systems old and new: left, the 'old cooler', now in the museum; right, the new plate heat exchanger.

Fermenting vats have regularly been replaced and during 1961 the erection of a new one was required. Quotes were requested from three suppliers and the company elected to purchase one made of Peroba wood, for the sum of £1,248 from Messrs Carty. By the following January it had been installed and awaited gauging by the Custom and Excise Officer.[21]

During a meeting of the Board in April 1951, the image projected by the appearance of the company's pubs came under scrutiny and Mary Gilchrist suggested that they should all be painted the same colour. To this end she suggested blue and primrose or black and yellow. Advice was sought but no decorator would recommend blue for exterior work and the alternative, black and yellow was adopted. Two pubs in the village were painted for the directors to see. The Chairman expressed herself well pleased and it was agreed other pubs should be painted in these two colours, but the impact on villagers and planning officers alike was dramatic. In February 1952, in response to this criticism, the Board agreed to 'tone down the colour scheme' as it was felt the colour scheme was not in keeping with the nature of old stone buildings. This was not the end of the matter and the colour scheme continued to draw criticism, particularly in Brailes and the company agreed to modify the colour scheme to meet the requirements of the recently implemented legislation.

It was not just the pub exteriors that needed work. In the decades immediately following the Second World War there were still rural properties without the essential services of running water and proper toilet facilities. The report of the Agricultural Economics Research Unit based at Oxford University highlighted the condition of rural properties. Its remit was to investigate the conditions of rural life in the country and was carried out during 1943. The investigation was based on 24 square miles of a 6 inch Ordnance Survey map which included the Hook Norton area.

The report found that most villages did not have running water; only four had piped water, supplied by the water company supplying Banbury. There were four other villages with small local systems which provided running water to stand pipes, from where villagers collected their water. For the other villages domestic water came from streams, springs, rainwater butts and wells. In two villages large galvanised tanks were supplied which were regularly filled, at least twice a week, by the local council's water tanker. The lack of running water meant there were none of the usual amenities. Properties lacked sinks; washing up was done in a basin on the table and the slops were thrown out on the garden. Even more modern properties which had sinks did not have taps; the waste pipe emptying into a bucket beneath which had to be emptied outside. Sanitary arrangements were primitive. All properties relied either on a bucket or an Elsan chemical toilet located in older properties in a shed at the bottom of the garden and in newer ones in a room within the house. Electricity may have been available in many villages, but not everyone could afford to pay for the wiring so candles and oil lamps were still prevalent. In some properties the downstairs was wired for electricity whilst more traditional methods of lighting were employed in the bedrooms.[22]

It was against this background that the Hook Norton Brewery was required, under the new post war legislation, to improve the sanitary arrangements in their public houses, having received a succession of reports from Sanitary Inspectors, and several local Rural District Councils requiring work to be done on the brewery's properties. In some pubs there was no provision for women, and Sanitary Inspectors required the provision of separate facilities for both sexes that complied with modern standards of hygiene. The general condition of the properties requiring renovation was in line with the deficiencies described by the Agricultural Economics Research Unit's 1944 report.

Improving sanitary arrangements was a particular priority. Six in particular were identified to be in need of urgent improvements in the provision of this facility. Work to upgrade facilities was carried out at the Elephant and Castle, Bloxham; the Sun Inn, Marston St Lawrence,

The Gate Hangs High, 1975.

the White Swan, Wigginton; the Great Western Arms, Aynho where Elsan chemical toilets were replaced by modern flush facilities and the Chandler's Arms, Epwell. At both the Red Lion and Albion Tavern in Chipping Norton facilities for washing glasses were non existent and the provision of running water was a priority. At the George Hotel in Brailes and both the Pear Tree and Gate Hangs High in Hook Norton the modernisation of the tenant's living quarters was given precedence. At the Chandler's Arms a bathroom was added and at the Fox Inn, Juniper the provision of running water and sewage disposal, at a cost of £500, was expedited.

The Board recognised that the company could not afford to finance all the work required 'at once', and between 1954 and 1966 eighteen licensed properties were renovated and upgraded. The work followed a cyclical pattern, while proposals for the necessary remedial work at a property were discussed and submitted to the appropriate planning authority, previously approved plans were being executed on one of the company's other pubs.

The programme of work carried out on the New Inn at Abthorpe is typical of that timetable. As part of a review of trade in April 1957, the Board discussed the future of the pub. Trade was poor and there seemed little prospect of any improvement. The future of the pub as a Hook Norton house seemed in doubt when it was agreed to approach the Northampton Brewery with a view of them taking on the licence. They were not interested and had in fact decided to close the only other public house in the village. It wasn't until March 1958 that the New Inn was again discussed and in view of the Northampton Brewery's decision, the Board visited the New Inn, to inspect the sanitary arrangements, which were found to be poor. It was, however, not until after a complaint from the Towcester RDC was received later that summer regarding the sanitary arrangements that Bill Clarke met a surveyor on site to discuss the project. By August 1958 plans for the New Inn had been drawn up which met the Sanitary Inspector's requirements and it was agreed to proceed with the project, providing not only new toilets for the pub, but also the provision of a bathroom with flush toilet at a cost of £700. In

February 1962 plans for further alterations to the pub to improve facilities were submitted to the Justices at the Brewster sessions.

The growing importance of the motor car as a means of personal transport was not overlooked as provision of car parks at Castle Inn, Chandler's Arms and Albion Tavern were included in the improvement plans for the company's properties. Not all work sanctioned was financed by the business. Alterations at the Butcher's Arms, in Kings Sutton were completed at the tenant's own expense. The completion of improvements to a property also brought the opportunity to sell the house. Having spent £500 at the Fox Inn, Juniper Hill, bringing the water supply and sanitary arrangements up to modern standards, the company were approached by the tenant, Mr Morris, who declared an interest in purchasing the property. A down payment £1,250 was suggested, with a mortgage of £750 at 5% to cover the remainder of the sale price. After some discussion a sum of £1,150 was accepted as the down payment. A trade agreement also became part of the deal and the pub was supplied by the Hook Norton Brewery. A proviso was added to the deal, if Mr Morris wanted to sell the pub in the future, the brewery were to have first option of purchasing it.

Pubs have been the currency of the brewing trade. In the past Brewers acquired pubs as a means of increasing their trade. The changing economic situation of the last years of the previous century and the early years of the twenty first, have seen many pubs become unviable and many have closed and been sold off. Operating in this climate the Hook Norton Brewery have sold several of their tied properties. The fate of these former Hook Norton houses has been mixed. The Albion Tavern has been demolished and the Wellington in Moreton in Marsh has been converted into apartments, while the Volunteer at Grove has been converted into a guest house. The Chandler's Arms in Epwell has been extensively refurbished by its new owners and re-commenced business in February 2014. Other pubs remain for sale and the proceeds from these sales being reinvested in the company's current tied houses. To date five have been extensively refurbished, the latest being the Castle at Edge Hill at a cost of around £260,000.[23]

The Brewing Family

In April 1978, Bill Clarke, now managing director, completed fifty years service with the company, a period in which he had also been involved with every facet of village life in Hook Norton. Traditionally brewers have not solely been concerned with the entrepreneurial activities of their businesses, but have taken a keen interest in the local politics and charitable affairs of the community in which they lived. This has certainly been true of the Clarke family who have actively contributed to village life in Hook Norton; as David Clarke explained in an interview in 1998,[24]

> "We've always been part of the village and we are the only major employer. We feel part of the village and like to support the village as we do. I suppose, one does tend to get involved in all these village organisations. It's just part of village life. The football club we sponsor, the band we sponsor, so that, the bit of sponsoring we do, we like to keep it locally in the village."[25]

The village fire brigade has been a focus for three generations of the Clarke family during the last seventy years. Bill, David and James Clarke have all served with the village brigade and risen to be the officer in charge. When in 1981 the County Council wanted to close the Hook Norton fire station, a heated response from the village and the local Brigade, led by David Clarke, successfully convinced the council to reverse their decision. Both Bill and David received recognition for their service of more than thirty years, being awarded the Queen's Medal (1951) and British Empire Medal (1992) respectively. It was Bill's involvement with the fire brigade that led to him being co-opted onto the Parish Council in 1932, as it was seen then as beneficial to have the officer in charge on the council. He served as a member of the Parish Council for more than thirty years, becoming the vice-chairman. With business at the brewery taking up more time he decided to stand down in 1964. The local church of St Peter has also played a major part in the Clarke family's life. Bill served as a sidesman, churchwarden and was a member of the PCC, while David, in addition to also being a sidesman, was for more than forty years a member of the Church bell ringing team. Being involved with village organisations is part of village life and both Bill and David Clarke have acted in various capacities with the village cricket and football teams, the Horticultural Society and the Band. Bill was President of both the Cricket Club and the Horticultural Society, where, on Flower Show Day he could be found selling programmes on the gate at Baker's Field and for many years he was the treasurer of the village brass band, while David became president of the band and the football club.[26]

Bill Clarke died in January 1982, he was 77 years old.[27] At a Board meeting held on the 8th January 1982, Ian Gilchrist paid tribute to Bill Clarke '[who] was a close friend as well as doing a splendid job at the head of the company [and] instead of standing in silence that we raise our glasses to him.' Percy Hemmings, also remembered Bill Clarke, the man with whom he worked for many years.

> "They say that everybody is replaceable in this world. Not Mr Clarke, he'll never be replaced. There'll be nobody to replace [him]. Not in matter of work. He was a good worker, but the personality of the man. He was a man, a perfect man. I was a worker but he didn't class me like that. If he met me at a place where there were a lot of 'up and ups' it made no difference to him, 'cos they were there and [he'd ask if I'd] have a drink? He was the same all the while. He never got in a flurry. He never swore at you and always called you by your name. And me, I never said 'Sir' it was always to me, 'Mr Clarke'. That was him, no other name whatever. Bill was his name, [but] I never called him Bill, [always] Mr Clarke."[28]

The responsibility for the day to day affairs of the brewery passed to Bill's son, David who had joined the company in April 1960 having completed his pupillage at the Burtonwood Brewery, and at first, like his father, he took charge of the bottling plant. In 1974 he became head brewer and was extremely proud that the company had 'never brewed keg'. At the end of the decade he succeeded his father as the managing director and presided over the emergence of the Hook Norton Brewery Company as a major producer of traditional English cask beers which has seen the brewery working at the capacity it was originally designed to do.

While business at the brewery blossomed, tragedy befell the Clarke family when their daughter Victoria was diagnosed as suffering from leukaemia. She was only 12 years old. Sadly Victoria lost her fight against the disease, but from this adversity the family united and became dedicated fundraisers for Leukaemia Research. What began as the family's response to their loss has now been embraced by the village and fund raising has become a community activity, with thousands of pounds being raised for charity each year. One of the most successful fund raising events has been the annual Hook Norton Festival of Fine Ales held at the Pear Tree Inn. In 2005 the Beer Festival donated £8,000 and a year later, £6,500. The event proved so popular that a new venue was needed. In 2009 it was moved to the 'Rural Fayre' field, a short distance from the Pear Tree, to accommodate the large numbers attending. Two years later the Festival donated a further £6,700 towards supporting long term research into Leukaemia and Lymphoma at the John Radcliff Hospital in Oxford. The annual village music festival 'Music at the Crossroads' has been another fund raising event that has supported the charity. The event is organised by the Hook Norton Charitable Association and like the Festival of Fine Ales has the leukaemia research in Oxford as its principal charity. To coincide with Ian Botham's 'Beefy Bowls Out Teenage Cancer' marathon walk in September 2006, the brewery produced twenty five barrels of a special beer 'Beefy's Bitter' in support of Botham's effort, the sale of which raised 10p from every pint sold to be donated to Leukaemia Research.

To date, eighteen years since its inception, fund raising for Leukaemia Research has raised in excess of £180,000 through the efforts of the brewery and the people of Hook Norton. This has not gone without recognition. In 2005 Leukaemia Research awarded Dr Graham Collins, based at John Radcliffe Hospital in Oxford, the 'Hook Norton

Fellowship', in recognition of the Hook Norton community's 'tireless' fund raising efforts. This allowed him to investigate DNA abnormalities in Hodgkin's Lymphoma, one of the commonest forms of lymphoma, affecting more than 1,000 people in the UK each year. In May 2006, the brewery were nominated and awarded the Banbury Guardian community project award, sponsored by Bartercard, in recognition of the village's Leukaemia fund raising efforts.[29]

The Sun Inn today.

In 1991 David's son, James joined the firm and, as had happened thirty years earlier, a father and son partnership again ran the brewery. With David as Managing Director and James as Head Brewer, a range of new beers were introduced. Twelve Days, the Christmas brew was the first of these new beers, introduced in 1992, followed by Haymaker, for the summer. Stout had been phased out by Percy Flick during the First World War but the recipe was revived and Double Stout was re-introduced, to be followed in 1997 by Generation to celebrate the birth of James's first child. These new beers were prize winning beers. In 1998, having already won a silver medal two years previously, Hook Norton

Best Bitter won the gold medal at the Brewing Industry International Awards, the brewing world's 'blue riband' award. These were the first of a succession of awards accrued by Hook Norton beers, including awards from the American Beverage Testing Institute for 'Old Hooky', Best Bitter and Generation.[30]

Three generations of the Clarke family, c1975.

This award winning partnership of father and son was severed by the untimely death of David Clarke in September 2004. Described in his *Times* obituary as 'One of the great names of the British "beerage", the dwindling band of independent brewers defying big-brand advertising to keep alive a unique British institution; traditional cask-brewed ale.' Shortly before his death, David was awarded a lifetime achievement award by the All-Party Parliamentary Beer Group in recognition of his contribution to brewing.[31] As Managing Director, David Clarke presided over the company at a time when the resurgence of 'Real Ale' saw demand for Hook Norton beer lead to a dramatic up turn in the company's business. Through his efforts the name of the Hook Norton Brewery became known beyond the bounds of 'Banburyshire' and references to 'a brewery in Oxfordshire' became synonymous with Hook Norton as its beer became more widely known.

David Clarke receiving his life time award from All-Party Parliamentary Beer Group.

James succeeded his father as managing director, being the fifth generation of the family to be involved with brewing in Hook Norton. Like his grandfather before him, he was a member of the Parish Council for a number of years as well as serving in the village Fire Brigade. Now his time is concentrated on meeting the demands of the business as the company moves into a new century.

The new century brought changes in the beer market with the emergence of the small independent brewer and the craft brewing movement. Brewers producing less than 60,000 hectolitres have benefited from 'the small breweries relief scheme' and are eligible to receive beer duty discounts. The aim of the craft brewing movement is 'to bring good, flavoursome, creative beers to the masses' and has generated a lot of interest and has helped to attract more drinkers, both male and female. In the spirit of this movement the Hook Norton Brewery is installing a five barrel brewing plant within the brewery to run alongside the production of session or pub beers. Initially plans to install a bottling line for their main beers were considered, but this proved to be cost prohibitive. The decision to install the pilot brewery had been under discussion for a number of years and was installed during the summer of 2014. Once operational, trials will be held, initially to carry out flavour matching on Hooky and Old Hooky. A small hand bottling line is also under consideration, providing an opportunity to produce small quantities of naturally conditioned bottled beer. It is planned that the new five barrel brewing plant will provide a new range of niche beers, only available at the Visitor Centre.[32]

While the pilot brewery offers new opportunities, the brewery's core business remains the brewing of their distinctive range of 'session' beers. The nature of that market has, however, changed and the high volume market of the past no longer exists. The heavy industry in Coventry that once supported the brewery following the First World War has gone. Drinkers are now more discerning and James Clarke recognises, 'they want to make sure they have a beer that is really good and different'.

He has a clear view of where the business stands in the brash modern world.

Certain changes [are] being made, but I'd like to think [these] are evolutionary rather than revolutionary. We must be very conscious to remember that we can live with the past, but we mustn't live in it. We live in a very dynamic world and in spite of being a very long established traditional company we still need to keep abreast of things.[33]

A brewing day at the Hook Norton Brewery 2011.

As one of the country's few remaining long-established breweries, The Hook Norton Brewery upholds an English brewing tradition that spans more than a thousand years. Long may it continue.

Cheers Hooky!

Notes

1   Gourvish. T. & Wilson. R. *The British Brewing Industry 1830-1980*. CUP. 1994. pp.364-6.

Monckton. H.A. *A History of English Ale & Beer*. Bodley Head. 1966. pp.189-9.

Burnett. J. *Liquid Pleasures*. Routledge. 1999. p.137.

2   Gourvish. T. & Wilson. R. 1994. pp.447-450. The 'Big Six' were, Allied Breweries, Bass Charrington, Courage, Scottish and Newcastle, Watney and Whitbread. See Chapter 11 for full account of 'Merger Mania'.

3   Gourvish T. & Wilson. R. 1994. pp.368, 370/71, 380/81.

4   Gourvish T. & Wilson. R. 1994. pp.474, 479, 484.

5   Oral Tradition. Conversation with James Clarke. November 2007.

See also Eddersdhaw D. *A Country Brewery Hook Norton 1849-1999*. Hook Norton Brewery Company Limited. 1999. pp.97-99.

6   Gourvish. T. & Wilson. R. 1994. p.484.

Clarke Family papers 1950.

Directors Meeting Minutes 16/11/1950.

7   Norman Gilchrist resigned as company secretary and director of the Company at a Board meeting on 22nd March 1955 as he was leaving for Canada. He was succeeded by Harold Wyton as secretary, whose salary was increased by £100. Wyton retired in 1969 after 60 years service with the company. He was succeeded by John Stratford, a grandson of F. Stratford one of the company's travellers at the beginning of the twentieth century. John Stratford held the position of company secretary on two separate occasions.

8   Hook Norton Village Oral Tradition 1972-1974.

9   Gourvish. T. & Wilson. R. 1994. p.446.

10 Conversation with James Clarke. 3rd August 2009.

www.the publican.com. 24th June 2009.

11 Oral Tradition: Conversation with James Clarke. 10th April 2014.

12 Oral Tradition: Conversation with James Clarke. November 2007.

13 Burnett. J. pp.137-138. Between 1959 and 1979 the growth in consumption of beer rose by 2% annually, wine by 7.4% and spirits by 5.2%.

Gourvish. T. & Wilson. R. 1994. pp.457-459, 566.

14 Protz. R., Millns. T. (Eds). *Called to the Bar*. CAMRA. 1992. pp.37-38, 45 (see pp.33-36 Michael Hardiman's account of the Irish holiday and the beginnings of the campaign.)

Gourvish. T. & Wilson. R. 1994. p567-8.

15 The keg was to be supplied by Gibbs Mew of Salisbury.

16 Radio Times: 19th August 1974. The programme was number six in the series and was screened at 7.35pm on BBC 2.

17 Young. F. *Beer Buffs' night out*. Oxford Times. 19th July 1974.

Hanson. T. *CAMRA. Drinking a toast to real ale*. Banbury Guardian. 12th December 1974.

Howarth. D. *Brewing up the Hooky Interest*. Banbury Guardian. May 1975.

Hook Norton Open Weekend Programme. June 1975. The brewery tours started at 11am and a charge of 15p was made per person.

18 Oral Tradition. Conversation with James Clarke. November 2007.

Oxford Times Online. *Anne has coffee at brewery event*. 10/9/1999. Archive. the oxfordtimes.net. 9th October 1999.

Oxford Mail. *Brewery in a time warp*. 11/9/1999. archive.oxfordmail.net/1999/9/11.

19 The Hook Norton Brewery Visitor Centre can be contacted by telephone on 01608 730384 or email at heritage@hook-norton.co.uk. Cost £9.50 per person.

The Visitor Centre is open Monday to Friday 9am-5pm and Saturday 9am to 3pm.

20 Oral Tradition. Conversation with Bill Clarke. 1974.

HNLHG: Oral Tradition Project. David Clarke Brewer. 8/4/1998.

HNLHG: Oral Tradition Project. Doris Cadd. 7/3/2006.

21 Oral Tradition: Conversation with James Clarke. November 2007.

Oral Tradition: Conversation with Bill Clarke. 1974.

The vertical fridges were retained and form part of the brewery museum.

22 Correspondence with Nancy Pargeter. 15th June 2009.

Email correspondence with Mrs Amanda Shaw. 2007.

Correspondence with Banbury RDC 7/5/1973. Piped water supply was available in Hook Norton from January 1956 and Mains Drainage Scheme in the village was completed in June 1968. Great Tew Primary School was still relying on a bucket lavatory during the mid 1970s.

Eddersdhaw D. 1999. pp.98-100.

23 email correspondence with James Clarke 22nd of April 2014.

24 Mathias. P. *The Brewing Industry in England 1700-1830*. CUP 1959. pp.330-338. Gourvish. T. & Wilson. R. 1994. pp.217-225.

A notable nineteenth century example was the first Lord Burton, who in addition to providing Burton with two large churches, its municipal buildings and a bridge over the river Trent, reputedly donated £200,000 to charity during his life time.

25 HNLHG: Oral Tradition Project. David Clarke Brewer. 8/4/1998.

Oral Tradition: Conversation with James Clarke. November 2007. In 2007 the village Cricket team was sponsored by the brewery. In 2009 James Clarke was President of the Band.

26 Oral Tradition: Conversation with Bill Clarke. 1974.

Hook Norton Horticultural Society: Annual Flower Show. 18/8/1973. President W.A. Clarke Esq.

HNLHG: Oral Tradition Project. David Clarke Brewer. 8/4/1998 Interviewed by Barbara Hicks and Nancy Pargeter. The Hook Norton Brass Band is now known as the Hook Norton and District Silver Band and is based in Banbury rather than the village.

The Times: Obituary. *David Clarke. Brewer*. 8/10/2004.

Clarke. J. (Ed) *Hook Norton Fire Brigade – A Celebration*. Hook Norton. 1996

27 Banbury Guardian. 7th January 1982.

28 Oral Tradition. Conversation with Percy Hemmings 29/10/1982.

29 Hook Norton Village Newsletter. *Hook Norton Beer Festival 2005*. December 2005.

Oxford Mail. Brewery backs Botham. September 29th 2006.

Inn Season. *Generosity of Hook Norton Villagers is honoured*. Hook Norton Brewery Winter 2005.

Leukaemia Research Annual Review. 2006. 4187 HN pdf.

www.cask-marque.co.uk. Hook Norton stands out as a beacon. 24/6/2006.

Hook Norton Fine Ales Prospectus. Saturday 21st July 2007.

www.banburytoday.co.uk. Village Festival helps charities. 15/12/2007.

Email correspondence with Roseanne Edwards of the Banbury Guardian. 25/2/2008.

www.hookybeerfest.co.uk

30 Bruning. T. *Hooked on fine ale and no towering ambitions*. What's Brewing 1998 Email correspondence with Barbara Hicks. 27/2/2008.

31 Register Obituaries: David Clarke. The Times. 8/10/2004.

32 Oral Tradition: Conversation with James Clarke. 10th April 2014.

33 Video: *Hooked on Tradition*. Hook Norton Brewery Company c1999.

Glossary of Brewing Terms[1]

Ale and Beer: These are fermented drinks made from malted barley. In mediaeval times ale was brewed without hops. From the fifteenth century hops were added to produce beer. From the eighteenth century ale and beer were terms used to denote beers with little or no colour and distinguish them from the '*black*' beers, porter and stout. This distinction between the two drinks has now been lost and the terms are often interchangeable.

Attemperation: Controlled fermentation.

Barrel: A measure of capacity for both liquids and dry goods. A beer barrel holds 36 gallons, and an ale barrel 32 gallons, as did Guinness's barrels until 1881.

'Standard Barrel': 'The *Standard Barrel* may be described as an imaginary or hypothetical unit of measurement adopted mainly for the purpose of levying the Beer Duty. It is taken to be a barrel of 36 gallons of beer of an original gravity before fermentation of 1055 degrees, and, though in practice exactly such a barrel of beer is seldom met with, it is in theory the

---

1   Gourvish T. & Wilson R. *The British Brewing Industry. 1830-1980.* 1994. pp.638-643
     Lynch P. & Vaizey J. *Guinness's Brewery in the Irish Economy. 1759-1876.* 1960. pp.251-254.
     The Shorter OED. Vol: 2 N-Z. Oxford. 1968. p1621.

barrel on which the brewer pays the duty of £5 and makes nearly all his calculations.' UK Beer Statistics taken from Brewers' Almanac Wine & Spirit Trade Annual 1928: www.europeanbeerguide.net

'Bulk Barrel': 'Any given barrel of beer which is not exactly the standard barrel as defined above is known as the *bulk* barrel. As the gravity or strength of the bulk barrel rises above or falls below the [standard gravity], so the charge for duty increases or diminishes ... per degree.' UK Beer Statistics taken from Brewers' Almanac Wine & Spirit Trade Annual 1928: www.europeanbeerguide.net

Beerhouse: Licensed to sell only beer. Some were limited to the numbers of days they could open. A product of the 1830 Beerhouse Act.

Brewing: To make ale or beer by infusion, boiling and fermentation, by which malt is converted into fermented liquor.

Bushel: A unit of measurement for barley and malt: 56lbs for barley, 42lbs for malt. Approximately two bushels of malt produced a barrel of beer. Eight bushels made a quarter.

Cask: A vessel for the storage and transport of draught beer. Casks came in a variety of sizes.

Cleansing: The removal of yeast from the beer when fermentation is complete.

Cooler: The shallow vessel in which hot wort is run after hops have been separated from it and allowed to cool before yeast is added.

Copper: The vessel in which the wort is boiled with hops.

Common Brewer: *'Commercial'* or *'Wholesale'* brewer as opposed to the public or beer-house brewer. Gourvish and Wilson classed brewers producing more than 1,000 barrels a year as *'common brewers'.* See Chapter 3. fn1.

Fermentation: The conversion of the wort sugars into alcohol. Carbon dioxide is given off during the process.

Good Trade Debts: Beer sent out but not yet paid for.

Grist: Malt grains ground ready for mashing. A quantity of ground malt sufficient for one mashing.

Hop-Back: A large vessel with a perforated false bottom to separate spent hops from the wort after boiling.

Hydrometer: An instrument which measures the density of a liquid by the level at which it floats in that liquid.

Inn: A public house for lodging and entertaining travellers. In 1577 only 12% of drinking houses in England were classed as inns.

Liquor: Water used in the brewing process.

'Long Pull': A generous over measure provided by certain publicans to attract trade. Banned during the First World War.

Malting: The process by which the barley grain is converted to starch under controlled conditions. This is done by immersing the barley in water, then spreading it on the floor of the maltings and under controlled temperature until the grains germinate. These grains are then heated on a kiln over a fire so as to stop further germination. Malt has to be kept dry before being used in brewing. Damp malt is known as *'slack malt'.*

Mashtun: The vessel in which malt is mashed and sparged to release the malt sugars. The mashtun has a false bottom of slotted plates, through which the wort will pass to the copper, leaving the malt grains for further mashing.

Mashing: The mixing of ground malt with hot liquor at a predetermined temperature in the mashtun.

Original Gravity: The specific gravity of the wort prior to fermentation, at a given temperature, compared with the density of water at 4°C – which is given the value of 1.000. It is the measure of the total amount of solids dissolved in the wort.

Porter: The eighteenth century term for *'black'* beer made from dark malt. It was the first mass produced beer and was brewed in London.

Pupillage: The state of being a pupil, in brewing terms when a prospective brewer is taken on by a brewery and taught the brewing trade.

Public House: A house in which the principal trade is the sale of alcoholic liquors to be consumed on the premises.

Quarter: A unit of measurement for barley and malt containing eight bushels.

Specific Gravity: The weight of any given substance (the wort) as compared with the weight of an equal volume of water.

Sparge: The practice introduced in the early nineteenth century of spraying the contents of the mash, after the wort had been run off, so as to extract as much fermentable matter as possible.

Saccharometer: A form of hydrometer used for estimating the amount of sugar in a solution by specific gravity.

Tavern: A public house where wine was retailed.

Treating: The practice of buying a round of drinks. Prohibited during the First World War.

Tun: Abbreviation for *'fermenting tun'*, the vessel in which the main fermentation takes place after yeast has been added to the cooled wort.

Vat: A vessel in which beer is stored before being racked.

Wort: It is the liquid run from the mashtun, containing malt sugars. Called *'sweet wort'* before it is boiled with hops. Afterwards called *'hopped wort'*. It is pronounced *'wert'*.

Yeast: A microscopic unicellular plant which is able to turn wort sugars into alcohol and carbon dioxide.

Bibliography

Manuscript Primary Sources

Documents of the Hook Norton Brewery Company:

Accounts prepared for the Surveyor of Taxes, 1895-1901.

Analysis of Trade, 1887-1891.

Analytical reports by F. Kendall & Sons, 1901.

Annual Report of Directors, 1907-1913. (Held at Companies House: Cardiff).

Balance Sheets, 1887-1891.

Brewery Deeds, 1849-1976.

Brewing Books, 1856-1874; 1887-1914.

Building Specifications, 1894.

Building Plans for: "New Malthouse" 1865; Pontifex Brewery 1872; Alterations by Alfred Kinder, 1880.

Conveyance of Business from John Harris & Co to the Hook Norton Brewery Company, 1900.

Diary of Alban Clarke, 1897.

Goods Purchased Ledger (2), 1901; 1904-1908.

Labour Account, 1904.

Letter Books, 1888-1895; 1896-1913; miscellaneous letters 1904; 1880 (re Brewery alterations), 1896, 1901 (Hoskins & Sons re valuation), 1905, 1912.

List of Agencies, 1900.

Malt Sales, 1892-1910/11.

Minutes of Director's Meetings, 1900-1951.

Mortgage agreements with Miss M.A. and Miss F.E. Harris, 1896.

Motor Dray Journeys, 1904-1909.

Notes on the running of the company agencies, 1892.

Private Trade Sales – comparison of traveller's sales, 1905-07. Summary.

Prospectus for 1st Share Issue, July 1900; Report of Messrs Thomas, Peyer & Miles, July 1900.

Prospectus for 2nd Share Issue, May 1903.

Sale of Beer, 1892-1895; 1895-1911.

Site Plans, c1856-1864.

Stock Books, 1855-1879.

Summary of Proceedings. The High Court of Justice-Chancery Lane, 1898.

Sundry Goods Purchased, 1896-1901.

Technical articles taken from the *"Brewers Journal"*.

Total Yearly Sales, 1892-1910/11; Analysis of Sales.

Trade at Hook Norton Brewery Licensed Properties, 1905-1907.

Trade Ledgers, 1901-1920.

Wages Book, 1895-1930.

Bodleian Library Oxford

Hook Norton – Seventeenth Century Wills.
John Haull, 1631.
William Hall, 1640.
William Prue, 1686.

Brighton History Centre: Brighton

Parish marriage records for St Nicholas's Church Brighton, 1858. Marriage of John Harris and Elizabeth Chaundy.

Companies House Cardiff

Hook Norton Brewery Company Records, 1900-1951.

Oxfordshire Country Record Office

Misc. Coleman 1/23 The Wykeham Arms – Sibford Gower, mortgage
agreement, 1886.
Electoral Registers: Hook Norton, 1841-1857.

Oxford City Westgate Library

Calendar of Wills.
Chipping Norton Advertiser, 1934.

Oxford County Museum: Woodstock

Oxfordshire County Trade Record Cards, 1637-1903.

Shakespeare Birthplace Trust Record Office. Stratford upon Avon

Papers of F. Kendall and Son. Stratford upon Avon, 1900.
Trade Directories for Banbury, Leamington, Chipping Norton and
Deddington, 1830, 1891, 1907.

Northamptonshire County Record Office:

Correspondence regarding population figures east of Banbury.

Banbury Library

Enumerator's Books for Census Returns for Hook Norton, 1851-1901.
Banbury Guardian, 1849, 1850, 1887-1888, 1917.

Probate Registry York

Probate Registry. Copies of Wills.
John Harris. ref. 01/04/1172.
Alban Clarke. ref. 01/06/2019.
John Henry Harris. ref. 01/06/2020.
Percy Flick. ref. 02/11/1251.

Primary Printed Sources

Barnard. A. *The Noted Breweries of Great Britain and Ireland. Vol 1-4.* Jos Causton & Sons 1889-91.

Bradford. W. *Notes on Malting and Breweries.* Oct 1889.

Bushnan. J.S. *Burton and its Beer.* 1853.

Dickens M. *History of Hook Norton.* Banbury Guardian. 1928.

Faulkner. F. *The Theory and Practice of Modern Brewing.* F.W. Lyon 1888. 2nd edition (A.A. Clarke's copy Feb 1889).

Gardener's Directory of Oxfordshire. 1852.

Ham. J. *The Theory and Practice of Brewing from Malted and Unmalted Corn.* c1850. c/1 (B.R.L).

Hawkes. S.M. The Swan Brewery. c1850.

Hunt Edmunds & Co Ltd. 1896-1946.

Kelly's Trade Directory 1891, 1903, 1907, 1920.

Lascelles & Co Directory and Gazetteer of Oxfordshire 1853.

Moritz. E.R. and Morris. G.H. *A Text Book of the Science of Brewing.* Spon. 1891.

Pigot & Co's Directory 1830.

Scammell. G. *Breweries and Maltings: Their arrangement, construction and machinery.* Fullerton & Co London 1871 (BL.7942K16).

Shadwell. A. *Drink in 1914-1922. A Lesson in Control.* Longman, Green & Co. 1923.

Sykes. W.J. & Ling. A.R. *Principles and Practice of Brewing.* Griffin 1907.

Tripp. C.H. *Brewery Management.* Lyon. 1892.

Tripp. C.H. Articles in the Brewer's Journal. 1899.

Collections of Newspapers, Videos and other Sources

Banbury Guardian. The Death of John Harris. 24/11/1887.

Banbury Guardian. Richard Howse. 15/8/1895.

Banbury Guardian. The Arsenic in Beer. 29/11/1900.

Banbury Guardian. Notice that beer of several locals brewers (including HN) was free of arsenic. 1/1/1901.

Banbury Guardian. Opening of the *'new'* Hook Norton Brewery Company Ltd. 20/3/1902.

Banbury Guardian. The death of Alban Clarke. 31/5/1917.

Banbury Guardian. CAMRA: Drinking Toast to real ale. 12/12/1974.

Banbury Guardian. Brewing up Hooky Interest. May 1975.

Central Office of Information: *'Twenty Four Square Miles'.* 1946. Issued as a video by Trilith, a media charity.

Country Life. Country Notes. Falling Consumption of beer. 20/2/1909.

Country Life. Country Notes. Children's Act and Pubs. 17/4/1909.

Daily Mail. 12/9/1905.

Deeds of *"The Wheatsheaf".* Courtesy of Mr R. Collins of Hook Norton.

Dumbleton. G. Poem *"Hooky".* 1970.

Financial Times. Brewing Supplement. 21/3/1979.

Guardian. *Do we think we've had enough? Beer sales plunge.* 20/11/2007.

Hook Norton Village Newsletter. December 2005.

Inn Season. Generosity of Hook Norton villagers is honoured. Winter 2005.

Oral Tradition: collected in Hook Norton between 1966 and 2006 relating to the village, including the brewery.

Oxford Mail. Brewery in time warp. 11/9/1999.

Oxford Mail. Brewery backs Botham. 29/9/2006.

Oxford Times. Beer buffs' night out. 19/7/1974.

Radio Times. 19/8/1976.

Shrewsbury Chronicle. 28/6/1895.

South Wales Echo. 1/5/1916.

Oral Tradition: collected in Hook Norton between 1966 and 2007 relating to the village, including the brewery.

The Times. David Clarke. Obituary. 8/10/2004.

Wellington Journal and Shrewsbury News. 10/3/1883.

Online sources

www.banburytoday.co.uk. Village helps charities.

www.cask-marque.co.uk. Hook Norton stands out as a beacon. 24/6/2006.

Leukaemia Research Annual Report 2006. 4187HN pdf.

Oxford Times online. Anne has coffee at brewery event. 10/9/1999.

Printed Secondary Sources

Barber. N. *Century of British Brewers 1890-2004*. Brewery History Society. 2005.

Bennett. J. *Ale, Beer and Brewsters in England 1300-1600*. O.U.P. 1996.

Billingham. C. *Home Brewing in the Black Country: The Billinghams of Pearson Street, Old Hill, 1934-1963*. Brewery History Society. Autumn 1998.

Bond. J. & Rhodes. J. *The Oxfordshire Brewer* Oxford Museum Services. 1985.

Burnett. J. *Liquid Pleasures: A social history of drinks in modern Britain*. Routledge. 1999.

British Beer & Pub Association. *A Wake-up for Westminster – Economic trends in the beer and pub sector*. September 2008.

Brown. M. & Willmot. B. *Brewed in Northants*. Brewery History Society. 1998.

Brown. M. *Oxon Brews*. Brewery History Society. 2004.

Child. J. Organisation: *A guide to Problems and Practice*. Harper & Row. 1977.

Clark. P. *The English Ale House 1200-1830*. Longman. 1983.

Collins. T. & Vamplew. W. *Mud, Sweat and Beers* Berg. 2002.

Dunn. M. Local Brew. *Traditional Breweries and their Ales*. Hale. 1986.

Eddershaw. D. *A Country Brewery Hook Norton 1849-1999*. Hook Norton Brewery Company. 1999.

Gourvish. T. and Wilson. R. *The British Brewing Industry. 1830-1980*. C.U.P. 1994.

Hardach. G. *The First World War 1914-1918*. Allen Lane. 1977.

Hawk. G.R. *Railways and Economic Growth in England and Wales. 1840-1870*. Clarendon Press Oxford. 1970.

Horn. P. *Labouring Life in the Victorian Village*. Fraser Stewart Books. 1995.

Ingle. R. *Thomas Cook of Leicester*. Headstart History. 1991.

Jennings. P. *The Public House in Bradford 1770-1970*. Keele University Press. 1995.

Lynch. P. & Vaizey. J. *Guinness's Brewery in the Irish Economy 1759-1876* C.U.P. 1960.

Mathias. P. *The Brewing Industry in England 1700-1830*. C.U.P. 1959.

Mathias. P. *The First industrial Nation*. Methuen. 1969.

McKenna. J. *Birmingham Breweries.* Brewin Books. 2005.

Monckton. H.A. *A History of English Ale & Beer.* Bodley Head. 1966.

Pearson. L. *British Breweries, an architectural history.* Hambledon Press. 1999.

Protz. R. & Millns. T. (Eds) *Called to the Bar.* CAMRA. 1992.

Rayner. D. *Steam Wagons.* Shire Publications. 2003.

Richmond. L. & Turton. A. *The Brewing Industry.* M.U.P. 1990.

Sambrook. P. *Country House Brewing in England 1500-1900.* Hambledon Press. 1996.

Shugborough. Information Sheet. *The Once a month Brewer.* Staffordshire County Museum Service. 1980.

Stapleton. B. & Thomas. J. *Gales: A study in Brewing, Business and family history.* Ashgate. 2000.

The Shorter Oxford Dictionary. 2 Vols Oxford. 1968.

Thirsk. J. (ed) *The Rural Landscape Ch.12: Hook Norton Oxfordshire – An Open Village.* Blackwell. Oxford 1998.

Thompson. F. *Lark Rise.* Folio Society London. 1979.

Trinder. B. *Victorian Banbury.* Phillimore. 1982.

Vaizey. J. *The Brewing Industry 1886-1951.* Pitman. 1960.

Victoria County Histories: Population figures for Oxfordshire, Warwickshire, Gloucestershire and Northamptonshire. 1851-1901.

Woolley. R.M. *Midland Tales 2: Hooky.* Woolley. 1978.

Woolley. R.M. *Midland Tales 3: Gi it sum 'ommer.* Woolley. 1979.

Journal Articles

Borthwick Papers No 31. *The Brewing Trade during the Industrial Revolution.* Borthwick Institute of Historical Research. University of York. 1967.

Dingle. A.E. *Drink and Working Class living Standards in Britain 1870-1914* Economic History Review Vol XXV No 4. 1972.

Fletcher. T.W. The great depression of English agriculture 1873-1896 Economic History Review. Vol XIII No 3. April 1961.

Gosling. L. *Trouble Brewing.* History Today. March 2008.

Harrison. B. and Trinder. B. *Drink and Sobriety in an Early Victorian Town: Banbury 1830-1860.* Longmans. 1969.

Horn. P. *Victorian Villages from Census Returns.* The Local Historian Vol. 15 No 1. 1982.

Keynes. J.M. *The City of London and the Bank of England August 1914.* Quarterly Journal of Economics Vol. 29 No 1 Nov 1914.

Knowles. T. and Howley. M. *Branding in the UK public house sector: recent developments.* International Journal of Contemporary Hospitality Management. 12/6/2000.

Knowles. T. and Egan. D. *The changing structure of UK brewing and pub retailing.* International Journal of Contemporary Hospitality Management. 14/2/2002.

MacDonagh. O. *The Origins of Porter.* The Economic History Review. Vol XVI. No 3. April 1964.

Mathias. P. *Agriculture and the Brewing and distilling Industries in the Eighteenth Century.* Economic History Review. 1952-53.

Mathias. P. *Industrial Revolution in Brewing.* Explorations in Entrepreneurial History. Vol 5. 1952-3.

Reinarz. J. *Flowers on Horseback.* Warwickshire History. Vol X. No 6 Winter 1998/9.

Reinarz. J. *Kendall & Son Ltd Stratford upon Avon. The business of a brewer's chemist in the Nineteenth and twentieth century.* Warwickshire History Vol XI. No 3. Summer 2000.

Reinarz. J. *Loyal and long serving Workers. Labour turnover in England's Provincial Brewing industry 1870-1914.* HSIR 17. Spring 2004.

Sigsworth. *Science and the brewing industry. 1850-1900.* Economic History Review. 1964/65.

Tann. J. Sources for industrial History: *Archaeology and the Factory.* Local Historian Vol 9. No 4. 1970.

University Theses and Dissertations

Plummer. C.W. *Economic History of the Highgate Brewery Co Ltd.* B.Phil Open University 1981.

Reinarz. J. *Flower & Sons Brewery 1870-1914.* PhD. Warwick 1998.

Roberts. N.C. *The Formation and Management of the local licensed trade in Crewe* 1830-1914. M.Phil. Keele 1999.

Woolley. R.M. *The Development of the Hook Norton Brewery 1849-1913.* M.Phil. Wolverhampton 2005.

Appendices

1. The death of Alban Albert Clarke of Hook Norton, Brewer. As reported by the Banbury Guardian.

Mr A.A. Clarke lived at Brooklyn House, Hook Norton, has died, we regret to say on Saturday evening as the result of a cycle accident in the afternoon on the hill between Hook Norton and Sibford near Temple Mill. Mr Clarke was 59 years of age and was the brewer and one of the directors of the Hook Norton Brewery Company, with which he had been connected all his life. Mr Clarke was an ardent fisherman and he was on his way out to enjoy an afternoon at his favourite sport when he met with an accident which caused his death later in the evening.

From the evidence given at the inquest which was held on Monday by Mr Coggins the Coroner for North Oxfordshire at the Bell Inn, Hook Norton, it transpired that Mr Clarke had been about his business as usual on Saturday morning, and after dinner he left his home on a bicycle to go to Traitor's Ford Brook and for some reason not clearly explained he was thrown from his machine on the hill between Hook Norton and Sibford, near Temple Mill.

He was first found by Miss Ada Pickering, driver of the motor mail between Brailes and Banbury who remained with him about an hour and whose kindness was

The Bell Inn: the venue for Alban Clarke's inquest.

referred to in terms of appreciation by the Coroner and jury. Dr Fielden of Sibford and Mr Michael Pettipher Bennett and other rendered assistance getting him home, but unfortunately, he was beyond human aid and he died at 9.30pm. The jury returned a verdict of accidental death. Mr J.W. Harris (Jun) was foreman of the jury. The other members were: Messrs Francis W. Phipps, H. Turnock, T. Smith, H.G.T. Peters, C. Stratford, E. Colegrave, G. Groves, W.H. Heritage, J. Timms, C.H. Hicks, W. Gasson.

Harry Haines said he was employed by Mr Clarke at the brewery and went out with him a great deal fishing. Mr Clarke had been fairly well in health and he had known him twelve years. He was not subject to fits and he was in the habit of riding a bicycle. He never complained of giddiness. He borrowed a bike from Mr Stafford [Stratford] on Saturday because his own was being repaired. Deceased asked the witness to go with him to Traitor's Ford Brook to assist him in his fishing. He had to meet him at his house after dinner, and the witness went at 1.45pm. Deceased handed him a basket to carry down to the ford, a distance of two miles, and told him what to do when he got there. Witness started off at once to walk and took a dog with him. He went on the road and down the hill where he was told the body was found. Mr Clarke did not turn up, but the witness remained at the ford till 6pm and then returned home. He heard of Mr Clarke's accident when he got back.

Ada Elsie Pickering, a single young woman, whose parents live at White Hill, Hook Norton, said she drove the royal mail from Banbury to Brailes, a distance of twelve miles. She had to be at Brailes at 7.45am and remained there till 5.30pm, when she returned to Banbury. She left Brailes on Saturday 26th May at 1.15pm to come home to Hook Norton and arrived there at 1.50pm. The house was locked up so she proceeded back to Brailes at once. When going back she found a man lying in the road about a quarter of a mile from her home. She was cycling down hill and she got off her machine. His head was pointing towards the bottom of the hill. He did not speak for half an hour and then she asked him his name and where he came from and he did not know.

There was a bicycle lying between his body and the grass and the front wheel was pointing up hill. His head was "fearfully cut", the worst wound seemed to be over the left eye. Blood was flowing from the wounds and he was groaning. He lay there apparently with his right arm under him and the left arm by his side. His cap was lying in the road a yard and a half further down the road. She did not notice anything unusual about the surface of the road. Had there been a big stone she would have noticed it. The first to pass was a boy with a butcher's cart and she suggested they should try and get the deceased into the cart, but she couldn't get any satisfactory answer. He said he was going to Sibford, and she told him to get a doctor. A gentleman then came along on a bicycle, and he went for a doctor. He was a stranger to her, and she thought he belonged to Sibford School. Shortly after two ladies came with towels with the Sibford School mark on. Two gentlemen then came up with a cart. She had already moved the deceased on to the grass at the side of the road to make him more comfortable. She was with the deceased an hour altogether.

Michael Pettipher Bennett farmer of Oatley Hill, Hook Norton said he had known Mr Clarke for forty years. Witness went to Temple Mill Sibford on Saturday afternoon. About 3pm Miss Pickering came down and said a man was up the road half dead. At that time he was at Temple Mill. Mr Sabin and himself started at once, but on second thoughts Mr Sabin said he would take some binders and he returned for home. Witness also returned and put his pony in the trap and they drove up together. On arriving at the place he found Mr Clarke in a kneeling position, on one knee and two young ladies from Sibford School were holding his hand and rendering other assistance. Mr C.H. Hicks was also there. Witness suggested they should lift Mr Clarke up and see if he could stand. He was partially conscious and he stood up on one leg. He said 'Oh my hip'. There was a considerable quantity of blood in the road near where he was. Then they lifted him into the witnesses trap and took him home.

During the journey home, he said, 'Pettipher are you sure the back is safe?'. When they reached Brooklyn they seated him in a chair and carried him upstairs. When they lifted him out of the trap he said, 'Pettipher you won't drop me will you'.

Nurse Dunkley said she belonged to the Nurses Home, Hook Norton and she was called in to see Mr Clarke on Saturday afternoon. She got there at 5.30pm. She ascertained he had met with an accident. He was in bed, but was not able to converse with her. He was unconscious and passed away at 9.30pm.

Dr W.H. Fielden, Sibford Ferris said that on Saturday afternoon, just after 3 o'clock, he received a message that a man was lying on the road above Temple Mill. He started at once and found Mr Bennett. Mr Bennett asked him to go forward and helped get the deceased to bed and then went down to consult Mrs Clarke and Mr J.H. Harris, his brother in law.

He told them if he were a patient of his he should want a consultant from Oxford at once. They decided to send for Dr O'Kelly, and he told them he expected to attend an inquest at Sibford at 4.30, and asked them if they were in any difficulty to let him know at once. He formed the opinion that there was a fractured skull, haemorrhage on the surface of the brain, and injuries to the left hip and shoulder. The pressure on the brain was the cause of death. The left collar bone was broken. The left eye was black and cut and so was his nose. His opinion was that Mr Clarke was trying to avoid a bad part of the road, put the brake on suddenly, and was thrown over the handle bars.

The Coroner, said they were distressing circumstances. There was no doubt the theory of the doctor was correct, but they would never know for certain. That he died as a result of an accident was certain. They did not want to consult in private on that point.

The jury returned a verdict of accidental death, and the Coroner said they appreciated the action of Miss Pickering in all she did. She acted the part of the good Samaritan.

Miss Pickering said she only did her duty. Mr J.W. Harris, jun, said they all wished to convey their respectful sympathy to Mrs Clarke in her bereavement. The Coroner said he would convey that expression of sympathy to Mrs Clarke. He was sure Mr Clarke would be missed very much in many activities. This concluded the proceedings. The funeral of Mr Clarke takes place at Hook Norton today (Thursday) at 2pm.
Banbury Guardian, 31st May 1917.

2. Hook Norton: Funeral of the late Mr A A Clarke.
As reported by the Banbury Guardian.

The funeral of the late Mr A.A. Clarke took place at 2pm on Thursday, and was the occasion of a large gathering of relatives and personal friends of the deceased and of sympathisers among the general public who assembled to pay their last token of respect to one who for many years had been very highly esteemed for his many excellent qualities by the community. The body was interred in the cemetery, and the first part of the service was held in the church and was conducted by the Rector, the Rev E.C. Freeman. The coffin was of polished oak with brass furniture which with the bier, was covered with floral wreaths. The bearers were six of the workmen at the brewery, of which the deceased had for many years been brewer and director, viz,: Messrs J. Hall, W. Coleman, Frank Beale, Frederick Beale, G. Hall and H. Matthews. The funeral procession from Brooklyn, the deceased's residence was preceded by the village special constables of whom the deceased was the local chief, and included Messrs F.L. Grant, W.H.T. Littleboy, J.W. Harris, junr, J. Clarkson, T. Bench, W. Heritage, C. Wyton, F. Padbury, H. Baker, E. Billing, J. Hayward, M. Osbourne, &c. The county constabulary were represented by Superintendent Allmond and PC Messenger. The chief mourners were: – Mrs Clarke, and Master Billy Clarke, Mr, and Mrs Harris (brother-in-law and sister-in-law), Mr Bowl (half brother), Mrs Smith (sister), Mr Smith (nephew), and Dr Broughton. Other mourners were: – Mr W. Toy, Mr P.W. Flick, Mr J. George, Mr E. Colegrave, Mr J.W. Hughes, Mr M.P. Bennett, Mr G. Groves, Mr F. Stratford, Mr W.A. Wilks, Mr J. Herring, Mr H. Allen, Mr W.J. Bloxham, Mr J.W. Harris, Mr C. Wilkins, Mr C.W. Twist, Mr E.H. Richardson, Mr C. Stafford, Mr A. Williams, Mr J. Jacques, Mr H. Dickins, Mr Allock and the workmen of the brewery. A large number of villagers assembled in the church and joined the procession on its way to the cemetery. The funeral arrangements were carried out by Mr G. White. In his sermon on Sunday the Rev E.C. Freeman paid a tribute to the excellent character of the deceased, especially referring to his uprightness and to the good relations which existed between him and the workmen under him, all of whom spoke highly of him and mourned his loss.
Banbury Guardian, 7th June 1917.

3. The death of John Henry Harris. 10th December 1934. Reported by the Chipping Norton Advertiser.

In the early hours of Monday morning the death took place at his residence 'Scotland Mount' of Mr J.H. Harris.

Mr J.H. Harris was the only son of Mr John Harris, who was the founder of the Hook Norton Brewery Company. [Mr J.H. Harris] was chairman of the Board of Directors. He leaves a wife to whom sympathy of all will go out also, to his other relatives. His loss will be widely felt for his never failing interest in the village was very helpful.

Chipping Norton Advertiser, 14th December 1934.

4. List of Licensed Houses owned by the Hook Norton Brewery Company in 1901.

Black Horse: Leamington Spa
Beer House: Chilson
Butcher's: Balscott
Pear Tree: Hook Norton
Kettle: Chipping Campden
Crown & Tuns: Deddington
Beer House: Greatworth
Sun Inn: Hook Norton
Wine Vaults: Stow on the Wold
Bell: Great Bourton
Gate Inn: Hook Norton
Beer House: Shenington
Reindeer Inn: Banbury
Coach & Horses: Banbury

Elephant & Castle: Rowington
Rose & Crown: Chipping Warden
Beer House: Down End Hook Norton
Blue Pig: Southam
Albion: Chipping Norton
Swan: Wiggington
Queen's Own: Woodstock
Red Lion: Chipping Norton
Beer House: Tadmarton
White Swan: Stratford upon Avon
Railway Hotel: Hook Norton
Elephant & Castle: Bloxham
Chandler's Arms: Epwell

5. Poem celebrating Bill Clarke's Golden Jubilee in 1978.

This year is the Golden Jubilee at the Brewery
Mr Clarke's fifty years at its Head.
He has built up its great reputation
All the pubs and clubs must be fed.
This beer is well known in the Midlands
Hooky Ale is the one they like best
No need to advertise in the papers
The drinkers will do all the rest.
Mr Clarke is well known wherever he goes
With that great big smile on his face
No matter what the company is
He is always in the right place.
The Navy all know him when they come here
They are some of the liveliest of men
When they meet in the pub they're all Good Friends
He joins in just like one of them.
Good luck to this fine English Gentleman
With pride he can stick out his chest
He comes from a long line of Gentlemen
And I know he is one of the Best.
George H Dumbleton. January 27th 1978
(First published in 'Hooky' 1978)

6. Brewing Awards won by Hook Norton beers.

1996. Brewing Industry International Awards – Best Bitter – Silver medal.

1998. Brewing Industry International Awards – Best Bitter – Gold medal.
Best Bitter Championship Trophy.

2000. BBI Ale and Lager Competition – Light Ale – Silver medal.
Old Hooky – Gold medal.
Beverage Testing Institute (USA) – Old Hooky – Exceptional.

2001. International Beer and Cider Competition – Generation – Silver Award.

2002. Brewing Industry International Awards – Best Bitter – Silver medal.
BBI Ale and Larger Competition – Light Ale – Diploma.
Old Hooky – Diploma.
Beverage Testing Institute (USA) – Best Bitter – Highly recommended.
Generation – Exceptional.
Old Hooky – Highly recommended.

2003. International Beer Competition – Haymaker – Silver medal.
Double Stout – Bronze medal.

7. Nineteenth century brewing advertisements.

FEBRUARY 15, 1889.　　　THE BREWERS' JOURNAL.　　　11

H. J. WEST & CO.,

MANUFACTURERS OF EVERY DESCRIPTION OF

BREWERS' & DISTILLERS' MACHINERY,

STAMFORD WORKS,

114—116—118, SOUTHWARK BRIDGE ROAD, SOUTHWARK, S.E.

Re **PONTIFEX & SONS** : *Dissolution of Partnership.*

WEST & CO., Brewers' Engineers and Coppersmiths, whose Senior, Mr. H. J. WEST, was recently in Partnership with Mr. C. Pontifex, at the address below, with offices at 331, Gray's Inn Road, King's Cross, as "PONTIFEX & SONS," beg respectfully to mention that the whole of the Brewers' Plant and Machinery (from a Filter Bag to a complete Brewery Plant) sold by PONTIFEX & SONS for the last 5½ years has been supplied by WEST & CO., and the Copper and other Metal Work has been actually Manufactured by them at their Works at Southwark.

Some 500 well known Firms have been supplied in this way, and WEST & CO. invite attention to this fact as sufficient evidence of their practical experience and success in this Department.

PONTIFEX'S CASK WASHERS.　FILTER BAGS.
BREWING COPPERS.　STEAM COILS.　STEAM PANS.　REFRIGERATORS.
CLEANSING APPARATUS.　RAKE MASHING MACHINES.　MASH TUNS.
SKIMMERS.　PIPE WORK, &c.

STAMFORD WORKS,

114—116—118, SOUTHWARK BRIDGE ROAD, SOUTHWARK, S.E.

From Frank Faulkner's 'The theory and Practice of Modern Brewing', 1888.

65

BRADFORD'S
PATENT MALT KILN COWL.

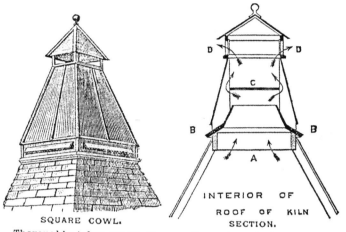

SQUARE COWL.

INTERIOR OF

ROOF OF KILN
SECTION.

Thoroughly takes off all Steam. Down draught impossible.
Direction of wind immaterial. Can be made to suit Kilns of
any shape. No moveable parts. Cannot get out of order.
The System can easily be applied to Kilns already having Louvre Ventilators.

The action of this Patent Cowl is as follows :—The hot air charged with
vapour from the Kiln rises to the outlet **A**, and there meeting the cold air
entering by the inlet **B** they pass and thoroughly intermix round the edge of
the diaphragm **C**, and a partial vacuum is obtained—due to the heated air
rising from the Kiln being cooled—causing a greater inrush of air through the
inlet **B**, and giving a velocity sufficient to carry the combined air and steam
rapidly through the exit **D**, this velocity is also greatly increased by the
partial vacuum produced at the exit **D**, by the wind from *any* direction passing
over the top of the cowl, which is made of such a shape as to produce that
result ; the diaphragm **C** thoroughly preventing the possibility of a down
draught even under the most adverse circumstances.

For full particulars apply to the Patentee,
MR. WILLIAM BRADFORD,
Architect and Brewers' Consulting Engineer,
CARLTON CHAMBERS, 12, REGENT ST., LONDON, S.W.

Advertisement for William Bradford's Patent Malt Kiln Cowl.

Index